Atlas of the
Pacific Northwest

Atlas of the
Pacific Northwest

Seventh Edition

Edited by
A. Jon Kimerling and Philip L. Jackson

Contributing authors

Robert E. Frenkel
Philip L. Jackson
J. Granville Jensen
Steven R. Kale
A. Jon Kimerling
Thomas J. Maresh
Gordon E. Matzke
Keith W. Muckleston
J. Kenneth Munford
Mary Lee Nolan
Ray M. Northam
James R. Pease
Charles L. Rosenfeld

Oregon State University Press

Third Edition © 1962
Fourth Edition © 1968
Fifth Edition © 1973
Sixth Edition © 1979
Seventh Edition © 1985

OREGON STATE UNIVERSITY PRESS
Corvallis, Oregon 97331

Library of Congress card catalog number: Map 62-50
ISBN: 0-87071-413-9 (paper); 0-87071-414-7 (cloth)

Printed in the United States of America

Contents

Maps and Graphs

Tables

Acknowledgments

This seventh edition of the Atlas of the Pacific Northwest carries on the over thirty year tradition of providing comprehensive information about the natural environment and human activities within the region. The guiding hand of Richard M. Highsmith, Jr., who applied his organizational talent, tireless energy, and enthusiasm toward producing the first six editions, is felt throughout. Once more the steadfast support given by the Department of Geography and the Oregon State University Press has made this up-to-date reference book and teaching aid possible. We are indebted deeply to Kenneth Munford and to the faculty of the Department of Geography, who unselfishly volunteered their time and talents to bring the most accurate information to this edition.

The content and organization of the sixth edition has largely been retained here, with individual sections on land use and energy resources included to reflect current concerns within the region. Maps, graphs, diagrams, tables, and text have been updated and are joined by 25 new maps and other graphics. Several maps have been redesigned for improved graphic clarity and increased aesthetic appeal. The number of pages printed in full-color has doubled to thirty-two, improving the readability of the complex maps in the middle sections of the book.

As with the sixth edition, all graphics were prepared using the facilities of the Department of Geography Cartographic Service. Special recognition for quality map revision work is due Suzanne M. Pierson. Other students involved in the project were Gary Bishop, Pamela Costa, Robert Evinger, Kathleen Golden, Andrew Herstrom, Mark Hicks, Thomas Kloster, Lorrie Meier, Phillip Nunemacher, Ibrahim Oroud, Richard Smith and Brian Young.

Professor Kimerling was responsible for the general layout, cartographic design, and graphics production, and Professor Jackson was responsible for the content and text editing. Oregon State University Press director Jeffrey Grass and managing editor Jo Alexander guided the atlas to completion.

A. Jon Kimerling
Philip L. Jackson

Map Notes

The state and county outline base maps, except for those at full-page size, and the river, relief shading, land use, general reference, and federal lands base maps were obtained from the United States National Atlas. Where sources of data displayed on maps are not indicated within the text, the respective authors have compiled their maps from data drawn from multiple sources.

A. Jon Kimerling, in addition to the maps in the section The Region, compiled as well as designed the following maps: Principal Indian Groups, Evolution of the Pacific Northwest States, Indian Land Cessions, Public Land Survey, Population, CCD Population Trend, Air Transport, Solar Power Resource, Geothermal Resources and Facilities, Manufacturing Employment in S.M.S.A.s, Business Centers and Trade Areas, and Resources for Wilderness Recreation.

The Landforms and Geology section is based upon physiographic regions prepared by Ira A. Allison that appeared in the first four editions of the Atlas. It has been further aided by the eloquent landforms map of the late Erwin Raisz and the suggestions of R. E. Lawrence, M. M. Miller, and J. E. Allen.

The Vegetation map was prepared from the sources noted in the text together with data from Küchler (1964) and, for Oregon, an analysis of 26 satellite images taken in the summer of 1973 by Landsat-1 from an altitude of about 910 km. Additional interpretation was based on existing vegetation maps and field experience.

Units of Measurement

English units of measurement are used throughout, with metric equivalents noted the first time a unit is used in each section. The editors regret any inconvenience caused by this solution to the ongoing problem of partial metrication.

Photo Credits

page 1—Oregon Department of Transportation; *page 3*—U.S. Department of Agriculture, Soil Conservation Service; OSU Publications Office; *page 4*—Jeff Grass; Tom Gentle; *page 9*—Oregon Historical Society; *page 14*— Oregon Historical Society; *page 16*—University of Washington; *page 28*—American Forest Institute; *page 29*—Oregon Department of Transportation; *page 34*—OSU Forest Research Lab; *page 39*—Photoart Commercial Studio; *page 41*—Oregon State Highway Department, Travel Division; *page 42*—Oregon National Guard; Idaho Department of Commerce and Development; *page 43*—Oregon Department of Transportation; *page 44*—John S. Shelton (two photographs); Phil Jackson; *page 48*—OSU Forest Research Lab; *page 52*— Oregon Department of Transportation; *page 54*—NASA; *page 55*—OSU Agricultural Experiment Station; *page 58*—Ed Jensen; *page 74*—*Oregon Department of Transportation; page 75*—U.S. Department of the Interior; *page 79*—Crown Zellerbach Corporation; *page 84*—Jeff Grass; *page 85*—OSU Agricultural Communications; *page 89*—AES Communications, OSU; *page 92*—AES Communications, OSU; *page 94*—OSU Agricultural Communications; *page 95*—AES Communications, OSU; *page 96*—AES Communications, OSU; OSU Agricultural Communications; *page 97*—U.S. Department of Agriculture, Soil Conservation Service; *page 99*—OSU Forest Research Lab; *page 100*—OSU Forest Research Lab; *page 102*—OSU Forest Research Lab; *page 105*—photographer unknown; *page 107*—OSU Publications Office; *page 115*—Fardell-Loren Photography; *page 121*—Jeff Grass; *page 122*—Steelcase Inc.; *page 124*—OSU Publications Office; *page 126*— Oregon State Highway Commission; *page 129*—Tom Gentle; *page 134*—Phil Jackson; *page 135*—Oregon Department of Transportation.

The Region

A. Jon Kimerling

The Pacific Northwest, as we define it, consists of the states of Idaho, Oregon, and Washington. Physically, parts of the region differ markedly from each other— the sagebrush desert landscape of eastern Oregon and Washington, the Rocky Mountains and lava fields of Idaho, the rugged coastline and sand dunes of the Oregon coast, the wheatlands of eastern Washington, the alpine landforms of the Wallowa Mountains of Oregon, Washington's northern Cascades, and the Olympic Range, the rainforests of the Olympic peninsula. The climate of the region also varies widely, including the mild wet coastal region, the dry sunny summers and wet mild winters of the western lowlands, and the wide temperature ranges and low precipitation totals of the intermontane region. Lifestyles, values, and politics differ widely, too.

The western portions of Washington and Oregon have more in common than the western and eastern parts of either state. Similar differences are apparent between northern Idaho and the more populous Snake River Plain. In Oregon and Washington, most economic development has occurred and most government institutions are located in the lowlands between the Coast Range and the Cascade Mountains. In Idaho, the Snake River Plain and the Boise region in particular have achieved governmental and economic dominance, creating a dichotomy between mountain and valley which parallels that between east and west in the coastal states.

Politically, too, the region is a mixed bag. Traditional conservative values, emphasizing independence and individual freedom, hard work and patriotism, are strong and widespread, reflecting the original pioneer spirit of early settlers and the geographical and cultural isolation of the region. Recently the region has acquired a more liberal reputation, particularly on environmental issues and "livability." Oregon is perceived as leading the nation in environmental legislation. The 1972 Bottle Bill, requiring a returnable deposit on certain bottles and cans, attempted to conserve resources, to reduce visual pollution, and to reduce solid wastes. A year later, the legislature mandated statewide land-use planning to guide urban development and to preserve agricultural and environmental values of the state. Both pieces of legislation have generally enjoyed support in the pop-

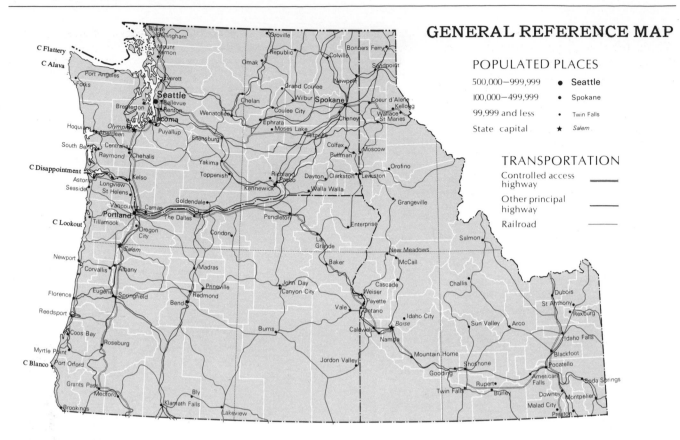

GENERAL REFERENCE MAP

POPULATED PLACES

500,000–999,999	● Seattle
100,000–499,999	● Spokane
99,999 and less	· Twin Falls
State capital	★ Salem

TRANSPORTATION

Controlled access highway

Other principal highway

Railroad

Table 1. Physical Dimensions of the Pacific Northwest

	Washington		Oregon		Idaho	
Land area	66,570 mi²	172,350 km²	96,184 mi²	249,020 km²	82,677 mi²	214,051 km²
Water area	1,622 mi²	4,199 km²	797 mi²	2,063 km²	880 mi²	2,278 km²
Coastline[a]	157mi	253 km	296 mi	476 km		
Tidal shoreline[b]	3,026 mi	4,869 km	1,410 mi	2,269 km		

[a] Length of general outline of coastline.

[b] Length of outer coast, offshore islands, sounds, bays, rivers, and creeks to head of tidewater.

ulous Willamette Valley. To some in Idaho, the establishment of one of the largest tracts of wilderness in the "lower 48" states is a source of intense controversy, while the presence of a Trident submarine base in the Hood Canal in Washington also causes disagreement between those who argue that the base means employment opportunities and those who fear that the Puget lowland has become a prime nuclear target.

Current economic problems are eroding the environmental lobby's support and strengthening calls for diversifying the region's economic base, which has traditionally relied on primary production, especially forest products and agriculture. Commercial timberlands cover 36% of the region's land area, producing about half the nation's softwood lumber and plywood. About 32% of land area is in farms, of which 59% is used for livestock grazing and the remainder as cropland. The leading

agricultural commodities by value are cattle, calves, and wheat, but specialty crops—including filberts, potatoes, apples, pears, grass seed, and mint—are locally important. With economic problems facing both the forest products industry and farming in the region, diversifying the economy to include high-tech industries is seen as the hope for the future. The Hanford Nuclear Reservation in Washington is, in 1985, one of three areas being considered as a national nuclear waste depository. And despite major cutbacks in the forest products industry, clearcuts scar the natural beauty of the region.

Nevertheless, much of the region is stunningly beautiful and remarkably unspoiled. Population density is low, despite four decades of net immigration. Though the total land area of the region is approximately 250,000 square miles (65 million hectares), representing 6.8% of the area of the U.S. (including Alaska), the region's population represents only 3% of the national total. Within the region, population is unevenly distributed, due in part to the high proportion of land in public ownership. More than half the region's population lives in the Seattle area or the Willamette Valley.

Geographically, the entire region is isolated. Portland, for instance, is 2,883 miles (4,642 kilometers) from New York by road, and less than twice this distance from Tokyo, Moscow, and Paris. And perhaps this explains the fact that there is an intangible cohesion to the region, an underlying characteristic that we recognize as the Pacific Northwest. Despite our differences, the gulf between us and everyone else is sufficiently great that we draw together. We share concerns even if we do not agree about solutions. Our issues are the opposing demands of employment for loggers and millworkers on the one hand and conservation of our forests on the other. Productivity in the forests and concern over toxic sprays. Energy supply and demand and the WPPPS fiasco. Fisheries disputes. Rajneeshpuram. And, for those of us west of the mountains, the rain. Our concerns mean little to those outside the region and this relative lack of interest draws us together, like members of a family.

Table 2. Distance from Geographic Center of the Pacific Northwest to Selected World Metropolis[a]

	Distance	
	mi	km
Auckland	7,117	11,461
Bangkok	7,633	12,291
Beijing	5,589	9,000
Berlin	5,054	8,138
Bombay	7,879	12,687
Buenos Aires	6,709	10,803
Cairo	6,842	11,018
Calcutta	7,398	11,913
Cape Town	10,047	16,179
Caracas	3,897	6,275
Djakarta	8,587	13,828
Essen-Duisburg-Bochum	4,956	7,981
Hong Kong	6,673	10,745
Istanbul	6,088	9,803
Leningrad	4,895	7,883
London	4,762	7,669
Manila	6,844	11,021
Mexico City	2,155	3,470
Montreal	2,137	3,441
Moscow	5,237	8,466
Nairobi	8,997	14,488
Osaka-Kobe	5,203	8,378
Paris	4,972	8,007
Rio de Janeiro	6,702	10,793
Rome	5,654	9,104
Sao Paulo	6,589	10,610
Shanghai	5,908	9,514
Sydney	7,871	12,675
Tehran	6,742	10,856
Tokyo	4,975	8,012

[a] Great circle distance.

PACIFIC NORTHWEST
COUNTIES

Table 3. Areas of Pacific Northwest Counties

Idaho County	mi²	km²	Oregon County	mi²	km²	Washington County	mi²	km²
Ada	1,043	2,701	Baker	3,068	7,946	Adams	1,894	4,905
Adams	1,371	3,551	Benton	668	1,730	Asotin	633	1,639
Bannock	1,122	2,906	Clackamas	1,884	4,880	Benton	1,722	4,460
Bear Lake	984	2,549	Clatsop	805	2,085	Chelan	2,918	7,558
Benewah	788	2,041	Columbia	639	1,655	Clallam	1,753	4,540
Bingham	2,084	5,398	Coos	1,604	4,154	Clark	627	1,624
Blaine	2,647	6,856	Crook	2,975	7,705	Columbia	853	2,209
Boise	1,910	4,947	Curry	1,627	4,214	Cowlitz	1,144	2,963
Bonner	1,733	4,488	Deschutes	3,031	7,850	Douglas	1,831	4,742
Bonneville	1,836	4,755	Douglas	5,063	13,113	Ferry	2,202	5,703
Boundary	1,275	3,302	Gilliam	1,208	3,129	Franklin	1,253	3,245
Butte	2,239	5,799	Grant	4,530	11,733	Garfield	709	1,836
Camas	1,054	2,730	Harney	10,166	26,330	Grant	2,675	6,928
Canyon	578	1,497	Hood River	523	1,355	Grays Harbor	1,910	4,947
Caribou	1,746	4,522	Jackson	2,812	7,283	Island	212	549
Cassia	2,544	6,589	Jefferson	1,793	4,644	Jefferson	1,805	4,675
Clark	1,751	4,535	Josephine	1,625	4,209	King	2,128	5,511
Clearwater	2,521	6,529	Klamath	5,970	15,462	Kitsap	393	1,018
Custer	4,929	12,766	Lake	8,231	21,318	Kittitas	2,317	6,001
Elmore	3,048	7,894	Lane	4,552	11,790	Klickitat	1,908	4,942
Franklin	664	1,720	Lincoln	986	2,554	Lewis	2,423	6,276
Fremont	1,864	4,828	Linn	2,283	5,913	Lincoln	2,306	5,973
Gem	555	1,437	Malheur	9,859	25,535	Mason	962	2,492
Gooding	720	1,865	Marion	1,166	3,020	Okanogan	5,301	13,730
Idaho	8,516	22,057	Morrow	2,060	5,335	Pacific	908	2,352
Jefferson	1,096	2,839	Multnomah	423	1,096	Pend Oreille	1,402	3,631
Jerome	595	1,541	Polk	736	1,906	Pierce	1,676	4,341
Kootenai	1,249	3,235	Sherman	830	2,150	San Juan	179	464
Latah	1,090	2,823	Tillamook	1,115	2,888	Skagit	1,735	4,494
Lemhi	4,580	11,862	Umatilla	3,227	8,358	Skamania	1,672	4,330
Lewis	476	1,233	Union	2,032	5,263	Snohomish	2,098	5,434
Lincoln	1,203	3,116	Wallowa	3,178	8,231	Spokane	1,758	4,553
Madison	473	1,225	Wasco	2,381	6,167	Stevens	2,481	6,426
Minidoka	750	1,943	Washington	716	1,854	Thurston	714	1,849
Nez Perce	844	2,186	Wheeler	1,707	4,421	Wahkiakum	261	676
Oneida	1,191	3,085	Yamhill	711	1,841	Walla Walla	1,262	3,269
Owyhee	7,641	19,790				Whatcom	2,126	5,506
Payette	402	1,041				Whitman	2,153	5,576
Power	1,413	3,660				Yakima	4,268	11,054
Shoshone	2,609	6,757						
Teton	457	1,184						
Twin Falls	1,947	5,043						
Valley	3,676	9,521						
Washington	1,462	3,787						

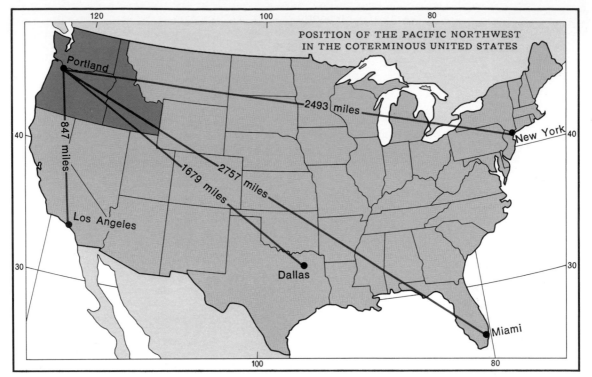

POSITION OF THE PACIFIC NORTHWEST
IN THE COTERMINOUS UNITED STATES

Table 4. Distances to Major U.S. Cities

	Boise				Portland				Seattle			
	Road[a]		Air[b]		Road		Air		Road		Air	
	mi	km	mi	km	mi	km	mi	km	mi	km	mi	km
Anchorage	3,007	4,843	1,829	2,946	2,716	4,373	1,509	2,430	2,544	4,097	1,386	2,232
Atlanta	2,172	3,498	1,834	2,954	2,599	4,185	2,218	3,572	2,616	4,212	2,252	3,627
Boston	2,637	4,246	2,256	3,633	3,044	4,901	2,582	4,158	2,973	4,788	2,560	4,122
Chicago	1,682	2,708	1,451	2,336	2,082	3,352	1,805	2,907	2,011	3,239	1,810	2,914
Cincinnati	1,905	3,067	1,664	2,679	2,331	3,754	2,029	3,268	2,298	3,701	2,041	3,287
Dallas	1,580	2,545	1,291	2,079	2,007	3,232	1,678	2,702	2,077	3,344	1,747	2,814
Denver	810	1,305	640	1,030	1,237	1,992	1,029	1,657	1,306	2,103	1,088	1,752
Detroit	1,941	3,125	1,662	2,677	2,347	3,780	2,006	3,231	2,277	3,667	2,000	3,221
Helena	486	782	290	467	658	1,059	563	907	587	946	563	907
Honolulu	-------	-------	2,833	4,562	-------	-------	2,552	4,109	-------	-------	2,616	4,212
Houston	1,777	2,861	1,495	2,407	2,203	3,548	1,879	3,025	2,272	3,659	1,954	3,147
Kansas City	1,381	2,224	1,163	1,873	1,808	2,911	1,544	2,486	1,838	2,959	1,577	2,539
Los Angeles	848	1,366	674	1,086	958	1,543	846	1,363	1,130	1,820	985	1,586
Memphis	1,831	2,948	1,510	2,430	2,257	3,635	1,895	3,052	2,288	3,685	1,934	3,115
Miami	2,827	4,552	2,365	3,809	3,253	5,239	2,755	4,436	3,270	5,266	2,804	4,515
Minneapolis	1,404	2,261	1,137	1,831	1,677	2,700	1,473	2,372	1,607	2,587	1,467	2,362
New Orleans	2,077	3,344	1,715	2,761	2,503	4,031	2,105	3,389	2,572	4,142	2,165	3,487
New York	2,476	3,987	2,151	3,464	2,883	4,642	2,491	4,011	2,813	4,529	2,479	3,992
Philadelphia	2,408	3,878	2,105	3,390	2,819	4,539	2,451	3,947	2,749	4,426	2,444	3,936
Phoenix	950	1,530	737	1,186	1,265	2,037	1,036	1,669	1,436	2,312	1,155	1,860
Pierre, SD	1,058	1,704	791	1,274	1,352	2,177	1,141	1,837	1,282	2,064	1,150	1,852
Pittsburgh	2,120	3,414	1,857	2,991	2,533	4,079	2,208	3,556	2,463	3,966	2,206	3,553
Raleigh, NC	2,425	3,905	2,052	3,305	2,852	4,592	2,422	3,900	2,795	4,500	2,437	3,924
Reno	428	690	338	545	540	870	458	738	712	1,147	594	957
St. Louis	1,631	2,627	1,389	2,237	2,059	3,315	1,766	2,843	2,079	3,348	1,790	2,883
Salt Lake City	340	547	299	481	766	1,234	680	1,096	835	1,345	760	1,224
San Diego	940	1,514	745	1,199	1,083	1,744	945	1,521	1,255	2,021	1,081	1,741
San Francisco	658	1,059	520	837	635	1,023	540	870	807	1,300	686	1,104
Santa Fe	957	1,541	799	1,287	1,377	2,217	1,170	1,884	1,456	2,328	1,260	2,029
Washington DC	2,3431	3,770	2,046	3,295	2,752	4,431	2,400	3,865	2,682	4,319	2,401	3,866

[a] Shortest major road distance.   [b] Great circle distance.

THE PACIFIC NORTHWEST IN THE WORLD

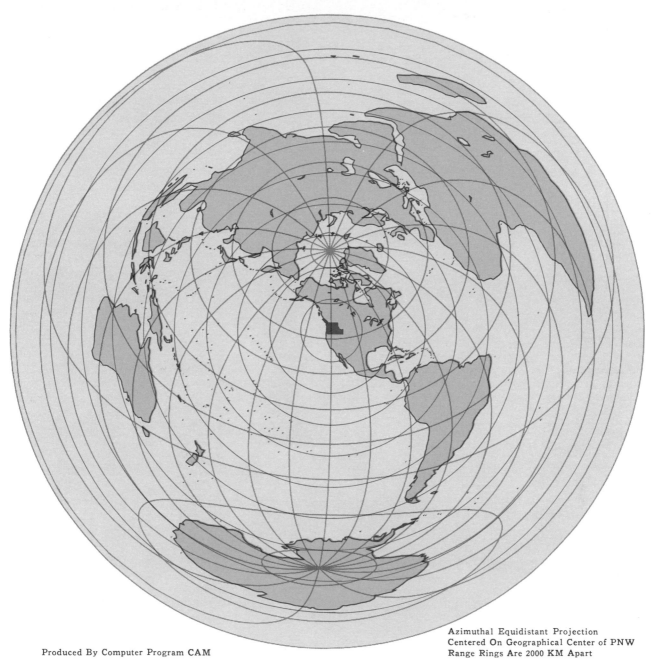

Produced By Computer Program CAM

Azimuthal Equidistant Projection
Centered On Geographical Center of PNW
Range Rings Are 2000 KM Apart

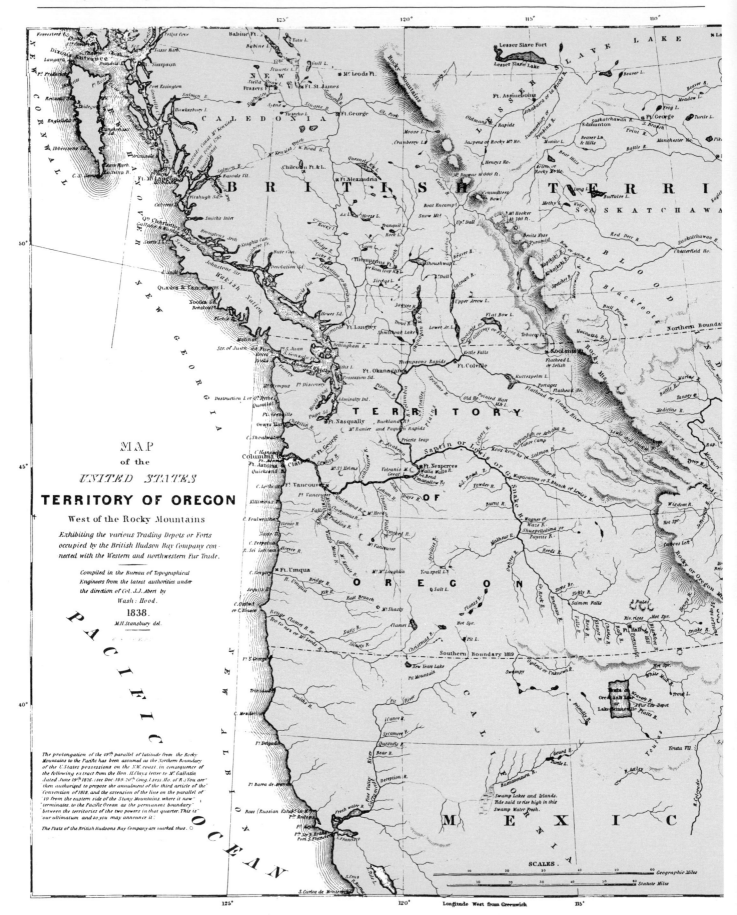

MAP
of the
UNITED STATES
TERRITORY OF OREGON
West of the Rocky Mountains

Exhibiting the various Trading Depots or Forts
occupied by the British Hudson Bay Company con-
nected with the Western and northwestern Fur Trade.

Compiled in the Bureau of Topographical
Engineers from the latest authorities under
the direction of Col. J.J. Abert by
Wash: Hood.
1838.
M.H.Stansbury del.

The prolongation of the 19th parallel of latitude from the Rocky
Mountains to the Pacific has been assumed as the Northern Boundary
of the U.States possessions on the N.W. coast, in consequence of
the following extract from the Hon. H.Clays letter to Mr Gallatin
dated June 19th 1826. (see Doc.199.20th Cong.I.sess.Ho. of R.)You are
then authorised to propose the annulment of the third article of the
Convention of 1818, and the extension of the line on the parallel of
19 from the eastern side of the Stony Mountains where it now
"terminates, to the Pacific Ocean as the permanent boundary
between the territories of the two powers in that quarter. This is
our ultimatum and so you may announce it.

The Posts of the British Hudsons Bay Company are marked thus . O

Historical Background: Discovery and Early Settlement

J. Kenneth Munford

Three prominent physical features, the Cascade Range, the Columbia River, and the Strait of Juan de Fuca, have had much to do with the cultural development of the Pacific Northwest.

The rugged Cascades have been at once a benefit and a barrier. They drain moisture from the westerly winds and give the seaward side of the region adequate rainfall, a mild climate, and lush vegetation. They shield this area from the extremes of the continental climate that sweep across the eastern part of the region. At the same time, they deprive the eastern part of moisture that would be gratefully received.

The Cascade Range has long also been a barrier to human movement. The earliest inhabitants no doubt found the jumble of cliffs, canyons, and dense forest difficult to traverse and inhospitable as a permanent abode. Fur trappers from Europe probed the streams on either side looking for beaver but made no well-worn trails. For the covered-wagon immigrants the Cascades were the most difficult barrier they had encountered in crossing half a continent—but they were also the last rampart to be overcome before entering the Willamette Valley and Puget Lowlands.

Long ago the Columbia River broke through this Cascade Range barrier almost to sea level, providing a passageway through the mountains and a network of waterways a thousand miles into the interior. Lewis and Clark, the first white explorers to cross the region, used the Columbia as their channel. So did David Thompson, who came a few years later over the Canadian Rockies and down the Columbia to its mouth.

To the experienced boatmen of these exploring parties and those of the fur traders who soon followed, the rapids, narrows, and waterfalls of the mid-Columbia were only a minor nuisance. To immigrants from the Oregon Trail who tried to get through them on rafts, they were a disaster. Equipment, cattle, and human lives were lost in the boisterous rapids of the Columbia Gorge.

Mariners approaching from the west likewise found the Columbia not always friendly. Where the silt-laden run-off from three states pours into the pounding surf of the Pacific, a shifting bar of sand made entry treacherous and dangerous in the early days. Many ships have been wrecked and many lives lost on the notorious Columbia Bar.

By contrast, the Strait of Juan de Fuca is a placid, sea-level channel leading into a deep, land-locked basin gouged out by glaciers in the Ice Age. A labyrinth of waterways winds among thousands of islands. Protected harbors, easy access to the sea, and vast resources provided the base for early commercial and industrial development.

Native People

Anthropologists tell us that the first human inhabitants of the New World reached Alaska from Siberia over a land bridge. These aborigines are believed to have pushed gradually southeastward through central North America, so that the people who came to the Pacific Northwest would have traveled westward over the Rocky Mountains, across Idaho and eastern Oregon and Washington, over the Cascade Range or through the Columbia Gorge to the western valleys. Some may have come into Puget Sound by water, through the inland passage along the coast of British Columbia.

The tribes into which they developed are classified by anthropologists according to the similarity of language of the different groups. Different cultural types developed in response to the particular locality in which they made their homes.

Unidentified ship (probably the *Commodore*) crossing the Columbia River Bar.

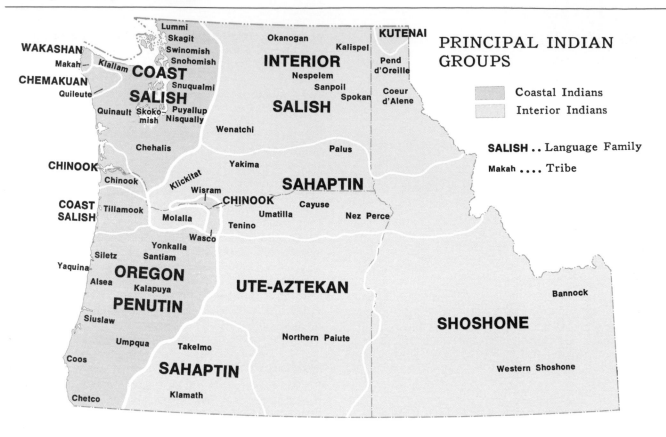

PRINCIPAL INDIAN GROUPS

Coastal Indians

Interior Indians

SALISH .. Language Family

Makah .... Tribe

When did these people arrive in the Pacific Northwest? New information—geological, climatological, biological, and cultural—gives fresh insight into the chronology of occupation. Carbon-dating and other scientific techniques indicate the presence of humans in the Snake River Plain 8,000 years ago, possibly as long ago as 14,500 B.P. (before the present). People fished along the Columbia 11,000 to 7,500 years ago. Families occupied Fort Rock sites in central Oregon for 11,000 years, one of them 13,000 years ago. Sites have been dated in the Willamette Valley at 8,000 B.P. and 4,000 B.P. and on the Oregon coast at 3,000 B.P. Archeologists believe the Puget Lowlands may have been occupied sparsely as long as 10,000 years ago.

These aboriginal people had no form of agriculture and no domesticated animals, except the dog, until the Spaniards introduced horses into America. They lived by hunting, fishing, and gathering. The people who lived west of the Cascade Mountains depended largely on seafood—salmon, shellfish, and seals—supplemented by berries and roots. They built substantial wooden houses, often big enough for a number of families, clustered into small villages.

East of the Cascades, hunting provided a larger proportion of the diet, though fish and roots were also significant, especially to the Nez Percé and other tribes with access to the salmon of the Columbia River. Surprisingly, since the climate is harsh in this region, housing was not substantial, though more clothes were worn by members of these tribes than by the Coast Indians.

Estimates vary greatly on how many natives were living in the Pacific Northwest when Europeans first came. There may have been 75,000 or twice that number, divided into perhaps 125 tribal groups. One thing is known for sure. Their numbers decreased rapidly in only a few decades, not so much from open warfare with the invading whites but from an insidious form of unpremeditated biological warfare. The Europeans brought with them new diseases, such as smallpox, cholera, and measles, to which they had developed resistance or partial immunity but to which the Indians had no immunity.

As early as 1788, Captain Robert Gray from Boston noted pock-marked faces among the natives. In the winter of 1805-1806, Captain Clark of the Lewis and Clark expedition wrote at Fort Clatsop, "The small pox has destroyed a great number of the natives of this quarter." The one-eyed Chinook chieftain Concomly, who befriended both the Lewis and Clark people and Astorians six years later, saw many of his people die and he himself succumbed in the epidemics of 1829-1830.

By the time the great migrations flowed into the Willamette Valley in the 1840s and 1850s, only a few scattered remnants of the native population remained in that vicinity. In the drier areas of eastern Washington and Oregon and southern Idaho, the horse-owning nomadic tribes offered greater resistance, not only to the white man's diseases but to the white man himself.

Contact of Cultures

As the two cultures met in the Oregon Country there were many instances of violence but also many friendly relationships with mutual assistance and respect. The first European explorers along the coast had no contact with the natives. As part of Spain's expansion throughout the western hemisphere in the 16th and 17th centuries, her ships cruised as far north as the Oregon border in 1542 and 1543 and farther north in 1603. Finding no indication of riches of the type they were draining from Central and South America, the Spaniards did not publicize or continue these explorations until many years later.

The English also kept their first voyage to the Pacific, that of Francis Drake in 1579, secret for a while, but eventually announced that he had landed on the west coast and taken possession of what he called New Albion for Queen Elizabeth. Mapmakers continued to use this name for the area north of California for more than 200 years (see 1838 map on page 8).

Spain and England took little interest in this remote wilderness for more than a century, but when news leaked out that the Russians had crossed Siberia and were trading in Alaska the Spaniards became concerned. They considered this entire region their possession and came again to explore, protect, and possibly to colonize it.

Juan Perez received a friendly reception among the natives on the west coast of Vancouver Island. He did not land on the Washington coast but did sail close enough to see Mt. Olympus and name it Santa Rosalia. That was in 1774.

The next year—while dramatic events occurred on the other side of the continent as the English colonists began their war for independence—two more ships, the *Sonora* and the *Santiago,* came up the west coast from Mexico. At Point Trinidad on the Washington coast they met congenial natives who watched them and even took part in the ceremony as the Spaniards erected a large cross and took possession of the land in the name of Carlos III, King of Spain.

The ships anchored southwest of the Olympic Peninsula. Early on the morning of July 14, 1775, Bruno Hezeta, captain of the *Santiago,* Father Sierra, twenty armed men, and others went ashore at what the English later named Point Grenville. The Hezeta party erected a cross and again proclaimed possession for King Carlos. Having completed the first landings by Europeans on what is now the Washington coast, they hurried back to the ship because of threatening weather. Later, on that same voyage, Hezeta recognized the mouth of the long-sought River of the West but did not attempt to enter.

Coming of the Traders

Next came the most significant voyage of the 18th century for the Pacific Northwest. In 1778, the English captain, James Cook, with two ships, came to chart the coast from Oregon to the Arctic and to determine whether or not a passage existed through North America to the Atlantic. He and his companions did not find such a passage, but what they did find was of immense importance. They discovered the Sandwich Islands (Hawaii), which in future years became a regular stopping place for ships plying between the Asiatic and the northwest coast. They also discovered by accident that furs they had purchased for clothing and bedding from friendly natives at Nootka Sound in British Columbia could be sold at immense profit in China.

The British Admiralty provided wide publicity for Cook's accomplishments. His journals, charts, and illustrations were published in 1784 and, earlier, two surreptitious accounts by crew members had appeared—Lt. Rickman's in London and Corporal John Ledyard's in Connecticut. News of the fortunes that could be made in the fur trade fired the imagination of adventurous merchants on both sides of the Atlantic.

The first trader to arrive was John Hanna in 1785. He sold 560 sea otter pelts in Macao, China, for 20,400 Spanish dollars. The next year a half dozen more English ships and one French expedition arrived.

The *Imperial Eagle,* a trading ship flying the Austrian flag but with an English crew, arrived in 1787. The young captain, Charles Barkley, 26, brought along his teenage bride, Frances Hornby Trevor, 17, who became the first white woman to visit the northwest coast.

They traded at Friendly Cove in Nootka Sound and at Barkley Sound—named for them—and made a discovery at the southern tip of Vancouver Island. "To our great astonishment," Frances Barkley wrote, "we arrived off a large opening extending eastward . . . which my husband immediately recognized as the long-lost Strait of Juan de Fuca, and to which he gave the name of the original discoverer."

The Juan de Fuca legend dates from 1622, when an unreliable account published in England told of a Greek sailor, Apostolos Valerianos, using the name Juan de Fuca, who had visited the northwest coast in 1592 on a Spanish ship. He told of discovering a passageway into an inland sea. Mapmakers began showing the Strait of Juan de Fuca at 48-49° north latitude as the opening into the River of the West. But until the Barkleys came along nearly two hundred years later no one had been able to find it.

Later Voyages

The first Americans. Robert Gray in the *Lady Washington* and John Kendrick in the *Columbia Rediviva* arrived from Boston in 1788. Merchants of the infant U.S., with their established patterns of trade disrupted by independence from England, were eager to establish new ones. The Americans had certain advantages in the Pacific fur trade because they were not obliged to respect the monopolies England had set up to protect its own merchants. Indeed, because of the mercantile system of the British, a number of enterprising Englishmen sailed under the flags of other nations, principally Austria and Portugal, to avoid obtaining licenses and paying

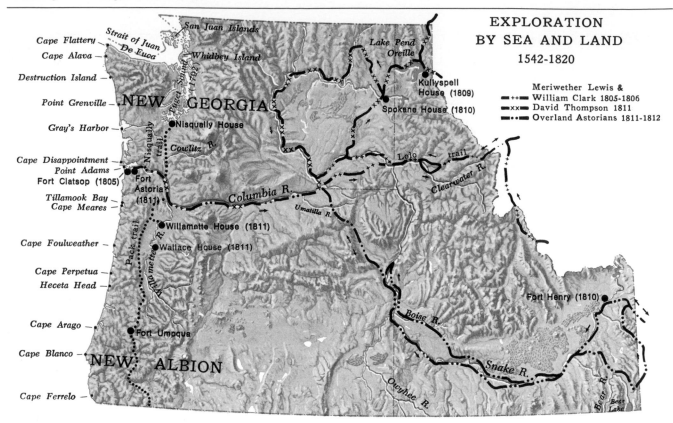

EXPLORATION
BY SEA AND LAND
1542-1820

Meriwether Lewis &
━━++━━ William Clark 1805-1806
━━xx━━ David Thompson 1811
━━••━━ Overland Astorians 1811-1812

duties to the East India Company or the South Sea Company. All the Americans or other privateers needed to do was to avoid the Spaniards on the southern coasts; trade for furs on the northwest coast; take the furs to China and trade them for tea, silks, porcelains, spices, and other Oriental products; and sell these goods at Atlantic ports, reaping a double profit in the process.

In August 1788, Robert Gray in the *Lady Washington* touched the Pacific coast just south of the Oregon border and did a little trading. It was here that he noticed pock-marked natives—a sign that they had already made contact with western civilization. Near the present Lincoln City on the Oregon coast, he set up "traffic on a very friendly footing" with natives who came out to the ship and "purchased a number of good sea otter skins for knives, axes, adzes, etca." When a party went ashore in Murderers' Harbor (Tillamook Bay), a scrap with the natives resulted in the death of Gray's personal servant, Marcos Lopez, the first black of record in the Pacific Northwest.

At Nootka Sound, Gray met the flamboyant John Meares, a former British naval officer, who that summer had confirmed Barkley's discovery of the Strait of Juan de Fuca. He had looked for the River of the West but found only Cape Disappointment. Meares had two ships at Nootka and was building a third. Gray was present for the launching of *North West America,* the first ship built on the northwest coast. Gray's partner John Kendrick soon arrived in the *Columbia Rediviva.* Trading was not too good. The Americans decided to remain for the winter at Friendly Cove.

The next year, 1789, Gray took the *Columbia* to China with the furs they had collected and sold them, but not at the high prices obtained by the previous traders because of the glutted market. In returning to the United States, Gray continued on westward and became the first to carry the Stars and Stripes around the world.

Spanish expeditions. In the interim between Gray's first and second voyages, Spaniards made their most extensive, and what proved to be their last, expeditions into Washington waters. Manuel Quimper explored the Strait of Juan de Fuca in the summer of 1790. Near Victoria, Indians to whom he had given presents told him in sign language that there was much water beyond, wide channels trending both northeast and southeast.

The next summer (1791) Francisco de Eliza explored the Strait. His ships penetrated through the San Juan Islands and entered Bellingham Bay. They did not explore far either north or south; Eliza still had the idea that there must be a navigable waterway through the American continent and kept probing eastward.

Later English and American surveyors disregarded most of the names the Spaniards gave to the places they had discovered, but a few reminders of this period remain, including Port Angeles, Cape Alva, Quimper Peninsula, and Lopez, Orcas, Patos, and San Juan Islands.

The voyage of the Discovery. In 1791 the British Admiralty sent George Vancouver, who had sailed earlier with Cook, to survey the northwest coast in the sloop *Discovery.* He arrived off the Washington coast in

April 1792, and early on the morning of the 29th sighted a sail, the first they had seen in eight months, which proved to be Robert Gray in *Columbia Rediviva.*

The two expeditions sailed north together to the entrance of the Juan de Fuca Strait, then Gray sailed south after trading with the natives. The English moved inland through the amazing labyrinth of waterways, naming many locations including Mt. Rainier, Bellingham Bay, and Puget Sound.

On board the *Discovery* was surgeon/naturalist Archibald Menzies, who identified new species of plants such as the madrona, the rhododendron that became the state flower of Washington, the flowering dogwood, and the Douglas-fir. Vancouver was enthusiastic: "The serenity of the climate, the innumerable pleasing landscapes, and the abundant fertility that unassisted nature puts forth, require only to be enriched by the industry of man with villages, mansions, cottages, and other buildings, to render it the most lovely country that can be imagined."

The River of the West. Meanwhile, to the south, Captain Gray with difficulty located the mouth of the River of the West—now the Columbia River—and with greater difficulty succeeded in crossing through the continuous breakers at the mouth. "The beach was lin'd with natives who ran along the shore following the ship," wrote John Boit, one of the crew members. "Soon after, about 20 canoes came off, and brought a good lot of furs and salmon, which last they sold two for a board nail. The furs we likewise bought cheap, for Copper and Cloth. They appear'd to view the ship with the greatest astonishment and no doubt we was the first civilized people that they ever saw."

Overland Explorers

The Napoleonic Wars (1800-1815) kept the Spanish, French, and English busy in Europe for two decades, and the maritime fur trade became mostly an American enterprise. Between 1794 and 1814, only a dozen British ships came to the northwest, while American merchants sent ninety.

Meanwhile, fur seekers and explorers approached the Pacific Northwest overland. In 1670 Charles II had given his cousin Prince Rupert and seventeen other English noblemen a charter extending to them the exclusive right to govern, control traffic in, and trade in the land that drained into Hudson's Bay. The corporation they founded—the Hudson's Bay Company—had set up posts throughout "Rupert's Land." Resisting this monopoly, a group of Canadians who had been gathering furs around the Great Lakes formed their own concern, the North West Company of Montreal. A partner in this company, Alexander Mackenzie, crossed Canada to the Pacific in 1793, with six French-Canadians and two Indians. This was the first crossing of the continent north of Mexico.

After the Louisiana Purchase, President Jefferson sent his secretary Meriwether Lewis and Captain William Clark as co-leaders of a Corps of Discovery to traverse the new purchase and if possible penetrate to the Pacific. Among those traveling with Lewis and Clark were French-Canadian interpreter and guide Charbonneau, his Indian wife Sacajawea, and their infant son who was born early on the journey. Their famous expedition to the mouth of the Columbia and back (1804-1806) gave the United States a good claim to the Oregon Country.

Competition Between the Traders

John Jacob Astor, whose American Fur Company had been operating successfully on the eastern side of the Rocky Mountains, sent two parties to the Columbia in 1810, one by sea, one overland.

Learning of the Astor enterprise, the North West Company tried to extend their operations to the west coast. A partner, David Thompson, who was a geographer as well as a trader, moved over the Canadian Rockies establishing posts and then sped down the Columbia by canoe with eight of his men, exploring and mapping as he went. By the time he reached the mouth of the Columbia in July 1811, however, he found the Stars and Stripes already unfurled at Astoria. Astor's ship, the *Tonquin,* had arrived in March. Thompson received a friendly welcome from Astor's men, many of whom were former associates in the Canadian company.

The overland Astorians, led by partner Wilson Price Hunt, were Americans, Scots, and French-Canadians. They too brought along an interpreter/guide, Pierre Dorion, and his wife, Marie, the second woman to cross the mountains from the Missouri to the Columbia. The Dorions brought along two young sons and Marie gave birth to a third after they reached eastern Oregon. Hunt's party, not as well prepared or equipped as the Lewis and Clark expedition, suffered many privations along the way. Most of them straggled into Astoria in the early months of 1812.

One of the overlanders, Donald "Perpetual Motion" McKenzie, a 300-pound Scot, took an exploring party into the Willamette Valley—"garden of the Columbia" —where he traveled as far south as the river named for him. Two of those accompanying him, Etienne Lucier and Joseph Gervais, twenty years later became the first independent farmers in the Pacific Northwest.

During the War of 1812 between America and Britain, Duncan McDougall, an Astor partner, feared that Astoria and the furs which the company had collected would be taken by force. He therefore sold them to the North West Company and many of the Astor employees went to work for the new owners. Although the treaty which ended the war provided that Astoria should be returned to the Americans, Astor was no longer interested and it remained in British hands.

Competition between the Hudson's Bay and North West companies was vicious and led to a state of virtual warfare between the rivals. Liquor was commonly used as a medium of exchange with the Indians, and destructive trapping practices were prevalent. Heads of the two

The *Tonquin* crossing the Columbia River Bar March 25, 1811.

companies finally agreed in 1821 to combine into a new Hudson's Bay Company, whose monopolistic privileges were extended to the Pacific.

Hudson's Bay Company in Control

At one time or another five nations claimed the Oregon Country—Spain, Russia, France, England, and the U.S. By 1818 only England and the U.S. remained in contention. They agreed at that time on "joint occupancy," which provided that west of the Rockies, north of Mexico and south of Russian Alaska, the area would be "free and open to the vessels, citizens, and subjects of both for ten years."

In the decade 1818-1828 the British—and the Hudson's Bay Company—remained in uncontested control. Traders spread out over the region, making friends among the natives by bringing them many desirable products: blankets, needles, awls, scissors, thread, beads, buttons, combs, yard goods, handkerchiefs, files, mirrors, fish hooks, knives, axes. Liquor was abandoned as a medium of exchange. Firearms were used only to a limited degree. In return the traders received the pelts of beavers, minks, bears, martens, otters, lynxes, raccoons, fishers, and wolverines.

The new Chief Factor for the Columbia District of the Hudson's Bay Company, Dr. John McLoughlin, a massively built Canadian of Scots, Irish, and French ancestry, moved the base of operations upriver to Fort Vancouver in 1825. He sent out brigades in all directions, along the Columbia and its tributaries, by pack trail to Puget Sound, south through the Willamette Valley, and through central Oregon to California. He reorganized a string of trading posts well up into British Columbia and east to the Continental Divide. He imported livestock and seed and started farms to produce food for local consumption and export to the Russians. He built mills to produce lumber and flour and industries to build ships, manufacture tools, and make clothing. Fort Vancouver became the industrial, commercial, political, and social center of the Pacific Northwest.

Settlements proliferated as McLoughlin permitted retiring employees to settle locally with their families rather than being returned to their place of recruitment. In 1829 Lucier and Gervais, who had come with the overland Astorians in 1812, were the first to move their families onto farms on French Prairie along the Willamette River. Others, mostly French-Canadians, followed. Thirty families were listed as living there in 1836, speaking French and still loyal to and somewhat dependent on the Old Company.

McLoughlin sent out brigades north into British Columbia, east into Idaho, southeast as far as Utah, and south as far as central California. He established purchasing and selling agencies at Yerba Buena (San Francisco) and in the Sandwich Islands (Hawaii).

Trade rivalry. In the ten years after renewal of the joint occupancy treaty in 1828, Americans began to take more interest in the Oregon Country. However, McLoughlin was very much in control and refused to permit the establishment of trading rivals in the region.

One attempt was made by Nathaniel Wyeth, a merchant from Massachusetts, who tried to establish a commercial operation along the Columbia in 1832. He sent a ship around Cape Horn and himself led a party across the continent. McLoughlin received the Americans graciously and gave one of them, John Ball, a Dartmouth graduate, a job teaching in the first school in the region. He gave Wyeth no help in establishing a rival business, however, and when his supply ship failed to arrive, Wyeth returned to New England.

Wyeth did not give up. He returned in 1834 and built Fort Hall (near Pocatello) and Fort William on Sauvie Island at the mouth of the Willamette. This time his supply ship arrived and for a time it looked as if he might gain a foothold, but overwhelming control of the region by Hudson's Bay Company finally discouraged him. He sold Fort Hall to Hudson's Bay Company, abandoned Fort Williams, and left the region.

Another group of Americans also arrived in 1834. Ewing Young, a Tennessean who had trapped and traded in the southwest, came north from California with fifteen others driving a herd of 150 horses and mules. Believing that the horses had been stolen, McLoughlin refused to let Young trade at any of the Hudson's Bay Company posts. Young was angered by this treatment and embarked on a project to make

whiskey. There were protests from, among others, the Methodists' Oregon Temperance Society and Hudson's Bay Company officers. Young was diverted from this project by a young naval lieutenant, William Slacum, whom President Andrew Jackson had sent to report on the American settlement. He encouraged the formation of the Willamette Cattle Company to buy livestock in California and drive them north to the Willamette Valley. Slacum subscribed $500 to the company and many of those who had protested the whiskey project also contributed. Ewing Young, his men, and others contributed their share by going to San Francisco with Slacum and driving back 630 cattle—the first of the long cattle drives that became legend in the far west.

Missionaries and Priests

When Wyeth returned to the Pacific Northwest in 1834, he brought with him Jason Lee and four other Methodist missionaries, who set up a school and mission in the Willamette Valley.

American settlement east of the Cascades began with another missionary group of five in 1836, including the first white women to come to the Pacific Northwest overland. Dr. Marcus and Narcissa Whitman, Reverend Henry H. and Eliza Spalding, and W. H. Gray built first among the Walla Walla and Cayuse tribes at Waiilatpu (near Walla Walla). The Spaldings then moved 90 miles east to start a school and farm among the Nez Percé at Lapwai (near Lewiston).

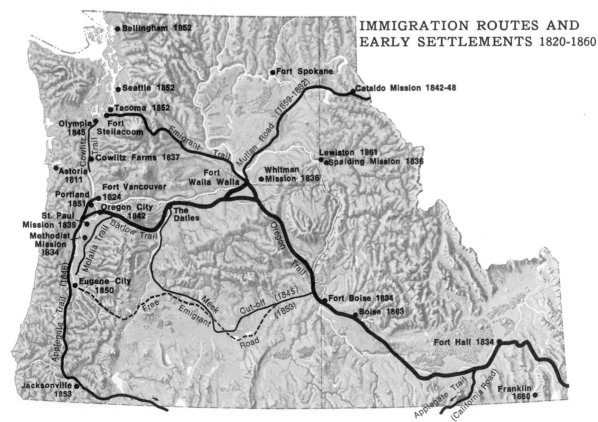

IMMIGRATION ROUTES AND
EARLY SETTLEMENTS 1820-1860

The Catholic French-Canadians had long desired the services of a priest. They had built a log chapel at St. Paul on French Prairie. In 1838 Hudson's Bay Company provided transportation for two priests who came with a brigade overland from eastern Canada, performing marriages, baptisms, and last rites along the way. A committee waited upon them at Fort Vancouver and invited them to come to the French settlement. They visited St. Paul in January 1839 and selected that location for their district headquarters.

The two priests and their reinforcements built chapels and designated cemeteries along the Hudson's Bay Company land and water routes. In 1863 a priest with the assistance of a skilled lay brother and unskilled Indians erected at Cataldo a remarkable church, the oldest building still standing in Idaho.

A Unique Population Pool

Catholic church records of the period reflect the intermixing of Caucasian, Indian, and Polynesian races occurring in the Pacific Northwest. Fur company personnel coming overland from the east—Scots, French-Canadians, and Iroquois Indians—were frequently joined by Cree and Chippewa wives from central Canada or took wives from western tribes. Among McLoughlin's shrewd and brilliant traders, Peter Skene Ogden was twice married to Indian women; the wives of James Douglas and John Work were half-Indian.

Ships which came through the Sandwich Islands often brought Hawaiian natives (called Owyhees or Kanakas at this time) to the Pacific Northwest. A few of them were women. Two Owyhee women came to Nootka Sound on the *Jenny,* apparently as stowaways, and were returned safely to their home islands. Other women may have come later as wives or as employees, but mostly the Owyhees were single men, as many as 300 by 1825 and many more later.

The missionaries hired Owyhees as reliable servants and laborers; they were also skilled boatmen and hunters. Some returned home after their period of service was completed. Others remained and intermarried. The Owyhee River near the Idaho-Oregon border was named in memory of two who were murdered by Indians while with a Hudson's Bay Company brigade in the region. To accommodate the large number of Hawaiians in the vicinity of Fort Vancouver, the Owyhee Church was built inside the fort walls, and the Reverend Kanaska William here ministered to his fellow Islanders from 1844 to 1848.

The blend of races encountered and recorded by the Catholic priests consisted of "French-Indian, Scots-Indian, Owyhee-Indian, French-Owyhee, Iroquois-Western Indian, and an occasional Negro-Indian, for a black now and then jumped ship or came with his master across the Plains" (Munnick 1972).

This unique population pool did not grow to lasting significance, however. Within a few decades the Americans, mostly of Anglo-Saxon lineage, overwhelmed it.

Wagon Wheels

The 1840s were a period of mass migration into the Oregon Country. The first settlers in this period were independent American trappers known as "mountain men" who were ready to give up their nomadic wanderings now that furs were no longer bringing high prices. Col. William Craig became the first permanent resident in Idaho in 1840 when he settled down with his family on a land claim south of Lapwai. Because his wife was Nez Percé, they were safe when others in the vicinity were driven out in the Indian uprisings.

Other mountain men, William Doughty, George Ebberts, Joseph Gale, Joseph Meek, Robert "Doc" Newell, and Caleb Wilkins—all of whom took an active part in the formation of an American government—and others settled in the Willamette Valley. Most had wives from the Nez Percé or other western tribes. The famous Joe Meek had three—the first one died in battle, the second deserted him, and the third outlived him.

The newcomers who began arriving overland in large numbers in the 1840s were different. The men brought white wives with them or married their fellow immigrants' daughters, and were of a different sort in other ways.

EVOLUTION OF THE PACIFIC NORTHWEST STATES

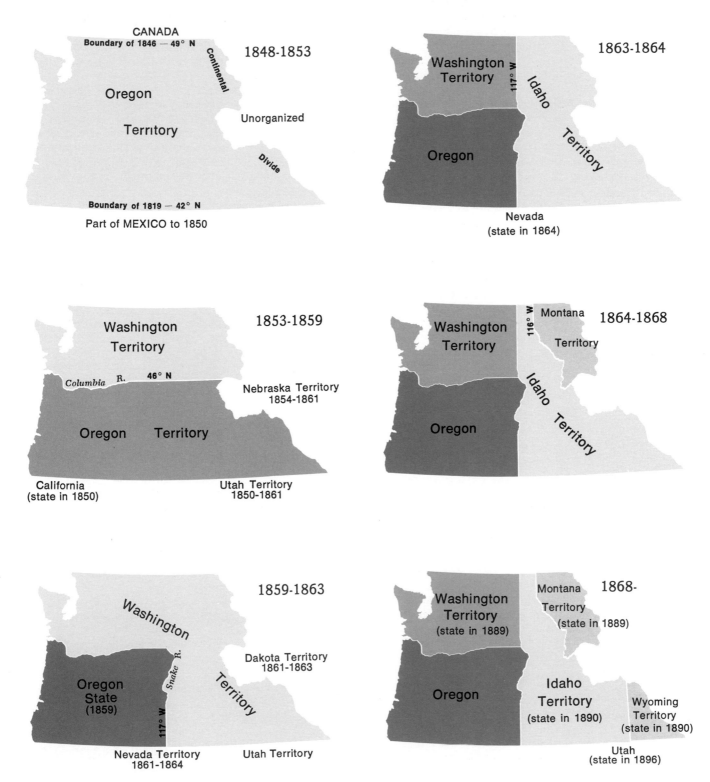

1848-1853

CANADA
Boundary of 1846 — 49° N
Continental
Oregon
Territory
Unorganized
Divide
Boundary of 1819 — 42° N
Part of MEXICO to 1850

1863-1864

Washington Territory
117° W
Idaho Territory
Oregon
Nevada
(state in 1864)

1853-1859

Washington Territory
Columbia R. 46° N
Nebraska Territory 1854-1861
Oregon Territory
California (state in 1850)
Utah Territory 1850-1861

1864-1868

Washington Territory
116° W Montana Territory
Oregon
Idaho Territory

1859-1863

Washington
Snake R.
Dakota Territory 1861-1863
Oregon State (1859)
117° W
Territory
Nevada Territory 1861-1864
Utah Territory

1868-

Washington Territory (state in 1889)
Montana Territory (state in 1889)
Oregon
Idaho Territory (state in 1890)
Wyoming Territory (state in 1890)
Utah (state in 1896)

For years they had been hearing wonderful stories of the Oregon Country—its healthy climate, its fertile soil, its opportunity for development and—most of all—its free land. They came to build new homes, towns, denominational churches, schools, colleges, and industries. They came to "make good" but had no illusions of getting rich quickly as did the immigrants who rushed to California for gold a few years later. This new breed of immigrants avoided the natives and did not intermarry with them.

The missionaries and early businessmen had come primarily from New York state and New England, but these people came from the heartland of the continent—Missouri, Tennessee, Kentucky, Ohio, Indiana, and Illinois. They represented many occupations—craftsmen, lawyers, teachers, ministers—but all of them had to supplement their professional income by owning land and carrying on an agricultural enterprise. They were educated, intellectually curious, and well-read. They believed in orderly government under law.

Many came from slave states and some brought blacks with them, although more often than not with the idea of freeing them. Oregonians rejected the idea of slavery in legislative actions and referenda, but they also tried to restrict black population.

In 1841, Hudson's Bay Company made an attempt to increase the number of British citizens north of the Columbia by sending James Sinclair with 120 part-Indian settlers over the Canadian Rockies and down the Columbia to Fort Vancouver. Most of these were assigned to the lonely farms at Cowlitz and Nisqually, and the colonization was only partially successful. Malcontents tended to drift away to the more congenial Willamette Valley settlements.

The first American wagon train, with more than one hundred people in sixteen to eighteen wagons, came in 1842, led by Dr. Elijah White, who had previously served with the Methodist mission. He had been appointed Indian sub-agent and in this capacity sought to lessen the friction between the native population and the encroaching whites.

The so-called "Great Migration" of 1843 brought 875 immigrants and 700 cattle, mostly to the Willamette Valley, and set the pattern for greater ones to come: 1,400 newcomers in 1844, 3,000 in 1845. The first census of the Oregon Territory in 1849 listed 5,410 males and 3,673 females, for a total of 9,083.

Years of Decision

When Ewing Young, wealthiest of the settlers, died in 1841 with no known heirs, the other settlers met to decide how to administer his estate. Other meetings followed in May 1843 and they decided by a vote reported to be 52-50 to form a provisional government along the lines of an American state and completely independent of Hudson's Bay Company. Judicial, legislative, and executive branches were set up at Oregon City.

The international struggle for ownership of the Oregon Country was coming to a climax. England was willing to withdraw claim to the area south and east of the Columbia but intended to keep what is now the western two-thirds of Washington as part of Canada. In 1844 American voters elected President James K. Polk, whose campaign slogan, "Fifty-four forty or fight!" indicated he was willing to go to war rather than give up any of the territory between Mexico and Alaska. When Polk's negotiators and Queen Victoria's ministers got together, however, they compromised on extending the boundary between the United States and Canada along the 49th parallel to the Pacific. Ports remained open to the British, and Hudson's Bay Company property rights were respected.

Hudson's Bay Company decided to move its headquarters to Victoria, B.C., but continued trading through its network of posts. Dr. McLoughlin resigned and moved to Oregon City, where he built a house (still preserved) and applied for U.S. citizenship.

INDIAN LAND CESSIONS

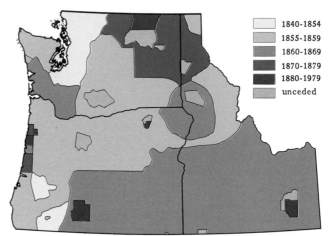

	1840-1854
	1855-1859
	1860-1869
	1870-1879
	1880-1979
	unceded

INDIAN RESERVATIONS

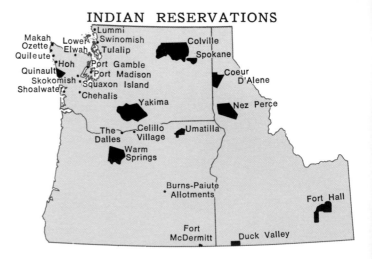

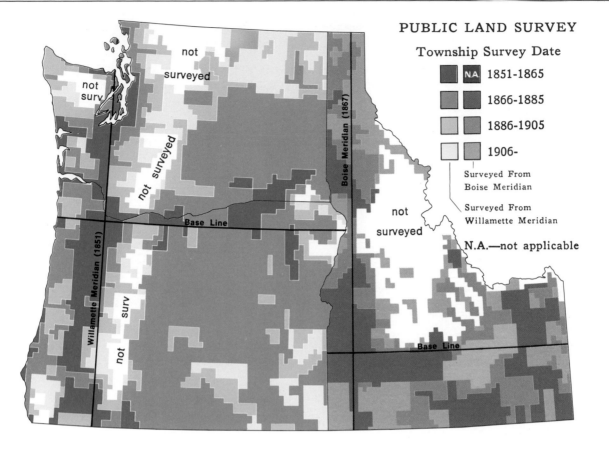

PUBLIC LAND SURVEY
Township Survey Date

1851-1865
1866-1885
1886-1905
1906-

Surveyed From
Boise Meridian

Surveyed From
Willamette Meridian

N.A.—not applicable

Indian Wars

At the same time, the Indians began a series of piecemeal attacks and ambushes on the whites who had been taking their lands and women, cheating them in trade, and spreading measles among them. The first blow came at Waiilatpu in 1847. Cayuse visitors to the Whitman mission fell upon Marcus and Narcissa, murdering them and twelve others and holding 53 captive until ransomed by Hudson's Bay Company. Thus began the Cayuse War. Indians in southern Oregon violently resisted settlers and gold seekers and the Rogue River War of 1850-1855 resulted.

Superintendents of Indian Affairs, Governor Isaac I. Stevens in the Washington Territory and Joel Palmer in the Oregon Territory, and their successors, negotiated treaties with various tribes, arranging for payment for land taken, providing protected reservations for displaced persons, and restrained those advocating extermination. Despite their best efforts, uprisings occurred throughout the region. Traders were driven out of many posts. Military campaigns of retaliation became known as the Yakima War of 1855-1859, the Modoc War of 1872, and finally Chief Joseph's War of 1877.

In many instances the Indians fought with courage and determination to preserve their old way of life, but the end was inevitable. The surging mass of settlers and gold seekers could be delayed only temporarily. By treaty, sale, or force the natives lost their land except for the reservations (see map of Indian Reservations on page 18). The resisting Indians came in the end to agree with their last great leader, Chief Joseph, who concluded, "I will fight no more forever."

POPULATION—1980

Each brown dot represents 500 people living either in unincorporated places, in the immediate vicinity of incorporated places with less than 500 people, or in rural residences in the general vicinity of the dot.

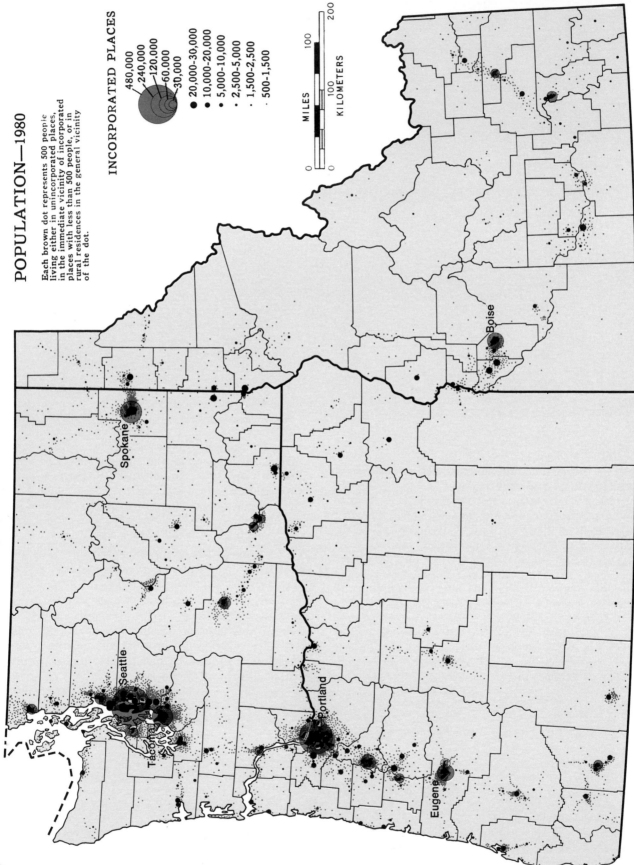

Population and Employment

Ray M. Northam

The population of the Pacific Northwest continued to increase in the 1980s as it has since the 1940s, and has become still more localized in relatively few major concentrations.

The regional rate of population increase was 19% in the decade 1950-1960, 11% from 1960-1970, and 24% from 1970-1980, while the national population increased by 19%, 13%, and 11% in the same periods. Of the approximately 7.7 million residents of the Pacific Northwest in 1980, 53.5% lived in Washington, 34.2% lived in Oregon, and 12.3% resided in Idaho. One should note, however, that about three-tenths of the land area of the State of Washington, one-half of the land area of Oregon and two-thirds of the land area of Idaho is in federal ownership and not available for human occupancy. The population of the Pacific Northwest has constituted just over 3% of the national population since World War II, a percentage which is increasing slowly as a function of net immigration. Projections of future population in the region are as varied as the projection techniques and/or the projectors, but one of the more realistic is that the regional population in 1995 will be 8.7 million—Washington with 4.6 million, Oregon with 2.9 million, and Idaho with 1.2 million.

Population Distribution

The distribution of population in the region is exceedingly concentrated in a few areas with high population densities. The Puget Lowland including Seattle contains about one-third of the region's people and the Willamette Valley nearly another one-quarter. These two areas account, then, for more than one-half of the people in the Pacific Northwest, although there are other clusterings of population in the Spokane, Yakima, Tri-cities (Pasco, Richland, and Kennewick, Washington) and Boise areas, plus significant nodes in the Rogue River Valley and the Snake River Valley upstream from Twin Falls. King County, Washington includes over 16% of the regional population and Multnomah County, Oregon accounts for another 7%, which means that nearly one-fourth of the people in the Pacific Northwest reside in only two of the 119 counties in the region. With the addition of Pierce, Spokane, and Snohomish counties in Washington plus Lane, Clackamas, Washington, and Marion counties in Oregon, nine counties contain approximately one-half of the regional population. All but one of these counties (Spokane County) are west of the Cascade Mountains, a fact which illustrates the concentration of population in the west of the region. One can also distinguish between rural population and the population residing in urban centers, with the highest percentage residing in metropolitan areas. Thus, 214 urban places in the Pacific Northwest with populations of 2,500 or more (incorporated and unincorporated) accounted for about two-thirds of the regional population in 1980, with this share still greater at present.

Table 5.   Population of Incorporated Places in the Pacific Northwest, 1980

Population	Number of places	% of places
<2,500	514	61
2,500-10,000	207	25
10,000-25,000	83	10
25,000-50,000	26	3
>50,000	10	1
total	840	100

Net Migration and Density

A factor that greatly influences the population of the Pacific Northwest is net migration, which varies considerably between decades. Net migration, which is the difference between immigration and outmigration, has contributed much to the population increase in the Pacific Northwest in each of the decades since World War II, and accounted for a greater share of population increase in the decade 1970-1980 than did natural increases in resident population. For that period the net immigration rate of increase was 11% in Oregon, 17% in Idaho, and just 3% in Washington, while the rate of natural increase was 7% in Oregon, 11% in Idaho, and 8% in Washington. Because of Washington's larger base population, these rates represent a greater absolute number of additional residents. Census reports of population in the decade 1970-1980 show an increase of 700,087 in Washington, 541,130 in Oregon, and 230,614 in Idaho.

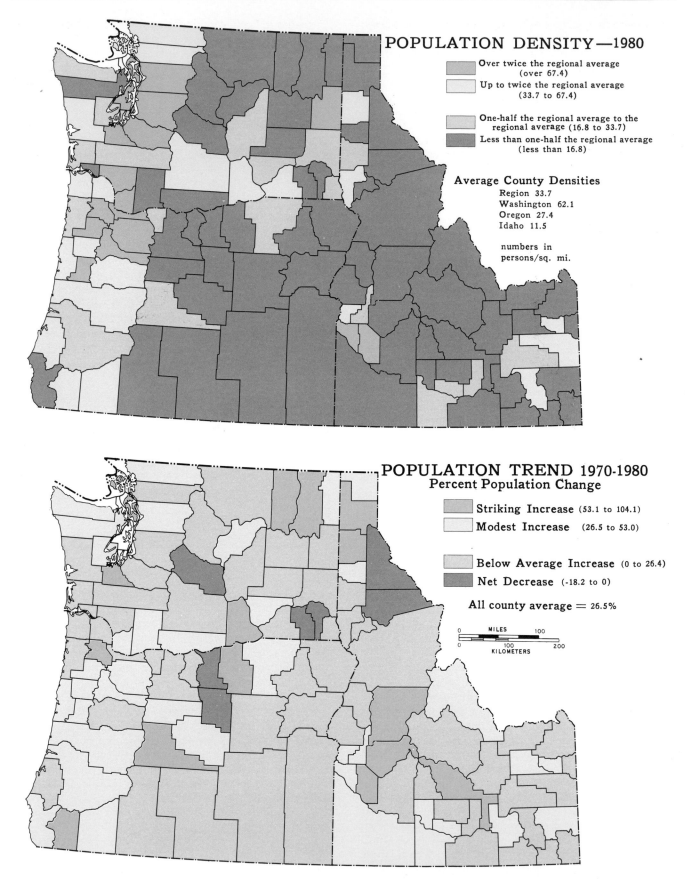

POPULATION DENSITY—1980

Over twice the regional average
(over 67.4)

Up to twice the regional average
(33.7 to 67.4)

One-half the regional average to the
regional average (16.8 to 33.7)

Less than one-half the regional average
(less than 16.8)

Average County Densities
Region 33.7
Washington 62.1
Oregon 27.4
Idaho 11.5

numbers in
persons/sq. mi.

POPULATION TREND 1970-1980
Percent Population Change

Striking Increase (53.1 to 104.1)

Modest Increase (26.5 to 53.0)

Below Average Increase (0 to 26.4)

Net Decrease (-18.2 to 0)

All county average = 26.5%

MILES
0   100
0   100   200
KILOMETERS

As more people have taken up residence in the Pacific Northwest, population densities have risen in 1980 to 62 per square mile (160 per square kilometer) in Washington, 27 in Oregon, and 12 in Idaho, compared with 51, 22, and 9 in 1970. Present densities in all three states would be higher since their populations have increased since 1980. These are still lower, however, than the national 1980 density of 64 persons per square mile. The degree of "crowdedness" in the region is made greater, though, by the high degree of population concentration and the fact that much of the land area is in public ownership and is not available for human settlement.

Census County Divisions

Reports on changes in population and population densities generally consider population residing in county units or in states. Since the Pacific Northwest includes some extremely large counties with considerable physical variations within them, a population characteristic may not apply to all parts of a county. Therefore, it may be desirable to examine characteristics and change in smaller areal units such as census county divisions (CCDs). The 119 counties in the Pacific Northwest are divided into 948 CCDs and population data are reported for each as part of the decennial census. Study of these data shows that groupings of non-metropolitan CCDs in some areas have rates of population growth that rival those of metropolitan centers.

Sectors of rural CCDs with rapid percentage increases in population can be found in certain foothill areas and river valleys on the windward side of the Cascades in both Washington and Oregon. Inland from Everett and Seattle and extending across the Cascades to the Wenatchee Mountains and the Yakima Valley is a sector of rural CCDs with high rates of population increase. A similar sector is found in Oregon eastward from the Portland-Vancouver metropolitan area and eastward from Salem and Eugene. The most striking sector of rural population growth in Oregon is centered on Bend, extending from the Madras area southward toward Crater Lake and Chiloquin, with an additional mode of accelerated growth in the Boardman area in northeastern Oregon. The major rural growth sector in Idaho is in the Snake River Valley from the vicinity of Twin Falls upstream to Pocatello and Idaho Falls.

This phenomenon appears to be associated not with extension of the commuter range of metropolitan centers, but with two other circumstances. The first is that a minor increase in the base population of a rural CCD produces a high percentage increase, while the same absolute increase in an urban CCD would pass unnoticed. In addition, there is a tendency for the growth industries of outdoor recreation and retirement to locate in these frequently attractive rural areas.

Urban Population

When the 1980 census was completed, the proportion of the population of the Pacific Northwest considered urban was 70%, compared with 69% in 1970, 57% in 1960, and 55% in 1950. The figures for each state in 1980 were Washington 74%, Oregon 68%, and Idaho 54%, while the figure for the nation as a whole was

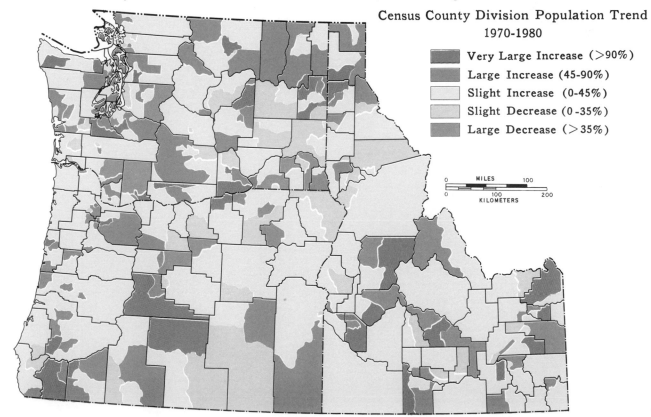

Census County Division Population Trend
1970-1980

- Very Large Increase (>90%)
- Large Increase (45-90%)
- Slight Increase (0-45%)
- Slight Decrease (0-35%)
- Large Decrease (>35%)

MILES 0 100
KILOMETERS 0 100 200

URBAN POPULATION BY COUNTY —1980—

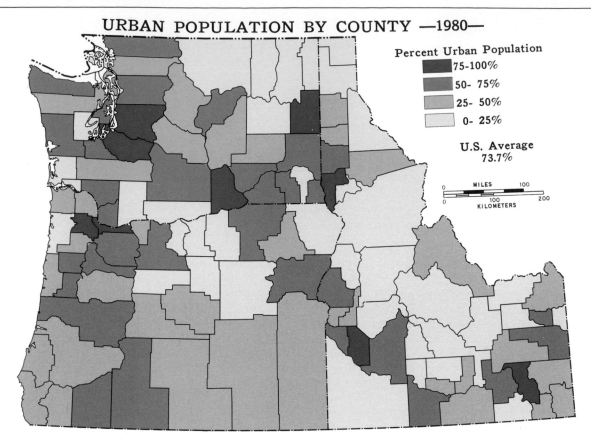

Percent Urban Population
- 75-100%
- 50- 75%
- 25- 50%
- 0- 25%

U.S. Average
73.7%

74%. These figures reflect a definition of "urban" that includes only incorporated and unincorporated places of 2,500 persons or more (see Table 5). The ten largest centers with populations greater than 50,000 accounted for 22% of the regional population, and most of these have increased in population size since 1970. By contrast, the places with populations of less than 2,500 accounted for only 6% of the regional population and many have experienced population loss since 1970.

Age and Sex Demographics

The population in any area can be divided into discrete groupings, based upon age and sex, and shown graphically with a population pyramid. The population pyramids on the opposite page show population age groups in five-year intervals on the vertical axis and male and female populations to the left and right, respectively, of the center line of the pyramid. Two different calibrations of the horizontal axis of the pyramid are utilized. The regional pyramid shows male and female populations as percentages of the total: the area to the right of the center line, for example, represents the percentage of the total female population in each age group. The state pyramids are calibrated to show absolute numbers of persons in each age group by sex. Therefore, the area included in each of the pyramids is different since each is proportionate to the total population of the state. The internal structure of the population of each state still is disclosed, as is the magnitude of

the total population and the role of each age group in the population structure.

In the pyramids for Washington and Oregon, there is a discernible "pinching-in" of the age group 45-49 which likely reflects the reduced birth rates during 1930s and the Great Depression. Reduction of birth rates may also help explain the "pinching-in" of the pyramids of age groups 1-4 and 5-9, since birth rates were slackening

URBAN AND RURAL POPULATION 1900—1980

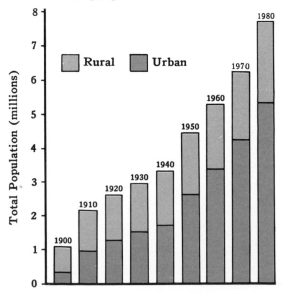

WASHINGTON

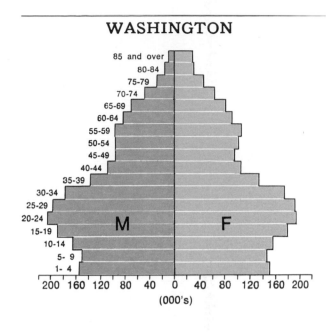

OREGON

IDAHO

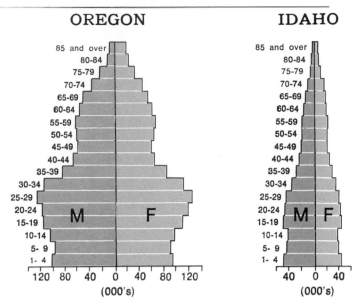

PACIFIC NORTHWEST

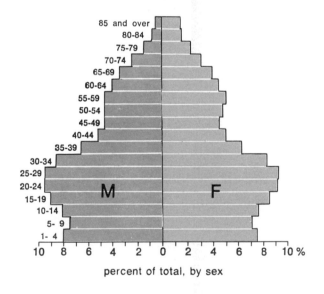

percent of total, by sex

in the 1970s. The bulge for the age group 20-24 likely reflects both the effects of high birth rates and a considerable net migration of young and relatively mobile persons to the Pacific Northwest. One additional point of commonality pertains to the sex structure of the population in the post-70 age groups. In each population group, females outnumber males by a considerable margin, as a result of higher survival rates.

Racial Minorities

The Pacific Northwest is an overwhelmingly white region. Of the 7,709,196 people recorded by the 1980 U.S. Census, 7,171,421, or 93%, were white, 145,350 (nearly 2%) were black, 98,639 (1%) were American Indians, 50,980 (less than 1%) were Asians, and 222,478 (nearly 3%) were defined as "of Spanish origin."

Idaho has the highest percentage of whites of the three states—96%—and Washington has the lowest —92%. Washington also has the highest percentage of racial minorities except for those of Spanish origin.

In all three states—as throughout the U.S., with the exception of the southeastern states—more blacks live

Table 6. *Population by Major Racial Groups Living in Major Metropolitan Areas in the Pacific Northwest, 1980*

	Boise		Portland		Seattle	
	% total state population[b]	% total city population	% total state population	% total city population	% total state population	% total city population
Whites	18.64	97.13	39.08	92.67	38.24	90.00
Blacks	25.18	0.39	85.54	3.02	55.08	3.62
Indians	8.51	0.52	26.76	0.70	27.30	1.03
Asians	25.08	0.86	62.33	2.06	62.05	3.96
Spanish origin[a]	10.50	2.22	32.32	2.03	26.72	0.30

Source: U.S. Census 1980

[a] Persons of Spanish origin may be of any race; hence totals for each column are slightly more than 100%.

[b] Percent of state total for racial group living in metropolitan area.

Table 7. *Counties in the Pacific Northwest with the Highest Percentage of Total Population in Major Racial Groups, 1980*

	Idaho		Oregon		Washington	
	County	%	County	%	County	%
Whites	Adams	99.43	Wheeler	99.34	Garfield	99.31
Blacks	Elmore	3.75	Multnomah	5.30	Pierce	6.14
Indians	Bingham	5.90	Jefferson	17.15	Ferry	16.92
Asians	Elmore	1.52	Benton	2.50	King	4.62
	Washington	1.52	Multnomah	2.50		
Spanish origin[a]	Minidoka	15.16	Malheur	14.13	Adams	22.26

Source: U.S. Census 1980.

[a] Persons of Spanish origin may be of any race; hence totals for each column are slightly more than 100%.

in major metropolitan areas than in other, more rural, parts of the state. This figure is particularly striking in Oregon, where 86% of the state's blacks live in Portland, where they comprise 3% of the city's population, more than twice the percentage for the entire state. Similarly, Asians also form a higher percentage of the population of these major urban areas, but this is not true of either American Indians or those of Spanish origin (see Table 6).

The most racially homogeneous county in the region is Adams County in west central Idaho, where 99% of the population is white. Blacks comprise the highest percentage of the total population in Pierce County, Washington (6%), while the highest percentage of Indians live in Jefferson County, in central Oregon (17%). The highest percentage of Asians is found in King County, Washington (5%), and the highest percentage of people of Spanish origin live in Adams County, in eastern Washington, where they comprise 22% of the total population.

Metropolitan Areas

There were thirteen standard metropolitan statistical areas (S.M.S.A.s) in the Pacific Northwest in 1980. These areas contained 76%, 72%, and 18% respectively of the populations of Washington, Oregon, and Idaho, and 68% of the regional population. Each S.M.S.A. is comprised of one or more counties that are metropolitan in character and consists of: (1) one or more central cities with a population exceeding 50,000; (2) an urban fringe (built-up area) peripheral to the central city; and (3) outer, less densely populated portions of the metropolitan area. In the period since 1970 six additional population concentrations have qualified for S.M.S.A. status, five in Washington—Richland-Kennewick, Yakima, Bellingham, Bremerton, and Olympia—and one in Oregon—Medford. It can be expected that still more localities will reach this status in the future.

The general trend has been for relative stability or slight decline of central city populations, accelerated growth of the urban fringe populations, and modest increases in portions of the outer metropolitan areas as the commuting range of central cities is extended by improvements in private and public transportation.

Table 8. *Population of the Pacific Northwest States by Major Racial Groups, 1980*

	Idaho	Oregon	Washington
		%	
Whites	95.52	94.59	91.46
Blacks	0.29	1.41	2.59
Indians	1.11	1.04	1.47
Asians	0.63	1.32	2.48
Spanish origin[a]	3.88	2.50	2.90

Source: U.S. Census 1980.

[a] Persons of Spanish origin may be of any race; hence totals for each column are slightly more than 100%.

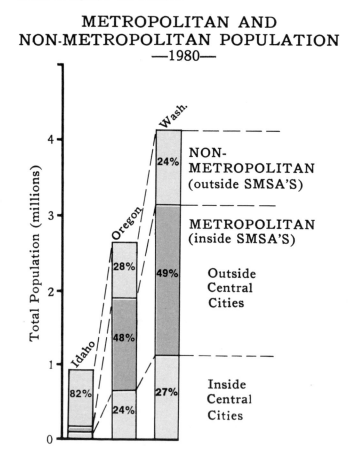

METROPOLITAN AND NON-METROPOLITAN POPULATION
—1980—

Labor Force

The non-agricultural labor force employed in the Pacific Northwest included 2,943,000 people in 1981, which was slightly less than the 2,983,000 in 1980 but appreciably more than the 2,336,000 in 1975. These values are modified by the number of unemployed, which reached 352,000 in 1981 for a regional unemployment rate of 9%. The numbers of unemployed in 1981 were 189,000, 131,000, and 32,000 in Washington, Oregon, and Idaho respectively. Many of these jobless had been employed in forest products industries and their unemployed status may be either temporary or permanent. Development and/or expansion of modern "high-tech" industries as well as worker retraining programs could be effective in dealing with regional unemployment problems.

The labor force can be grouped into the primary, secondary, and tertiary sectors. The primary sector includes activities based upon direct exploitation of the natural resource base, including agriculture, logging, commercial fishing, and mining. The secondary sector includes manufacturing industries that process, assemble,

STANDARD METROPOLITAN STATISTICAL AREAS
(S.M.S.A.'s)—1980

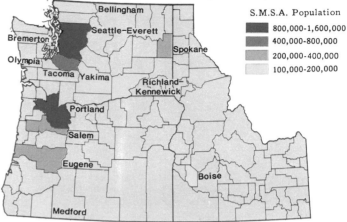

S.M.S.A. Population

■	800,000-1,600,000
▨	400,000-800,000
▦	200,000-400,000
☐	100,000-200,000

POPULATION BY SIZE OF PLACE—1980

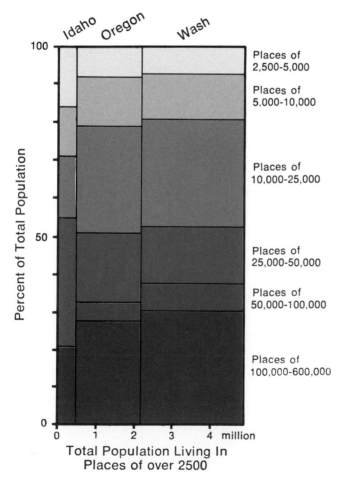

EMPLOYMENT IN NON-AGRICULTURAL ESTABLISHMENTS—1980

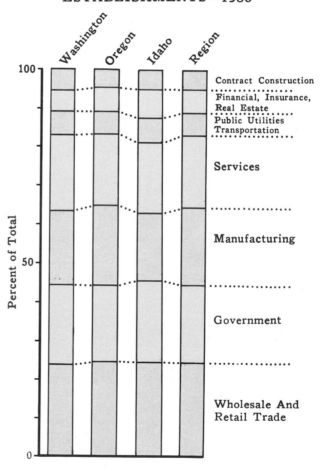

or fabricate materials derived from the primary sector and contract construction. The tertiary sector encompasses activities dealing with the distribution of tangible goods such as the transportation and retail and wholesale trades as well as those that support all sectors such as professional and personal services, and public administration and governmental services. Employment in the tertiary sector is dominant in the Pacific Northwest, as it is in the nation, and involves over two-thirds of the regional labor force. The secondary sector generally accounts for about 25% of the regional labor force and the primary sector about 5-6%. Recent years have seen an increase in employment in the tertiary sector, especially in the service activities; a general stability in the secondary sector; and a decline in primary sector employment caused both by a relative decline in employment opportunities in agriculture and logging and by a general improvement in labor productivity through advancement and technology.

It is estimated that the greatest share of the output of workers in the region satisfies local or regional demands. Only about 26% of the labor force in Washington and Oregon and 30% of the work force in Idaho produce goods and services to meet non-local demands. The continued growth of employment in the tertiary sector does little to change this situation.

STRUCTURE OF LABOR FORCE BY STATE AND ECONOMIC SECTOR

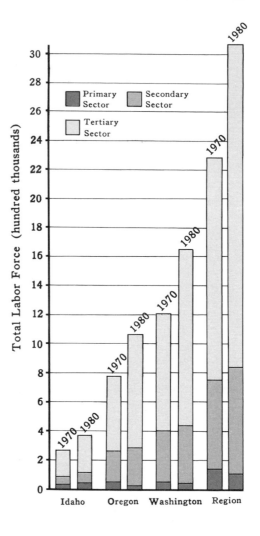

UNEMPLOYMENT RATE
1962-1982

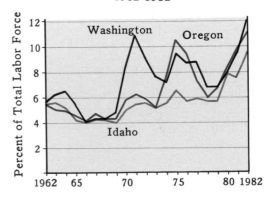

Transportation

Ray M. Northam

The Pacific Northwest is approximately 1,000 miles (1,600 kilometers) from Los Angeles, 2,000 miles from Chicago, and 3,000 miles from New York and, therefore, transportation linkages with other sections of the nation must overcome considerable friction of distance. Even within the region there are relatively long distances between regional nodal points, yet systems of transportation involving a variety of modes have been developed and serve the region well.

Terrain has been a limiting factor in the development and operation of transportation routes and terminals. The mountainous topography of the region has led to a distinct channeling of land transportation routes through a limited number of natural corridors. The strategic inportance of Stevens, Snoqualmie, Chinook, Santiam, and Willamette passes for railroads and/or highways is noteworthy. Probably of greater strategic significance, however, is the Columbia River Gorge—the only water-level route through the Cascades. This gap in the mountains provides a transportation corridor between the intermontane areas, the western valleys, and the Pacific shoreline that is utilized for rail, highway, and inland waterway transportation. It serves a vital link between the Columbia Basin and Portland. This transportation route is especially important at present for railroads operating in an era of energy shortages and escalating costs. Use of a water-level route is more energy efficient than the use of high mountain passes where greater motive power is needed to overcome steep grades and circuitous routes.

Passenger Transportation

Local and commuter transportation within the region relies overwhelmingly on the private automobile. Mass transit alternatives are generally available only in urban centers and are under utilized and heavily subsidized. Taxpayer subsidies to automobile transportation in the form of urban highway construction and maintenance costs are, however, also high (Table 10).

Table 9 shows that auto and truck travel dominates regional as well as local passenger transportation. Eighty-nine percent of all person-trips to destinations in Washington were by automobile or truck; for Oregon and Idaho the figure was 90%.

In large part these figures reflect the lack of available alternatives and the low priority in terms of investment given to transportation alternatives to the private automobile by states in the region. According to U.S. Department of Transportation figures, Idaho will be spending 92% of its total projected capital investment in transportation on highways by 1990, while the figures for Washington and Oregon will be 68% and 80%, respectively. Intercity bus services are available, but are criticized by users and potential users as slow and inconvenient. Nevertheless, intercity bus travel is the most fuel efficient transportation method available, providing 300-400 seat miles per gallon, compared to 200-350 for rail, 70-120 for automobiles, and 30-60 for air.

Air and particularly rail services are available from and to a limited number of cities. Air transportation is continuing to take a larger share of this travel market, and this trend is likely to intensify if federal subsidies to the Amtrak rail system are reduced or removed.

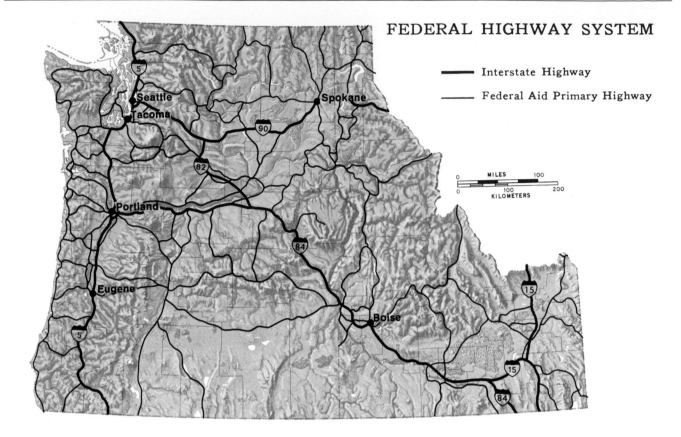

FEDERAL HIGHWAY SYSTEM

— Interstate Highway

— Federal Aid Primary Highway

Table 9.   Travel to Destinations in Pacific Northwest States

	Washington	Oregon	Idaho
		thousands of person-trips	
Mode of Transportation			
Auto/truck	9,525	6,747	2,364
Airplane	892	543	205
Bus	168	154	46
Train	117	52	3
Purpose of Trip			
Visit relatives or friends	4,581	2,313	1,002
Business	2,044	1,367	341
Personal or family affairs or medical	1,434	1,141	539
Outdoor recreation	930	1,508	504
Entertainment	873	476	69
Sightseeing	372	366	13
Shopping	247	59	-------
Convention	122	174	72
Round Trip Distance			
200 to 299 miles (322 to 482 km.)	5,043	3,332	881
300 to 399 miles (483 to 643 km.)	2,757	1,306	469
400 to 599 miles (644 to 965 km.)	1,185	1,372	407
600 to 799 miles (966 to 1,287 km.)	391	232	288
800 to 999 miles (1,288 to 1,609 km.)	118	274	107
1,000 to 1,199 miles (1,610 to 3,219 km.)	574	649	393
2,000 + miles (3,220 + km.)	999	519	116

Source: U.S. Department of Transportation, *National Travel Survey,* 1977.

A number of major airlines operate scheduled passenger services from major air terminals in Seattle, Portland, Spokane, Boise, and Eugene. Connections are provided with other U.S. cities, with the Far East and Australia, and with Western Europe using over-the-pole routes. Seattle dominates in passenger traffic, largely because it is the point of departure for overseas flights and for flights to Alaska. There is a high volume of passenger movement between major urban centers in the region, especially between Seattle and Portland and Seattle and Spokane. A number of passenger commuter flights connect several smaller cities in the region beyond the automobile commuting range with large centers, particularly Seattle, Portland, Spokane, Boise, and Eugene. The volume of air passengers traveling to both domestic and overseas destinations has been increasing steadily, leading to expansions at major air terminals in the region.

Table 10. Percentage of Projected Urban Transportation Costs Allotted to Highways and to Public Transportation Systems, 1980 and 1990

	Idaho	Oregon	Washington
Urban highways			
Capital costs[a]	39.80	51.19	80.63
Annual costs[b]	77.52	48.12	49.55
Urban public transportation			
Capital costs[a]	60.20	48.21	19.37
Annual costs[b]	22.48	55.88	50.45

Source: U.S. Department of Transportation *National Transportation Trends and Choices (To the Year 2000)*, 1977.

[a] Costs projected to 1990.
[b] Costs projected to 1980.

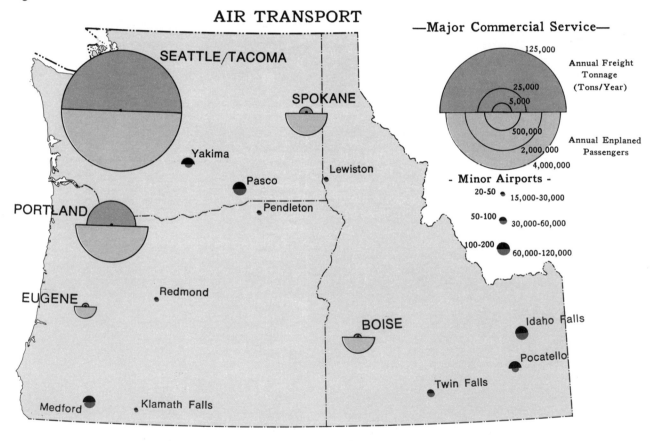

AIR TRANSPORT

—Major Commercial Service—

SEATTLE/TACOMA

SPOKANE

Yakima

Pasco

Lewiston

Pendleton

PORTLAND

Redmond

EUGENE

BOISE

Idaho Falls

Pocatello

Twin Falls

Medford

Klamath Falls

Annual Freight Tonnage (Tons/Year)

125,000

25,000

5,000

500,000

2,000,000

4,000,000

Annual Enplaned Passengers

- Minor Airports -

20-50   15,000-30,000

50-100   30,000-60,000

100-200   60,000-120,000

Freight Transportation

The railroads dominate in interstate shipment between distant points, whereas truck transport is of major significance for shorter distance movements because of faster and more flexible service. Air carriers are also important for the movement of high-value, low-bulk freight while waterways move commodities of high bulk and/or low value per unit at relatively low cost.

About 23,442,000 tons (21,262 million kilograms) of freight originated and was transported in Idaho in 1977 (most recent available figures), for a total of 8,293 million ton/miles. More than three times as much freight was transported in Oregon—75,957,000 tons—for a total of 22,216 million ton/miles. The figures for Washington are higher: 81,559,000 tons of freight transported a total of 28,666 million ton/miles.

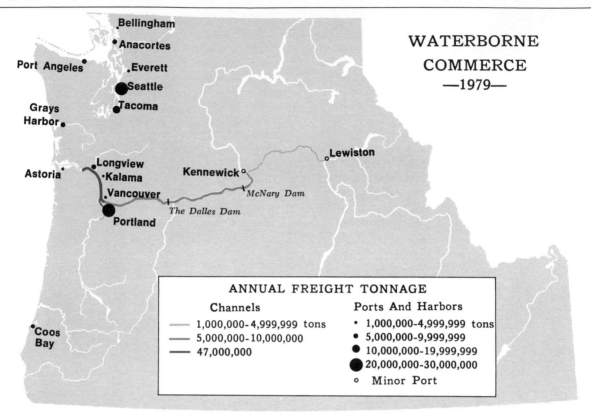

WATERBORNE
COMMERCE
—1979—

ANNUAL FREIGHT TONNAGE

Channels
— 1,000,000-4,999,999 tons
— 5,000,000-10,000,000
— 47,000,000

Ports And Harbors
· 1,000,000-4,999,999 tons
● 5,000,000-9,999,999
● 10,000,000-19,999,999
● 20,000,000-30,000,000
○ Minor Port

Table 11 shows that transportation methods vary significantly between the states in the region. In part this reflects the availability of alternatives to trucking. Washington, where the most extensive rail and water transportation facilities are available, transports more than half its freight by these means. Air freight, however, retains a similarly low percentage in all three states.

Two air carriers dominate in movement of air freight in the region, one of which transports air freight exclusively. Air freight is especially important to Seattle and Portland and the volume of air freight moved through these major air terminals has been increasing steadily.

Inland waterway transportation is mainly on the Columbia River, with the predominant movements downstream of Portland-Vancouver where a channel depth of 35-40 feet (10-12 meters) is maintained with the aid of dredging, especially at the entrance to the Columbia

River estuary. Upstream from Portland-Vancouver barges are used, especially for grains from the intermontane plateaus. Barge movements occur as far upstream as Lewiston, Idaho on the Snake River, taking advantage of a number of lockages and slack-water reservoirs associated with the large dams built on the Columbia-Snake system.

Taking advantage of its coastal location, the Pacific Northwest engages in important maritime trade consisting of both coastwise and foreign shipping. This activity involves development and maintenance of deepwater ports that are accessible to both American and foreign flag merchant ships. Regular dredging of inland ship channels must be conducted to maintain critical depths, especially of the lower Columbia River.

Ocean-going vessels utilize a number of ports in the Pacific Northwest in three different settings: (1) the Columbia River estuary; (2) Puget Sound/Strait of Juan de Fuca; and (3) coastal Oregon and Washington. Portland leads in total tonnage of foreign trade handled, mainly the export of grains from the Columbia Basin, followed in order by Seattle, Tacoma, Longview, Anacortes, Coos Bay, Astoria, Everett, Port Angeles, Grays Harbor, and Vancouver. Seattle dominates in ocean-going barge traffic to Alaska, while Portland leads in barge and small ship construction and in ship repair.

Three railroads serve the region—Union Pacific, Burlington Northern, and Southern Pacific—concentrating on interstate shipment of bulky items such as lumber, wheat, and other grains.

In all three states, the number of trucks used for personal rather than freight transportation has increased

Table 11.   *Transportation Methods for Freight by State of Origin*

	Idaho	Oregon	Washington
		%	
Truck	60.70	71.32	49.26
Rail	39.07	19.51	30.50
Water	0.19	9.14	20.19
Air	0.04	0.03	0.05

Source: U.S. Department of Transportation, *Commodity Transportation Survey Summary,* 1977.

Table 12. Waterborne Freight Traffic, 1980

Ports handling one million or more short tons, in rank order of total tonnage (000's of short tons)

	Foreign			Domestic				Local
				Coastwise		Internal		
	Total	Imports	Exports	Receipts	Shipments	Receipts	Shipments	
Portland	29,314	2,087	11,674	4,805	336	5,315	2,997	2,100
Seattle	21,289	4,521	5,081	2,222	1,721	5,292	1,603	849
Tacoma	17,162	2,454	9,433	644	739	2,116	688	1,088
Longview	9,956	761	5,967	214	24	2,066	901	23
Anacortes	9,166	5,155	117	633	1,295	302	1,585	79
Coos Bay	6,804	2	4,951	358	193	942	7	351
Everett	4,359	539	1,458	-------[a]	10	1,055	426	871
Port Angeles	4,278	787	1,433	293	5	830	684	246
Grays Harbor	3,249	5	2,754	9	34	5	-------	442
Vancouver	2,911	841	478	6	6	1,182	340	58
Astoria	2,437	205	1,046	1	-------	1,122	61	2
Bellingham	2,047	292	274	63	224	852	297	45
Kalama	1,466	25	503	8	12	804	114	-------

Source: Corps of Engineers, *Waterborne Commerce of the United States, 1980.*

[a]------- no data reported.

significantly in the decade 1967-1977 (most recent figures available). In Idaho this use rose from 42% to 60% and Oregon and Washington figures are comparable. Truck use for transportation of agricultural products—the second highest use—fell correspondingly from 35% to 18% in Idaho, from 21% to 15% in Oregon, and from 20% to 13% in Washington.

Most trucks are used for local transportation—82% of trucks in Idaho are so used, as are 86% of those in Oregon and 72% in Washington. Similarly, 90% of all

trucks in Idaho and Oregon and 92% of trucks in Washington drove at least 75% of their annual mileage within the state. The average truck in each state drove 10,000 miles in a year.

Pipelines provide another important mode of land transportation, especially in the movement of petroleum products and natural gas. This is an especially vital service since the Pacific Northwest is completely reliant upon external sources for these forms of energy.

RAIL LINES

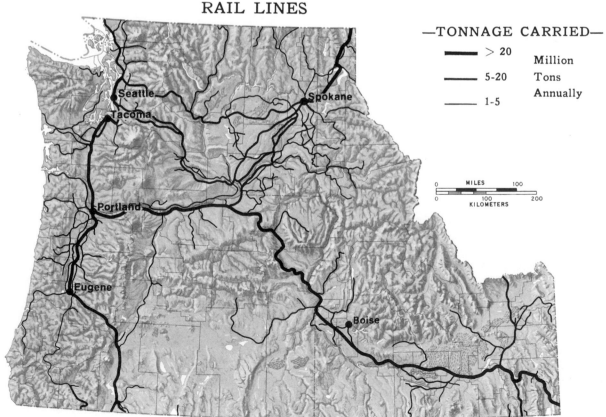

—TONNAGE CARRIED—

━━━ > 20	Million
── 5-20	Tons
─ 1-5	Annually

Land Use and Ownership
James R. Pease

Land use in the Pacific Northwest is closely linked to land ownership and soil quality. The predominant land cover throughout the region is forest, comprising 46.6% of the total land base. About 79% of this forest land is managed as commercial timberland, which is defined as land capable of producing at least 20 cubic feet per acre per year (0.22 cubic meters/hectare/year) of industrial wood. As indicated in Table 16, much of this forest land is in public ownership.

The Forest Service controls 47% of the forest land base, the Bureau of Land Management 5%, state governments about 6%, and Indian reservations about 3.5%. The forest industry owns and manages 19% of the commercial timberland base. Another 18% of timberlands is in farm and other private ownership (see Commercial Timberland section, page 98). These forest areas are predominantly classified as soil capability class VI (see the map of Land Capability Classes on page 38).

Grazing lands account for the second major land use, and are particularly important in Oregon and Idaho. As shown on the land use and land capability maps that follow, the high lava plains of southeastern Oregon and southern Idaho outside of the Snake River Plain support subhumid grassland and desert shrubland. Most of this area is administered (under grazing permits) by the Bureau of Land Management.

Irrigated and dry cropland accounts for significant land use in all three states, with 23.5% of non-federal lands devoted to this use. Although Oregon's percentage of cropland (14.8%) is less than that of Washington (25.8%) and Idaho (32.8%), two-thirds of Oregon's billion dollar agriculture industry is provided by crop sales.

Changes in Land Use

As a percentage of total land area, urban uses make up only 2.1% of the regional land base. However, public concern over urbanization of resource lands has resulted in state legislation to protect these lands in all three states. The pressure for land conversion from agriculture to urban uses has occurred on some of the most productive lands, including the Puget Sound Lowlands, the Willamette Valley, and the middle Snake River basin. One projection estimates 210,000 acres (85,000 hectares) of agricultural land in the Pacific Northwest will be converted to urban uses between 1980 and 1990, and another 150,000 acres by the year 2,000. Most

Table 13. Land Use in the Pacific Northwest

	Pacific Northwest		Oregon		Washington		Idaho	
	acres (000's)	%	acres (000's)	%	acres (000's)	%	acres (000's)	%
Non-Federal Lands[a]								
Cropland	18,538.7	23.5	4,356.4	14.8	7,793.4	25.8	6,388.9	32.8
Irrigated land	6,777.3	8.5	1,563.6	5.3	1,653.4	5.4	3,560.3	18.3
Forest lands, ungrazed	20,325.1	25.7	8,050.4	27.4	9,774.0	32.4	2,500.7	12.8
Forest lands, grazed	8,231.5	10.4	3,838.8	13.0	2,916.3	9.6	1,476.4	7.5
Pasture & rangeland grassland & desert shrubland	26,346.6	33.4	11,357.9	38.7	6,981.6	23.2	8,007.1	41.1
Urban & built-up land	1,704.5	2.1	525.5	1.7	990.2	3.2	188.8	0.9
Total Non-Federal Lands	78,872.0		29,332.1		30,091.7		19,448.2	
Federal Lands[b]								
Commercial forestlands[c]	28,587.0	36.3	13,811.0	42.8	5,214.0	43.0	9,562.0	27.8
Other forestlands[c]	16,324.7	20.7	4,886.9	15.1	4,260.3	35.1	7,177.5	20.9
Rangelands[d]	30,485.8	38.7	13,135.8	40.7	1,667.6	13.7	15,682.4	45.7
National Parks	2,070.0	2.6	168.9	0.52	1,811.0	14.9	97.1	0.28
Total Federal Lands	78,637.9		32,251.7		12,104.3		34,281.9	

[a] Source: Table 2a, Preliminary Data, 1982 National Resources Data, USDA Soil Conservation Service, April 1984.
[b] Source: Public Land Statistics, April 1984.
[c] Source: Table 3.4, *Forest Resource Report No. 23,* USDA Forest Service, 1981.
[d] Source: Table 2.3, *Forest Resource Report No. 22,* USDA Forest Service, 1981.
Note: Figures may vary from Census and other sources due to differences in definitions and data gathering methods.

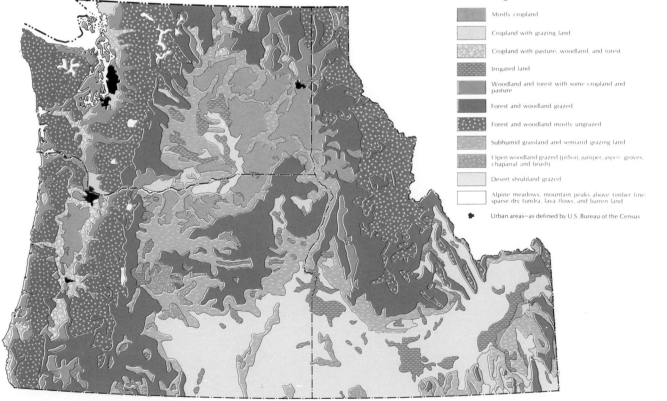

MAJOR LAND USES

- Mostly cropland
- Cropland with grazing land
- Cropland with pasture, woodland, and forest
- Irrigated land
- Woodland and forest with some cropland and pasture
- Forest and woodland grazed
- Forest and woodland mostly ungrazed
- Subhumid grassland and semiarid grazing land
- Open woodland grazed (piñon, juniper, aspen groves, chaparral and brush)
- Desert shrubland grazed
- Alpine meadows, mountain peaks above timber line, sparse dry tundra, lava flows, and barren land
- Urban areas—as defined by U.S. Bureau of the Census

Table 14. *Estimated Acreage of Agricultural Land Converted to Urban Uses, 1980-2000*[a]

	Total agricultural land		Total cropland		Irrigated cropland		Pasture land	
	acres	%[b]	acres	%	acres	%	acres	%
Idaho	128,500	(0.8)	94,900	(1.4)	74,200	(2.1)	19,100	(2.1)
Oregon	76,000	(0.4)	43,000	(0.9)	18,100	(1.1)	15,900	(1.7)
Washington	159,500	(0.9)	92,200	(1.1)	64,200	(3.5)	32,100	(5.9)

Source: Table IV-15, Northwest Economic Associates, *Report No. 13,* 1979.

[a] Based on medium population projections and the historical level of land conversion.

[b] Percentage of 1975-1977 base period non-federal acreage.

of this conversion will occur on irrigated cropland. Table 14 shows projected converted acreage and the type of agricultural land affected.

Forest land conversion is also a public policy issue. In western Oregon, between 1961 and 1976, 262,000 acres of timberland in private ownership were converted to non-forest land while 50,000 acres of non-forest land reverted to forest land for a net decrease of 212,000 acres of the 1961 timberland of 6.4 million acres. This is an average of 16,000 acres a year. In 1975 Oregon adopted land use laws severely restricting the conversion of forest lands.

Land Ownership

Land ownership in the region is dominated by two federal agencies, the Forest Service (Department of Agriculture) and Bureau of Land Management (Department of the Interior), although, as indicated on the map of Land under Federal Management below and Table 16, land is also administered by a variety of other federal agencies. Federal lands are primarily managed for timber production and grazing, followed by recreation, fish and wildlife habitat, and mineral and energy rights leasing. In addition, the Bureau of Land Management in Oregon administers Oregon and California railroad grant lands that reverted to federal management. Fifty percent of the revenues from these lands are shared with the counties.

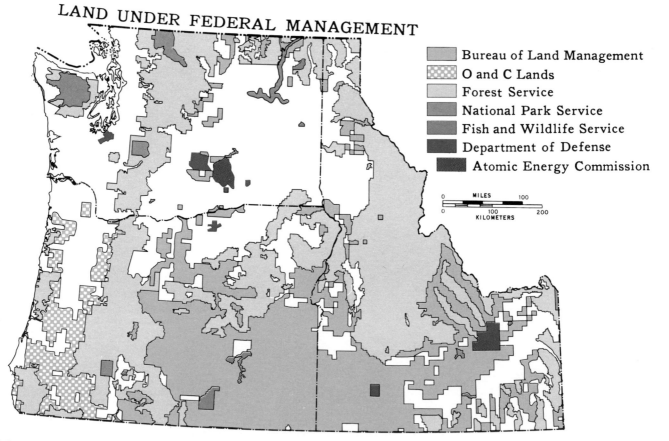

LAND UNDER FEDERAL MANAGEMENT

Bureau of Land Management
O and C Lands
Forest Service
National Park Service
Fish and Wildlife Service
Department of Defense
Atomic Energy Commission

Table 15. Public Land Ownership

	Oregon		Washington		Idaho	
	acres	%	acres	%	acres	%
Owned by federal government	32,251,744.0	52.3	12,104,326.1	28.4	34,281,911.6	64.9
Owned by state government	1,662,059.5	2.7	3,618,198.4	8.5	2,426,209.2	4.6
Total land area	61,557,760.0	100.0	42,567,040.0	100.0	52,743,680.0	100.0

Source: Public Land Statistics, April 1984.

State governments own 2.7% of the land base in Oregon, 8.5% in Washington, and 4.6% in Idaho. The land management agency in Oregon is the Division of State Lands, in Washington the Department of Natural Resources, and in Idaho the Department of Lands. Each of these agencies is directed by a land board made up of elected officals, including the governor of the state. The state lands were acquired by federal grants when each state entered the Union. Oregon has disposed of about 60% of its lands, while Washington and Idaho have disposed of 27% and 30% respectively.

Lands under state ownership are managed for timber production, grazing leases, mineral and energy rights leasing, and recreation. While the state land agencies manage public lands for maximum long-term economic gain, the multiple use concept must also be accommodated. Like the federal public land managers, state land management agencies have come under increasing pressure from special interest groups concerned with how and for whom the public lands should be managed.

In the private sector, well over 75% of farmland is owned by families as proprietary farms or family corporations. Non-family incorporated farms tend to be larger than proprietary farms but account for only about 5% of the agricultural land base. Foreign ownership, while increasing in recent years, includes less than one-half of one percent of farmland in the Pacific Northwest.

Table 16. Land Ownership by Federal Agencies

	Oregon	Washington	Idaho
		acres	
Department of Agriculture			
Forest Service	15,616,397.6	8,902,434.9	21,244,494.1
Other Agencies	14,607.8	394.0	32,462.8
Department of Commerce	9.3	123.5	-------
Department of Energy	4,889.5	370,872.1	572,442.8
Environmental Protection Agency	20.9	17.5	-------
General Services Administration	377.5	372.0	175.2
Department of Health, Education & Welfare	1.4	-------	0.5
Department of the Interior			
Bureau of Indian Affairs	401.7	102.7	32,816.5
Bureau of Land Management	13,572,654.8	310,674.5	11,906,668.9
O&C Lands	2,149,156.0	-------	-------
Bureau of Mines	43.8	21.0	-------
Bureau of Reclamation	66,308.0	100,818.0	283,391.6
Fish & Wildlife Service	479,062.8	128,713.5	44,218.3
National Park Service	168,993.6	1,811,070.5	97,153.2
Department of Justice	-------	4,456.0	4.1
Department of Labor	800.7	-------	-------
Department of Transportation	1,066.4	1,067.0	624.3
U.S. Postal Service	71.3	140.1	9.8
Veterans Administration	613.8	255.6	67.3
Department of Defense	176,267.1	472,574.0	67,382.2
TOTAL[a]	32,251,744.0	12,104,326.1	34,281,911.6

Source: Public Land Statistics, April 1984.

[a] Includes O&C Lands.

Note: Figures may vary from Census and other sources due to differences in definitions and data gathering methods.

LAND CAPABILITY CLASSES

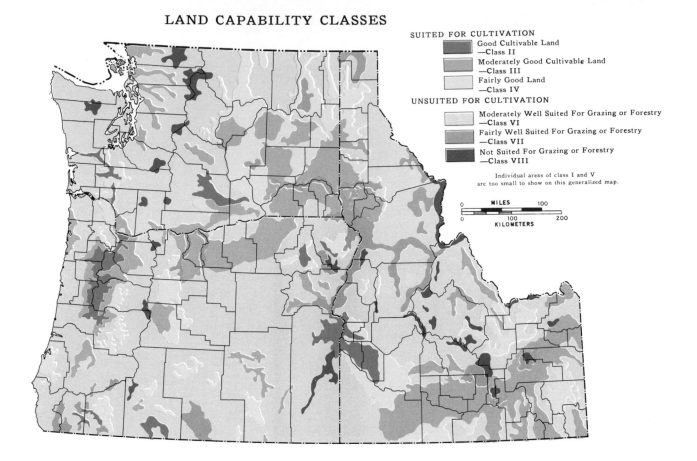

Land Capability

Land capability is a primary determinant of resource land use, while geographic and economic factors are more important for urban land use. The map of Land Capability classes above shows the general distribution of Soil Conservation Service land capability classes in the Pacific Northwest. This classification system grew out of a concern for the protection and enhancement of the nation's soil resources and groups soils according to erosion potential and limitations on use. This classification is not based on economic productivity. However,

Table 17. Summary of Land Characteristics in Soil Conservation Service Land-Capability Classes

	Class I	Class II	Class III	Class IV	Class V	Class VI	Class VII	Class VIII
Limitations for crops	Few	Some	Severe	Very severe	Impractical	Unsuited	Unsuited	Preclude
Required conservation	None	Moderate	Special	Very careful	NA	NA	NA	NA
Range improvements	NA[a]	NA	NA	NA	NA	Practical	Impractical	Impractical
Physical limitations								
Slope	Nearly level	Gentle	Moderate	Mod. steep	Nearly level	Steep	Very steep	Very steep
Erosion potential	Low	Moderate	High	Severe	Limited	Severe	Severe	Severe
Past erosion	None	Moderate	Severe	Severe	Slight	Severe	Severe	Severe
Hazard of overflow	None	Occasional	Frequent	Frequent	Frequent	Excessive	NA	NA
Soil depth	Deep	Moderate	Shallow	Shallow	Variable	Shallow	Shallow	Shallow
Soil structure	Good	Unfavorable	Mod. salinity	Severe salinity	Usually poor	Salinity	Salts	Salinity
Drainage	Good	Correctable	Wetness	Wet soils	Poor	Poor	Wet soils	Wet soils
Climatic limitations	None	Slight	Moderate	Mod. adverse	Short season	Severe	Unfavorable	Severe
Moisture capacity	Good	Fair	Low	Low	NA	Low	Low	Low
Stones	None	Few	Few	Few	Possible	Present	Severe	Severe

Source: Adapted from A. A. Klingebiel and P. H. Montgomery, *Land-Capability Classification;* Agriculture Handbook 210, SCS, U.S. Department of Agriculture, 1961.

[a] NA = not applicable.

because they require less care, lands in the highest categories (I-IV) of land capability often are the most productive. Deep, well-drained, nearly level, loamy soils are likely to have low erosion potential and high economic productivity.

Four broad categories of limitations are considered in the classification: erosion and runoff, excess water, root zone limitations, and climatic limitations. Integrating these limitations, eight land capability classes are recognized. These classes are summarized with their major characteristics and limitations in Table 17. Generally, lands in Classes I to IV are regarded as suitable for cultivation, while land capability classes of V and greater have limited use and are generally not suited for cultivation.

In the Pacific Northwest there are relatively few areas with Class I and Class II land; indeed, the areas of Class I land are so small that they have been generalized together with Class II land on the map. The Willamette, Yakima, Middle Snake, and Grande Ronde valleys have the most land in these top classes. Most of the Pacific Northwest is Class VI land, unsuitable for cultivation but used for pasture, range, and forestry. The area of Class V lands is small and is included as part of the Class VI mapping unit.

In the capability class system, soils are grouped at three levels: class, subclass, and unit. Soil surveys which classify and map soils at the series level relate this finer level of classification to land capability and management, as shown in Table 17.

While soil quality, to a large extent, determines potential resource use, ownership is often the deciding factor in formulating resource policies. Federal agencies, state governments, and the private sector each have objectives that may well differ, as may local city and county policies. In 1973, Oregon introduced land-use planning legislation to ensure that development conforms to statewide planning goals and guidelines. Nevertheless, the patterns and trends of land use reflect market demands and public policies, both of which are subject to change over time.

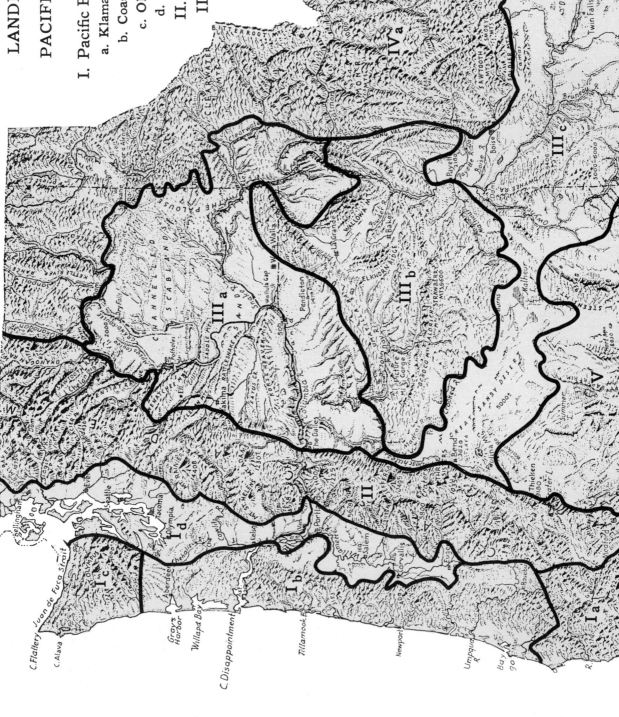

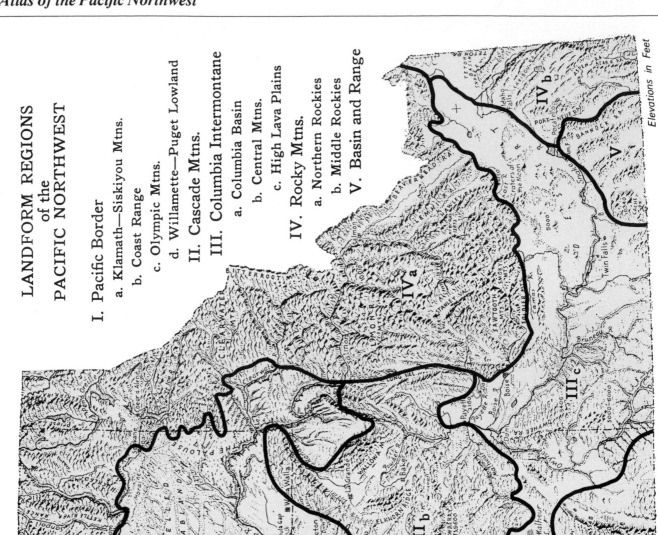

LANDFORM REGIONS
of the
PACIFIC NORTHWEST

I. Pacific Border
   a. Klamath—Siskiyou Mtns.
   b. Coast Range
   c. Olympic Mtns.
   d. Willamette—Puget Lowland
II. Cascade Mtns.
III. Columbia Intermontane
   a. Columbia Basin
   b. Central Mtns.
   c. High Lava Plains
IV. Rocky Mtns.
   a. Northern Rockies
   b. Middle Rockies
V. Basin and Range

Elevations in Feet

© Erwin Raisz

Landforms and Geology

Charles L. Rosenfeld

The Pacific Northwest is comprised of five physiographic provinces, which in turn are subdivided into one or more subprovinces as shown on the map of Landform Regions on the opposite page. The following is a brief description of the major physiographic features of each province.

Pacific Border Province

The Pacific Border Province includes the Klamath-Siskiyou section, Coast Range, Olympic Mountains, and Willamette-Puget Lowlands.

The Klamath Mountains section is defined on a partially geologic and partially topographic basis. The steep topography, dense vegetation, and structural complexity have produced a confusing geologic record. Metamorphic recrystallization masks much of the deposition history of the ancient sedimentary and volcanic strata of the region. This section has been folded, uplifted a few thousand feet, and dissected by erosion. Topographically these mountains merge with the younger Coast Range to the north and with the southern end of the Cascade Range.

The Coast Range of Oregon and Washington consists of moderately folded marine tuffaceous sandstones and shales together with basaltic volcanic rocks and related intrusives. These also have been uplifted 1,000-2,000 feet (300-600 meters) or more, and then eroded by streams to form rounded mountains of moderate relief. Resistant igneous rocks account for certain summits and for several capes projecting seaward. Sea terraces, sand dunes, and other shore features occupy narrow strips along the coast. Drowned valleys provide many harbors and the drowned lower course of the Columbia River offers a route through the Coast Range.

The Olympic Mountains consist of a mass of folded and metamorphosed rocks eroded into sharp, steep-sided ridges that stand 4,000-8,000 feet above sea level. The highest peaks bear perpetual snowbanks and several small glaciers. The mountains were severely glaciated during the ice age.

The Willamette and Cowlitz Lowlands are primarily stream valleys eroded to low elevations in belts of relatively nonresistant tilted or folded Tertiary rocks (see map of Geology on page 47). Resistant rocks locally form hills and watergaps. Both valleys contain alluvial terraces. The Puget Lowland, eroded by streams and Pleistocene glaciers, is a partially drowned system of valleys. Bordering Puget Sound are hummocky plains of till and fairly smooth sheets of glaciofluvial gravel.

Mt. St. Helens.

The Cascade Mountains

The Cascade Mountains of Oregon and the southern half of Washington are a broad upwarp composed of (1) underlying layers of early Tertiary tuffs, breccias, lavas, and mudflows, exposed in the Columbia River Gorge and other deep valleys; (2) a thick middle section of Tertiary basalts that form the deeply eroded Western Cascades; and (3) an upper section of Tertiary and Quaternary andesites and basalts that form the less dissected High Cascades lava platform, which is generally 15-25 miles (24-40 kilometers) wide and 4,000-6,000 feet high along the crest of the range. Crowning the range are a number of well-known, snowcapped volcanic peaks in various stages of dissection—Mt. Rainier, Mt. St. Helens, Mt. Adams, Mt. Hood, Mt. Jefferson, Three Sisters, Mt. McLoughlin, and others. Crater Lake occupies a caldera which resulted from the eruptive collapse of the summit of Mt. Mazama about 6,600 years ago.

The northern half of the Cascade Range of Washington is a dissected upland underlain mainly by upper Paleozoic sediments that have been folded, metamorphosed, and intruded by granites with ridges rising to elevations of 6,000-8,000 feet. Above them rise several volcanic cones (Mt. Baker and Glacier Peak). The northern Cascades were extensively glaciated, and the mountains now harbor many small glaciers.

Columbia Intermontane Province

The Columbia Intermontane Province, often inappropriately called the Columbia Plateau, includes the Columbia Basin, Central Mountains, Harney High Lava Plains, Malheur-Owyhee Upland, and Snake River Lava Plain.

The Columbia Basin is an irregular structural and topographic basin underlain by Tertiary basalt flows that have been depressed below sea level in the Pasco area and upwarped on the flanks of the surrounding mountains. Fluvial, lacustrine, eolian, and glacial sedi-

Hell's Canyon, the deepest gorge in the U.S., on the Idaho-Oregon border.

ments overlie much of the basalt, and locally form terraces or other subordinate physiographic features.

The portion in north central Oregon is partly a plateau incised by canyons and partly a low plain of sand and gravel. The portion in south central Washington is comprised of a series of anticlinal ridges (partly faulted) and synclinal valleys. The outstanding features include Horse Heaven Hills, Yakima Valley, Saddle Mountain, Kittitas Valley, and the Wenatchee Mountains-Frenchman Hill. The Columbia and Yakima rivers cross several of these ridges forming watergaps. Most of the remainder is a plateau with steeply incised stream valleys. Noteworthy are the Waterville Plateau, Quincy Basin (alluvium filled), Palouse Hills (loess covered), and Tristate Upland (on the southeast). The northern edge of the plateau was glaciated and the channeled scablands reflect the drainage ways of ice age floods. The Grand Coulee is the most spectacular of these channels.

The Central Mountains are comprised of a complex group of folded and faulted uplifts, including the Seven Devils, Wallowa, Elkhorn, Greenhorn, Aldrich, and Ochoco mountains. They rise 2,000-5,000 feet above their surroundings and reach elevations of 6,000-10,000 feet. They include various rocks of differing resistance to erosion. Because of orographic rainfall, the mountains are well dissected. The higher portions, especially the Wallowa Mountains, were glaciated. Alluvium filled fault troughs occur within the mountains, as at La Grande, Oregon.

The Harney High Lava Plains are situated between the Central Mountains, the Basin and Range area, the Cascade Mountains, and the Malheur-Owyhee Upland. They are mainly a flattish tract of recent lavas, ranging in elevation generally from about 4,000-5,000 feet. The surface is lower near the Deschutes River canyon, the only major stream in the area. Volcanoes are abundant in the western portion. Chief among them is Newberry Volcano (Paulina Mountain), with its breached caldera. Hundreds of faults, mostly of small throw, are present; they become more pronounced southward toward the Basin and Range Province.

The Malheur-Owyhee Upland occupies parts of southeastern Oregon and southwestern Idaho. It is a partly dissected, warped plateau, mostly 4,000-8,000 feet high and underlain mainly by Cenozoic lava flows, tuffs, and lakebeds. Most of the area is poorly mapped and little studied. The Owyhee River and its tributaries drain much of the area in deeply incised canyons.

The Snake River Lava Plain is an arcuate downwarp 30-60 miles wide and about 400 miles long. It descends gently from an elevation of about 6,000 feet above sea level at its east end to about 2,200 feet on the west. The eastern part is a more or less silt-covered recent lava plain, almost featureless except for low lava domes and occasional cinder cones. Very young lavas occur at Craters of the Moon, Hell's Half Acre, and elsewhere. The western part of the plain is underlain by lakebeds and alluvium as well as lava, and is partly dissected to terraces, box canyons, and open valleys.

Rocky Mountains Province

The Northern Rocky Mountains Province includes parts of northeastern Washington, northern and central Idaho, and western Montana. It is characterized by high mountain ridges and deep intermontane valleys eroded from rocks of moderately complex structure. Where the rocks have been folded and faulted, the ridges are aligned as in the Selkirk ranges. Some valleys (e.g., Bitterroot and Purcell) are 10-20 miles wide and favor settlement and transportation. The mountains of central Idaho, developed by erosion of massive granite rocks (the Idaho batholith), are irregular and resist exploration and settlement.

Most of the province drains into the Columbia River and its tributaries, although the eastern part outside the Pacific Northwest drains into the headwaters of the Missouri River system. Although much of this section is well dissected, as seen in the photograph of Soldier Mountains on page 44, Pleistocene glaciation has produced some of North America's most spectacular mountain scenery.

A part of the Middle Rocky Mountains section extends into southeastern Idaho, where northerly to northwesterly trending mountain ridges and valleys have eroded from folded, thrust-faulted, or tilted rocks. The valleys are about 6,000 feet above sea level, and the ridges reach 2,000-4,000 feet higher. Block faulting, characteristic of the Basin and Range Province, extends into this area also; therefore, the boundary is somewhat arbitrary.

The Owyhee Mountains of southeastern Oregon.

Basin and Range Province

The northern edge of the Great Basin section of the Basin and Range Province extends into south central Oregon and into southern Idaho. The part in Idaho consists of a series of tilted fault blocks and parallel stream valleys developed in a region of folded rocks. By contrast, the part in Oregon is a high lava plain interrupted by fault block mountains and by fault troughs. Representative of the high-standing blocks are Steens Mountain, Hart Mountain, Abert Rim, and Winter Ridge. Typical fault troughs are Alvord Basin, Warner Valley, and the basins of Abert, Summer, Goose, and Klamath lakes. The western part of this province is covered by the ash and pumice of the Mt. Mazama and Mt. Newberry eruptions, which greatly alter the appearance, drainage, and vegetation of the area. The presence of so many young faults attests to the recency of tectonic activity in the region, as do the numerous hot springs and geothermal areas.

Abert Rim in the Basin and Range Province.

A section of central Idaho's Rocky Mountains.

Fort Rock, in central Oregon. Native people lived in this region as long as 13,000 years ago.

Tectonic Setting of the Pacific Northwest

The geologic deformation of the earth's crust has undergone radical re-examination in light of discoveries linking such movement with sea-floor spreading and continental drift, which have been combined to form a body of theory called *plate tectonics*. Submarine volcanic activity produces new sea-floor material, forcing older oceanic crust to spread laterally away from the activity. In some cases the sea floor is thrust beneath the margins of a continent, back into the mantle of the earth. This process is called subduction. At present many earth scientists believe such a process is active in the Pacific Northwest; however, it appears to be a complex and rather special case.

The diagram of Plate Tectonic Relationships on page 46 illustrates the concept of subduction as applied to this region. The movement of the oceanic Gorda Plate has been indicated by seismic and paleomagnetic evidence, providing the source of tectonic stress and material which results in the continued volcanic activity of the Cascades and the moderate seismic activity of the region. The 1980 eruption of Mount St. Helens generated considerable scientific inquiry into the mechanisms of Cascade vulcanism and its relation to plate tectonics. The creation of the Cascades Volcanoes Observatory and the regional seismic network promise to yield new insights into the tectonic origins of the region.

Glacial Features

The complexity of the landscape history of the Pacific Northwest is well illustrated by the sequence and variety of landforms related to the Pleistocene ice ages. Lobes of ice pushed southward from the Cordillerian ice in western Canada, forcing their way along river valleys and lowland areas. Although we have identified several periods of glaciation during the Pleistocene, the complexity of glacial activity within the region has masked any simple sequence. For example, the large lobes were part of a continental ice sheet of great thickness which advanced by pressure flow, whereas the local glaciers in the mountains contained much less ice and moved down their valleys by gravity. The mechanics and volume of these different glacial systems indicate that they responded differently to changes in climate and their respective advances were not necessarily synchronous.

Glacial features also include all the modifications brought about by glacial meltwater and associated climatic changes. These effects include glacially diverted rivers, large inland lakes, and the effects of frozen ground upon the landscape. Among the most dramatic effects were the sequence of mammoth floods which formed the Channeled Scabland of eastern Washington. Glacial Lake Missoula formed when the Clark Fork of the Columbia River was dammed by a Cordillerian ice lobe.

MAJOR TECTONIC FEATURES

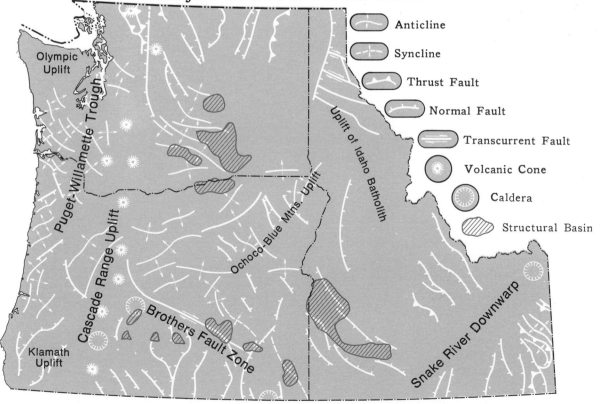

When the lobe began to melt, the ice dam burst, releasing up to 50 cubic miles (208 cubic kilometers) of water which rushed westward over the Columbia Plateau near Spokane. As the floods raged over the plateau, the water ripped off the soil cover and cut channels into the basalt bedrock.

Other features include the shorelines of lakes that were greatly expanded during the wetter, cooler glacial periods of the Pleistocene. Some of these lakes have dried up completely, while others, like Summer Lake and Goose Lake in Oregon, remain as small remnants of their former extent.

PLATE TECTONIC RELATIONSHIPS IN THE PACIFIC NORTHWEST

GLACIAL AND PERIGLACIAL FEATURES

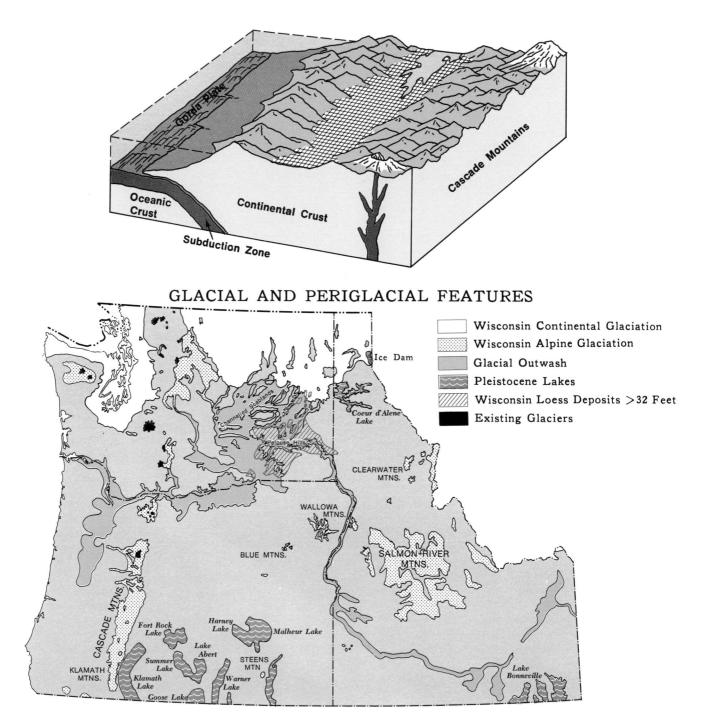

Legend:

- Wisconsin Continental Glaciation
- Wisconsin Alpine Glaciation
- Glacial Outwash
- Pleistocene Lakes
- Wisconsin Loess Deposits >32 Feet
- Existing Glaciers

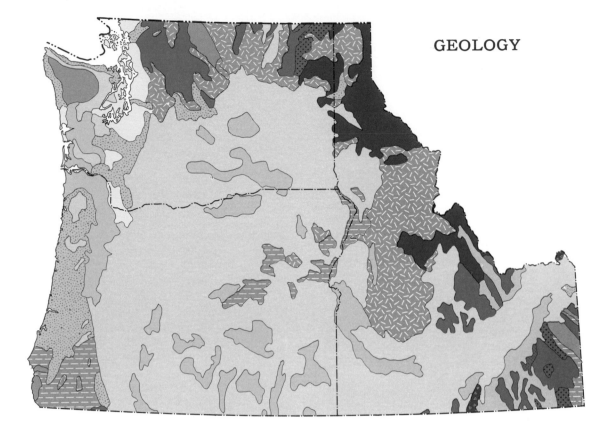

GEOLOGY

SEDIMENTARY ROCKS

 QUATERNARY
Recent and Pleistocene

UPPER TERTIARY
Pliocene and Miocene including Recent
and Pleistocene

LOWER TERTIARY
Oligocene, Eocene, and Paleocene

CRETACEOUS
In parts of Rocky Mountains includes
Jurassic and Triassic

JURASSIC AND TRIASSIC

 UPPER PALEOZOIC
Permian, Pennsylvania, and Mississippian, parts
of Rocky Mountains - middle and lower Paleozoic

 MIDDLE PALEOZOIC
Devonian and Silurian

 LOWER PALEOZOIC
Ordovician and Cambrian

YOUNGER PRECAMBRIAN

OLDER PRECAMBRIAN
Metamorphic and igneous rocks

VOLCANIC ROCKS

 QUATERNARY AND TERTIARY
Includes small areas of intrusive rocks

INTRUSIVE ROCKS

 **LOWER TERTIARY AND
MESOZOIC** – Chiefly granitic rocks

Climate

Philip L. Jackson

Climatic diversity is the hallmark of the Pacific Northwest. The several climates found in the region reflect geographic circumstances that, in human terms, provide a unique mosaic of varied living environments. The climatic characteristics of the region favorably support a broad spectrum of human activities including forest resource use, crop and animal agriculture, and a wide variety of outdoor recreation activities. Climatic moderation is said to be characteristic of the Pacific Northwest, but extremes are here too. While the region is relatively free of violent weather phenomena, there are sufficient local occurrences of windstorms, ice storms, blizzards, floods, and droughts to keep the subject of weather and climate high on the list of conversational topics.

Throughout the Pacific Northwest, distinctive seasonal changes in temperature and precipitation occur, due in part to geographic circumstances that include a west coast position astride the mid-latitude cyclonic storm belt, oceanic and continental influences, and the effect of surface form and elevation. Dominance of one or more factors produces subregional climatic differences. In combination, these features translate into a distinctive climatic regime characterized by relatively dry, warm summers and cooler, wetter winters. This distinctive winter seasonality of precipitation is the unifying factor in a region of climatic diversity.

Climatic diversity in the Pacific Northwest is largely attributable to the Cascade Mountain chain, which creates a major east-west moisture divide and shields the higher elevation interior from the moderating temperatures of the Pacific Ocean. Sharp vertical temperature and precipitation gradients are also induced by the Olympics, the Blue Mountains, and the mountain complexes of Idaho. In general, there are more rainy days and mean annual precipitation totals are highest west of the Cascades. Annual temperature ranges are low and freeze-free periods are generally long, especially in those locations influenced by marine air. To the east, in the rain shadow of the Cascades, precipitation totals are low, there is a greater seasonal temperature range, and a greater variability in the length of the freeze-free period.

Climate Elements

The latitudinal location of the Pacific Northwest, from 42° to 49° north, is primarily responsible for seasonal temperature and precipitation contrasts. Because the region is situated roughly halfway between the equator and the north pole, summer days are long and insolation is more direct, producing higher average temperatures than during winter months. Atmospheric circulation and the seasonal temperature lag of ocean waters have a moderating influence and serve to make winter temperatures milder and summer temperatures cooler west of the Cascades. Landforms play a major role in directing the flow of surface air movement. Marine and continental air masses are both influenced by terrain barriers. Temperatures of coastal stations are moderated by marine air which penetrates some distance inland through river valleys and terrain gaps in the Coast Range.

The Cascades form an effective barrier to marine air, and contrasts between winter and summer temperatures are most apparent east of the mountains. The relative length of the freeze-free season illustrates this contrast between marine and landmass influences. Above freezing temperatures persist from 240-300 days from north to south along the coastal margin and the western lowlands. East of the Cascades, except for the Columbia River borderlands and the Snake River Plain, the freeze-free season is generally less than 120 days, and it is less than 30 days in the Cascades and the mountains of Idaho.

Atmospheric circulation varies from summer to winter producing important temperature and precipitation variations throughout the region. Summer windflow is generally from the northwest, the result of high pressure domination in the region of the northeastern Pacific. Cooler, dryer air flow from the north Pacific contributes to mild summer temperatures west of the Cascades. With clear skies and long hours of sunshine, eastern areas have higher summer temperatures, a result of rapid land mass heating. The generally higher elevations to the east moderate summer extremes, but low eleva-

tion stations along the Columbia and Snake Rivers often experience some of the highest summer temperatures in the region.

Winter precipitation in the Pacific Northwest is associated with cyclonic storms embedded in the atmospheric flow across the Pacific. In late fall and winter, warm moisture-laden air travels northeasterly across the Pacific, paralleling the pressure gradient between the subtropical high and the north Pacific low pressure systems. This generally southwest air flow meets contrastingly cooler and drier air, creating frontal zones that move through the Pacific Northwest. Vast cloud sheets form as air is drawn into low pressure cyclonic disturbances and is forced to rise up over frontal surfaces. As the moisture-laden air cools, clouds form and precipitation results. During December, January, and February precipitation is widespread and incessant throughout much of the Pacific Northwest, but totals are greater on the west side of mountain barriers that force air moving inland from the Pacific to rise and cool. Rain falls abundantly on the Coast Range and lower slopes of the Olympics and Cascades. At higher elevations, winter snowfall generally exceeds 300 inches (750 centimeters). In parts of the Cascades, as much as 1,000 inches has been recorded, producing the pattern of comparatively wetter windward (western slope) locations with drier conditions at leeward (eastern slope) locations. Air descending the leeward slopes inhibits the precipitation process, because air warms as it descends, a condition that contributes to aridity. Some distance to the east of the Cascades annual amounts of precipitation increase on the southwestern flanks of the mountains of northeast Oregon, southeast Washington, and southwestern and northern Idaho.

July and August are the driest months over most of the Pacific Northwest, but because of the contrast between total amounts of precipitation, western stations show a more dramatic seasonal regime than do the stations to the east. Some stations in Idaho show a spring precipitation peak caused by mountain ranges that produce atmospheric instability and convective thunderstorm precipitation.

GENERALIZED PRESSURE AND WINDS

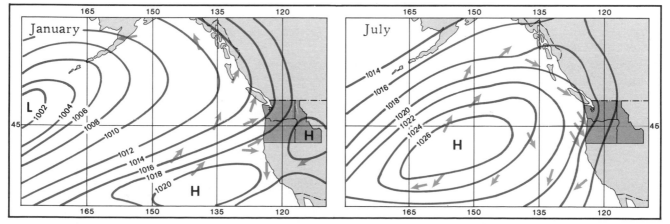

Climatic Regions

Climatic diversity in the Pacific Northwest is strongly influenced by two factors: distance from the Pacific Ocean, and physiographic relief. Five broad regional climates result. A marine climate exists along the western margin of the continent, reflective of temperature and moisture characteristics of offshore waters. The relief and orientation of the Coast Ranges of Oregon and Washington inhibit the free flow of marine air inland, producing a modified marine climate in the western lowlands leeward of the Coast Range. This area includes the Puget Lowland, the Willamette Valley, and the Rogue Valley. A dramatic change in climate is produced by the north-south trending Cascade Mountains, characterized by a complex mountain climate that varies with the elevation, slope, and aspect of surface features. The "rain shadow" effect of the Cascades is clearly shown in the arid climate regions to the east. Moisture bearing winds are effectively blocked from the dry interior, known as the Intermontane Region. Over this broad region, continentality begins to dominate, and it is only in the higher elevations that precipitation totals increase due to orographic lifting of eastward-flowing air. Finally, the high mountains and valleys of north-

eastern Oregon and central Idaho exhibit a climate that contrasts sharply with the Columbia Plateau and Snake River Plain of the Intermontane Region. Within the mountain complex, annual precipitation is greater, and summers are short, due to higher elevation and landmass effects.

Climographs have been prepared to assist in the visualization of the specific regions described. Stations selected are representative of a region, but it should always be kept in mind that climatic statistics from nearby stations may differ considerably due to the influence of local terrain features. Maps of climatic elements are necessarily generalized to depict broad regional patterns.

The Coast Region. A mild and wet marine climate extends along a narrow coastal strip and into the river valleys of the Coast Range. The freeze-free season for frost sensitive crops varies from 300 days at Brookings, Oregon to 240 days at Tatoosh, Washington. However, stations more than 30 miles inland show a reduction of a month in the average freeze-free season.

Summer temperatures peak in August, with maximums rarely exceeding 70°F (21°C), although Astoria, Oregon has recorded 100°F temperatures. Average tem-

PREVAILING SURFACE WIND DIRECTION AND SPEED

—January—

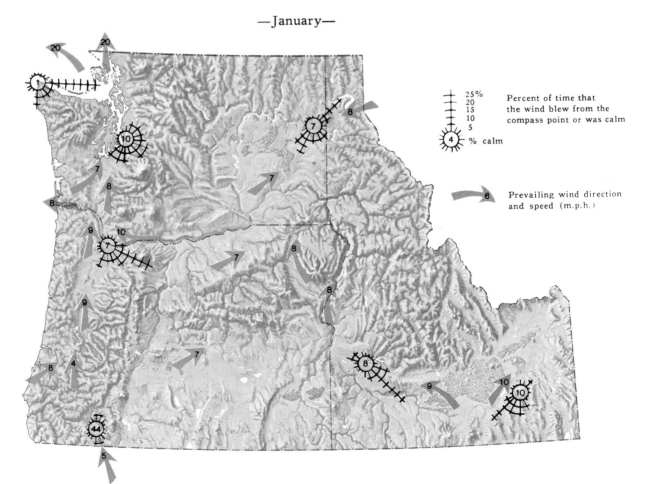

peratures are in the range of 55-59°F, but, while winters are mild on the coast, they are also raw, windy, wet and cloudy. Summer coolness and reduced sunshine are related to the frequency of fog in the coastal zone. Indeed, fog and cloudiness are common during the summer; sunshine duration is only about one-half of that possible.

Evergreen forest growth is highly favored in the coastal mountains where rain falls over 200 days of the year and annual totals may exceed 125 inches. Average precipitation ranges from 60-80 inches in the south to 80-100 inches in the north. Summer is relatively drier than winter. Stations receive on the average only about 10% of the total annual precipitation during June, July, and August.

The windward slope of the Coast Range receives the most rain at elevations from 500-2,000 feet (150-600 meters) due to orographic lifting. Snow during winter is not uncommon in higher elevations. The Olympic Mountains of Washington contain peaks ranging from 4,000-8,000 feet above sea level, and cause east-moving cyclonic storms to deposit copious amounts of rain and over 100 inches of snow during winter months. Summer precipitation amounts are also higher in the Olympics due to orographic lifting and convective disturbances.

The Western Lowlands. The Western Lowlands, extending from the Rogue Valley in the south to the Willamette Valley and Puget Sound Lowlands in the north, have dry, sunny summers and moist, mild winters. The north-south orientation of the Coast Range produces a lee effect and consequently slightly larger annual temperature ranges with higher maximums and lower minimums. In the southern valleys, hot summer days in excess of 90°F are not unusual whereas to the north daytime average temperatures are more moderate. The average July maximum for Portland is 78°F and 75°F for Seattle. Since precipitation is primarily a winter season phenomenon, summer daytime humidity averages 50% or less, a delightful situation favorable to human comfort. Cool nights are also more likely in summer, with average July minimums from 50-55°F. Dry, hot winds occasionally invade the lowlands, funneling through the Columbia Gorge from the east. On these occasions, clear, hot and dry conditions may last for several days, greatly increasing irrigation requirements, electricity demand, and forest fire hazard.

Dry spells may last 30-60 days in the summer, especially during July and August, but the dry summer merges into the rainy season in late September and early October. Winter is mild, cloudy, and moist. Cloud cover

PREVAILING SURFACE WIND DIRECTION AND SPEED

—July—

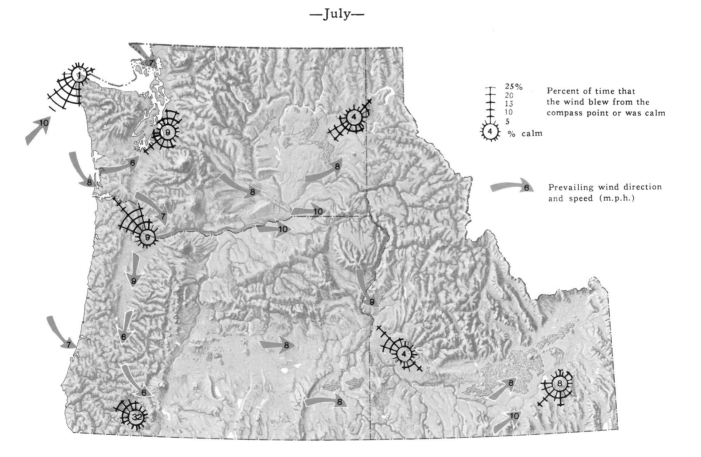

reduces possible sunshine to 25-30% and low intensity, gentle rains last an average of 16-18 days in each month during December and January. The highest monthly precipitation is in December, usually from 6-9 inches. To the south, the Rogue Valley is shielded from marine influences by the Siskiyou Mountains and receives only about one-half the monthly totals of the northern lowlands. Throughout this region some winters may pass without snowfall, but it is not uncommon for winter snows to total 10 inches. Total annual precipitation ranges from 35-45 inches, a relatively small amount considering the large number of rainy days.

The Cascades. Sharp temperature and precipitation gradients are induced by the Cascade Range. The high mountains to some extent create their own microclimates that correspond with changes in elevation, slope, and aspect. With the exception of the Columbia Gorge,

the high average elevation and orientation of the range creates an effective orographic barrier, resulting in a major east-west moisture divide. Winter precipitation is dominant as in the other climatic regions of the Pacific Northwest. The Cascades receive copious amounts of rain on the western slopes, but it is the annual snowfall that sets the region apart. Total annual precipitation ranges from 70 to over 100 inches, with the highest amounts normally falling in the northern Cascades of Washington. Snowfall is heaviest at elevations from 5,000-7,000 feet, with winter totals of 200-600 inches, and ground accumulations of up to 25 feet. Crater Lake receives on the average over 100 inches each month during December, January, and February. Year-round snowfields and glaciers are found on the highest peaks. In other areas snowfields may last from April to the end of July. Winter temperatures are distinctly colder at higher

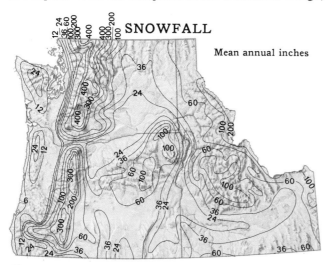

SNOWFALL

Mean annual inches

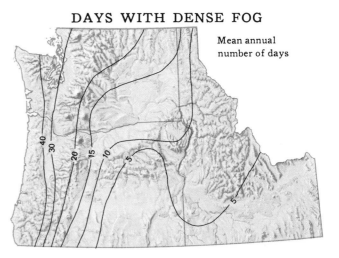

DAYS WITH DENSE FOG

Mean annual
number of days

elevations, but the lower Pacific slopes of the Cascades have mean minimum winter temperatures above 30°F. The average January temperature at Snoqualmie Pass, Washington (3,020 feet) is 27°F. The higher eastern slopes have less snow accumulation but there is a greater abundance of sunshine, enhancing winter recreational activities.

Summer is brief in the higher Cascades; in some areas the length of the freeze-free season is less than 30 days. The northern Cascades have a higher frequency of summer storms than do the more southerly mountains. Still, only about 8% of the total annual precipitation falls during the summer. Temperature maximums are generally from the 70s to 80s during the day but may drop to freezing at night due to the clear and relatively dry atmosphere found at higher elevations.

The Intermontane Region. The distinctive climatic characteristics of the intermontane region are low precipitation totals, large temperature ranges between summer and winter, and fewer cloudy days than to the west. This is a very large region, extending from the Columbia Basin in the north to the fault-block basin and range to the south. Average annual precipitation totals over the area range from 10-20 inches, with up to 30 inches falling in elevated locations. In general, precipitation amounts increase in response to elevation increases to the east. Pendleton, Oregon, for example, averages only 11-14 inches of precipitation, while Moscow, Idaho in the elevated Palouse Hills averages 22 inches. Boise, Idaho, to the east on the Snake River Plain at about the same elevation as Moscow, only averages 12 inches of annual precipitation.

The Blue Mountains of northeastern Oregon receive only one-third to one-half the precipitation that falls in the Cascades. Fall, winter, and spring precipitation totals here are nearly the same. Convective thunderstorms in spring contribute 1-2 inches of rain per month; an important climatic feature for dryland grain farming. The cool nights and dry sunny days of July and August provide ideal conditions for ripening wheat in the Palouse and the Snake River Plain, and foster the growth of orchard crops in Oregon's Hood River and Washington's Yakima and Wenatchee valleys.

During the winter, precipitation is generally in the form of snow, ranging from 10-30 inches depending on elevation and exposure. Snow tends to remain on the

ANNUAL PRECIPITATION

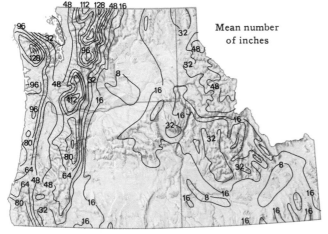

Mean number of inches

DAYS WITH PRECIPITATION

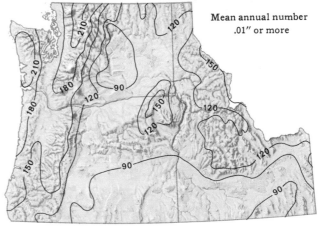

Mean annual number .01″ or more

WINTER PRECIPITATION

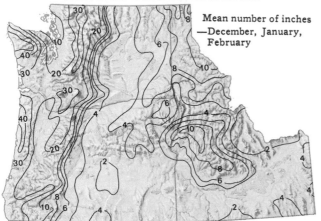

Mean number of inches —December, January, February

SUMMER PRECIPITATION

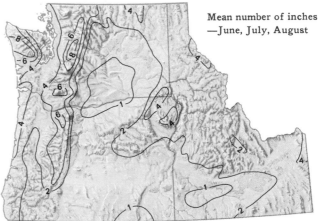

Mean number of inches —June, July, August

ground for some time due to colder winter temperatures than are experienced in the western part of the region. Except for areas along the Columbia and Snake Rivers, characteristic continental temperature ranges are experienced. July daytime temperatures in the 80s and 90s are common, dropping to the mid-50s at night. January mean temperatures average 20-30°F but in some locations daytime temperatures may not rise above 0°F. As cold, dry air masses flow into the region from the Rocky Mountains, temperatures may drop to –20 to –30°F. During the winter, strong winds flow across the plateau in response to pressure system movements. Soils of the Palouse and Columbia borderlands are particularly susceptible to severe wind erosion at this time of year if left unprotected.

Northeastern Mountains and Valleys. Continental influences dominate the highlands of northeastern Oregon and central Idaho. Within this region, the considerable elevation differences are responsible for strikingly different mountain and valley climates. Over the region, an average annual temperature range of 50°F or more is common. January temperatures average 19-21°F and temperatures below 0°F are not uncommon, with –40 to –50°F reported. Precipitation in winter is almost entirely snow, which falls seventy to eighty days a year. The higher mountains, such as the Wallowas, Bitterroots, and Selkirks, capture large amounts of moisture from winter cyclonic storms, but at moderate elevations snowfall totals are only 40-80 inches.

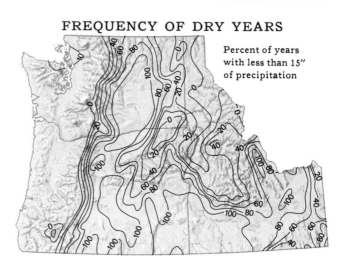

FREQUENCY OF DRY YEARS

Percent of years with less than 15″ of precipitation

The bright, clear days of summer are punctuated by thunderstorms. These local storms are short in duration but serve to cool down temperatures and contribute significantly to the 10-20 inches of precipitation at most valley stations. Summer is relatively short in the higher elevations, but in the valleys the freeze-free period is sufficient for forage and some small grain production. Temperatures may rise into the 80s on July days and drop into the low 50s at moderate elevations at night.

FREEZE-FREE PERIOD

Mean annual
number of days

LAST KILLING FROST OF SPRING

Mean date

FIRST KILLING FROST IN FALL

Mean date

JANUARY MAXIMUM TEMPERATURE

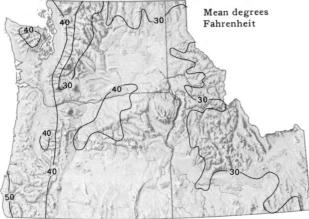

Mean degrees
Fahrenheit

JULY MAXIMUM TEMPERATURE

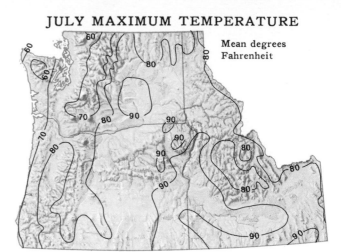

Mean degrees
Fahrenheit

JANUARY MINIMUM TEMPERATURE

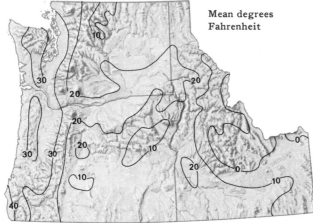

Mean degrees
Fahrenheit

JULY MINIMUM TEMPERATURE

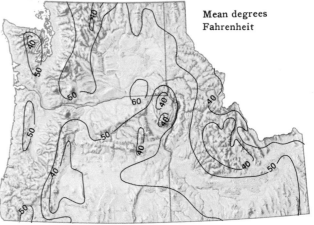

Mean degrees
Fahrenheit

JANUARY SUNSHINE

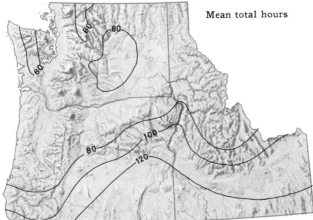

Mean total hours

JULY SUNSHINE

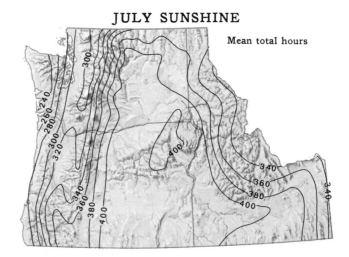

Mean total hours

VARIATIONS IN TEMPERATURE AND PRECIPITATION

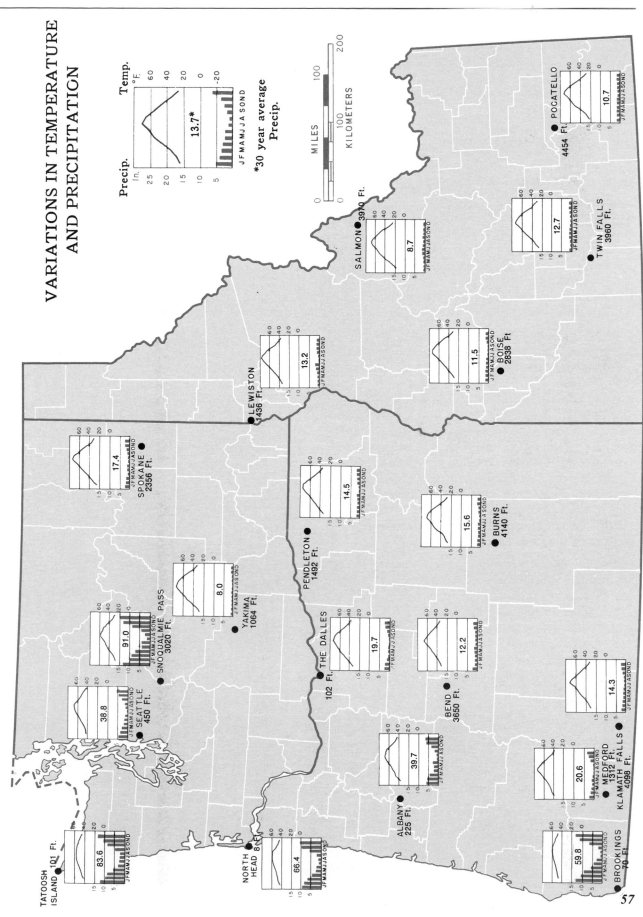

*30 year average Precip.

Vegetation
Robert E. Frenkel

The vegetation of the Pacific Northwest exhibits a complex pattern reflecting diversity in climate, soils, relief, incidence of fire, biotic interaction, and history. Recent impacts on pristine vegetation by logging, grazing, agriculture, industrial development, and urbanization have greatly altered the natural pattern. While it is possible to map this altered pattern, the map of Vegetation Zones on page 60 depicts plant cover as it might appear in the absence of human interference, if logging, agriculture, and urban-industrial use were not present.

Major vegetation differences, especially those determined by macroclimate, are displayed by three vegetation provinces—Forest, Shrub-Steppe, and Alpine—embracing fifteen vegetation zones or zone complexes. As used here, a vegetation zone is the area within which maturely developed soils (zonal soils)—support a particular climatic climax vegetation. A zone would therefore be a broad area within which one plant association is capable of becoming dominant under prevalent climatic conditions over a long period of time. In practice, alteration of plant cover has been profound. As a result, the potentially dominant species identifying the mapped vegetation zones may not currently prevail.

Within a given vegetation zone exist numerous plant communities which, when fully developed under localized environmental conditions, may be referred to as plant associations. The classification and description of these localized plant communities and related habitat types is well developed in the Pacific Northwest (see map of Plant Community Classification Status, 1983, on page 62).

The vegetation of the region is imperfectly known. A major review of the plant cover of Oregon and Washington was conducted by Franklin and Dyrness (1973). The major works which introduce the interested individual to the broad aspects of Pacific Northwest vegetation are Daubenmire's (1970) detailed studies of steppe vegetation of Washington and forest vegetation in eastern Washington and northern Idaho (Daubenmire and Daubenmire 1968); Steele et al.'s (1981) study of central Idaho forests; and Cronquist et al.'s (1972) review of the vegetation of the southeastern portion of the region.

Species and Ecotype Range

A quite different concept than that of vegetation zones concerns the distribution of individual plant species within the region of their occurrence, or a species' range. A plant species does not occupy all the area within its range owing to differences in soil, topography, and local climate. Plant species often consist of a series of races genetically adapted to localized ecological conditions, called ecotypes. The maps on the opposite page show the ranges of eight prominent tree species and some major ecotypes in the Pacific Northwest.

Douglas-fir *(Pseudotsuga menziesii).*

PONDEROSA PINE

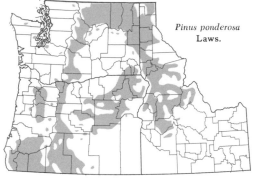

Pinus ponderosa
Laws.

SHORE PINE/LODGEPOLE PINE

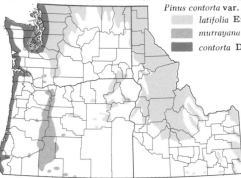

Pinus contorta var.

latifolia Engelm.
murrayana (Grev. & Balf.)
    Engelm.
contorta Dougl.

QUAKING ASPEN

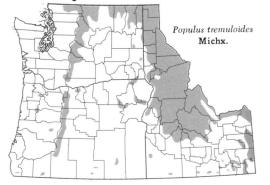

Populus tremuloides
Michx.

OREGON WHITE OAK

Quercus garryana
Dougl.

ENGELMANN SPRUCE

Picea engelmanii
Parry

WESTERN JUNIPER

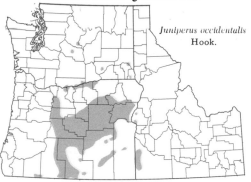

Juniperus occidentalis
Hook.

WESTERN HEMLOCK

Tsuga heterophylla
(Raf.) Sarg.

DOUGLAS-FIR

Pseudotsuga menziesii var.

glauca (Beissn.) Franco
menziesii (Mirb.) Franco

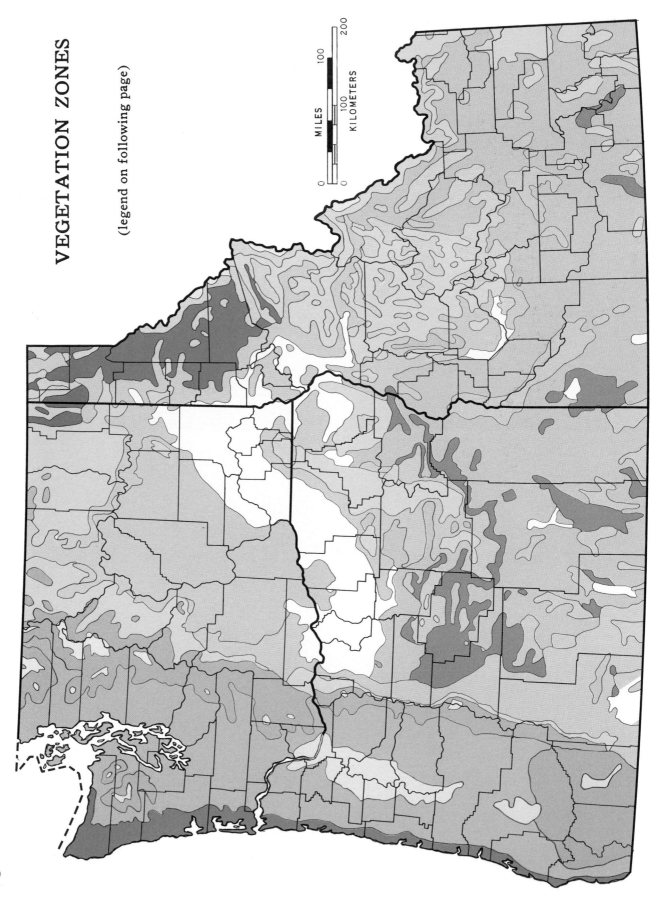

VEGETATION ZONES

(legend on following page)

MILES

KILOMETERS

0 100 200

0 100

Forest Province.

Sitka Spruce Zone. Confined to the coast, this coniferous zone extends from Alaska to southwestern Oregon and has been extensively altered by logging and fire. Sitka spruce (*Picea sitchensis*) characterizes the zone although in many places western hemlock (*Tsuga heterophylla*) and Douglas-fir (*Pseudotsuga menziesii*) dominate. Red alder (*Alnus rubra*) often forms patches in disturbed areas and riparian situations, while western redcedar (*Thuja plicata*) characterizes swampy habitats. Besides stabilized dune communities in which shore pine (*Pinus contorta*) is a prominent successional species, there are salt marsh communities in estuaries and communities associated with shifting dunes. The Sitka Spruce Zone grades into the Western Hemlock Zone to which it is closely related.

Western Hemlock Zone. Mantling both the Coast Range and western slopes of the Cascades, this zone is one of the most extensive in the region, stretching from British Columbia to California. Although named for the shade-tolerant western hemlock (*Tsuga heterophylla*) characterizing the persistent vegetation, the dominant tree is often the seral Douglas-fir. Extensive logging has occurred throughout the area. Communities within this zone have been studied in detail and have been related to site characteristics. Some important species are western redcedar in moist sites and, in the south, ponderosa pine (*Pinus ponderosa*) and incense cedar (*Calocedrus decurrens*). In disturbed moist sites, red alder and bigleaf maple (*Acer macrophyllum*) are common. Western hemlock gives way to Douglas-fir in drier sites and Pacific silver fir (*Abies amabilis*) at higher elevations.

Western Redcedar Zone. At moderate altitudes in moist locales in the northeastern portion of the region, this zone occurs between the more xeric Grand Fir and Douglas-fir Zones and the spruce-fir type. Dominant trees include western redcedar, western hemlock, and western white pine (*Pinus monticola*), but grand fir and western larch are found in drier sites. Understory unions in this zone are often similar to those of the Grand Fir and Douglas-fir zones.

Engelmann Spruce and Subalpine Fir Zones. Confined to higher elevations to the east, this type is the counterpart of the Cascade Subalpine Forest. Varying from dense to open parklike stands of subalpine fir and Engelmann spruce (*Picea engelmannii*), the zone has occasional intrusions of subalpine larch (*Larix lyallii*) and whitebark pine (*Pinus albicaulis*) at higher elevations and Douglas-fir at lower elevations.

Cascade Subalpine Forest Zone Complex. A group of zones marked by heavy snow flanks the Cascades and Olympics and extends into British Columbia. This group includes the Pacific Silver Fir Zone marked by *Abies amabilis*. At higher elevations, silver fir gives way to a more stunted forest of mountain hemlock (*Tsuga mertensiana*) and subalpine fir (*Abies lasiocarpa*) and forms a parklike pattern of open meadow and forest stringers. In areas of volcanic ash or areas recently disturbed by fire, even-aged stands of lodgepole pine (*Pinus contorta* var. *murrayana*) prevail. In southern Oregon, the zones bear close relationship to the California red fir forest.

Grand Fir and Douglas-fir Zones. Mesic coniferous forests occur in interior areas and exhibit a broad distribution. Often both grand fir (*Abies grandis*) and Douglas-fir (*Pseudotsuga menziesii*) occur in mixed stands, although Douglas-fir tends to be more prevalent in Idaho. Other trees of importance, in order of increasing moisture tolerance, are ponderosa pine, western larch (*Larix occidentalis*), and lodgepole pine; the latter two species are fire-responsive pioneers. In northern Idaho, western redcedar and western hemlock are prominent. Oregon boxwood (*Pachystima myrsinites*) and common snowberry (*Symphoricarpos albus*) dominate two prevalent understory communities.

Ponderosa Pine Zone. In a broad belt below the Grand Fir and Douglas-fir zones is an open coniferous forest dominated by *Pinus ponderosa*. Understory vegetation varies from shrubby mats of bitterbrush (*Purshia tridentata*) and snowbrush (*Ceanothus velutinus*) in central Oregon to meadows of Idaho fescue (*Festuca idahoensis*) further to the east. This zone has been severely altered by timber harvest.

Mixed Needleleaf-Broadleaf Forest Zone Complex. A highly intricate set of zones closely related to plant communities in California, this mixed evergreen forest straddles the Siskiyou Mountains in southwestern Oregon. Edaphic, fire history, and climatic contrasts lead to sharp breaks in plant cover. Douglas-fir dominates the upper canopy, but various sclerophyllous trees and shrubs are found in the understory including tanoak (*Lithocarpus densiflorus*), canyon live oak (*Quercus chrysolepis*), Pacific madrone (*Arbutus menziesii*), and golden chinquapin (*Castanopsis chrysophylla*). Serpentine soil bears a distinctive flora and sparse vegetation, and other dry rocky areas support sclerophyllous broadleaf chaparral.

Rogue-Umpqua Forest-Shrub Zone Complex. Occupying valleys in the rainshadow of the Siskiyou Mountains is a vegetation mosaic exhibiting many xeric characteristics. Woodlands are dominated by Oregon white oak (*Quercus garryana*), with California black oak (*Q. kelloggii*) on mesic sites. Pacific madrone, ponderosa pine, sugar pine (*P. lambertiana*), and incense cedar distinguish this zone from Willamette Valley. On shallow soils, south slopes, and recently burned areas, sclerophyllous shrub communities are found with narrow-leaved buckbrush (*Ceanothus cuneatus*) and white-leaved manzanita (*Arctostaphylos viscida*).

Willamette Forest-Prairie Zone Complex. Confined to bottomland and adjacent slopes of the Willamette Valley is a mosaic of forest, woodland, open savanna, and prairie. Prairie and oak savanna at the time of first settlement was maintained by aboriginal burning. Woodlands dominated by Oregon white oak have since been invaded by Douglas-fir and grand fir, with bigleaf maple important on north-facing slopes. Grasslands maintained by grazing include many introduced species and occupy drier sites. Lacing this mosaic of forest and prairie are bands of riparian woodland in which Oregon ash (*Fraxinus latifolia*), black poplar (*Populus trichocarpa*), and willow (*Salix* spp.) are prominent.

Western Juniper Zone. This open woodland dominated by western juniper (*Juniperus occidentalis*) is the northern counterpart of the Pinyon-Juniper type of the Great Basin. Shrub-steppe dominated by big sagebrush (*Artemisia tridentata*) and Idaho fescue typically comprises the understory of this zone. Throughout the arid regions of interior Oregon, juniper woodland characterizes rimrock habitat where local moisture supplies permit establishment of this xerophytic tree.

Shrub-Steppe Province.

Steppe Zone Complex. Grassland without shrubs mantles areas of north-central Oregon and the Palouse of southeastern Washington and adjacent Idaho. Much of this grassland has been converted to farming with circle irrigation. Among the various communities within this grassland is the *Agropyron-Festuca* type characterized by bluebunch wheatgrass (*Agropyron spicatum*) and Idaho fescue. In moister situations, Sandberg's bluegrass (*Poa sandbergii*) and Idaho fescue are prominent together with many forbs and shrubby common snowberry. The steppe type is intermediate between ponderosa pine forest and more xeric shrub-steppe, and the communities of the Steppe Zone Complex form understory unions in these adjacent vegetation types.

Big Sagebrush Zone. The most widespread vegetation zone in the Pacific Northwest extends from Canada to Nevada and from the Cascades to the Rockies. Dominated by big sagebrush, the zone intermingles with juniper woodland in central Oregon and supports nonintensive grazing. Plant communities have been identified based on understory grasses, shrub cover, soils, and slope. Two prominent communities are *Artemisia tridentata/Festuca idahoensis* and *Artemisia tridentata/Agropyron spicatum* associations, the former with greater moisture requirements. Low sagebrush (*Artemisia arbuscula*) frequently replaces big sagebrush in eastern Oregon on shallow stony soils. Other prominent shrubs include several species of sagebrush and rabbit brush (*Chrysothamnus* spp.). Commonly referred to as "high desert," the shrub-steppe in this zone consists of nondesert species and exhibits a shrub-grass structure which is distinct from true desert.

Desert Shrub Zone Complex. Occupying pockets within the Big Sagebrush Zone, the Desert Shrub Zone Complex is the most xeric of the region. Frequently the type occupies playas where saline conditions prevail, but also occurs in the rainshadow of several mountain ranges in southeastern Oregon and southern Idaho. Important shrubs, most of which are halophytic, include shadscale (*Atriplex confertifolia*), salt sage (*A. nuttalli*), greasewood (*Sarcobatus vermiculatus*), and spring hopsage (*Grayia spinosa*). Grasses and forbs are occasionally found in this open vegetation.

Alpine Province.

Alpine Zone Complex. Found near and above the tree line, this zone complex is narrowly represented in the Cascades and more extensively in the Rocky Mountains. Mainly comprised of herbaceous plants and low shrubs, these zones contain a few trees displaying krummholz form and occupying protected habitats. Alpine heath communities of the subalpine park land extend into the alpine zones, and glaciers, permanent snow fields, and extensive areas of talus and rock cover much of the area.

Habitat Type Status in the Pacific Northwest

Over the past thirty years a regional approach to classifying land has been developed. While broad expanses of vegetation may be classified and mapped as vegetation zones, most detailed vegetation classification is based on the concept of habitat type.

A habitat type is the lowest level of ecosystem classification and is defined as the aggregation of landscape components supporting, or capable of supporting, a relatively stable plant community in the absence of disturbance. A habitat type is therefore the physical and biotic base for the development of a climax association. Like vegetation zones, habitat type vegetation represents a site's potential natural vegetation; because of prior alteration, most land units are occupied by developmental (seral) vegetation. Habitat types are named for the ultimate stable plant communities at a site; for example, a widespread habitat type for middle elevations of the Oregon western Cascades is the western

hemlock/rhododendron/Oregon grape (*Tsuga heterophylla/Rhododendron macrophyllum/Berberis nervosa*).

Extensive areas of the Pacific Northwest have been classified by habitat type, but few have been mapped at this level. The classifications are especially useful in prescribing site specific management practices.

Ecoregions

Regional variations in climate, vegetation, soil, and landforms in the Pacific Northwest are integrated into a single map of ecoregions. An outgrowth of regional planning at the federal level, ecoregion mapping helps with (1) planning where broad management problems must be considered; (2) organizing and retrieving resource inventory data; and (3) interpreting and analyzing resource data. This system has been useful in assessments required by the Resources Planning Act, in the U.S. Forest Service Roadless Area Review and Evaluation (RARE II) program, and in the National Wetlands Inventory conducted by the Fish and Wildlife Service.

PLANT COMMUNITY CLASSIFICATION STATUS—1983

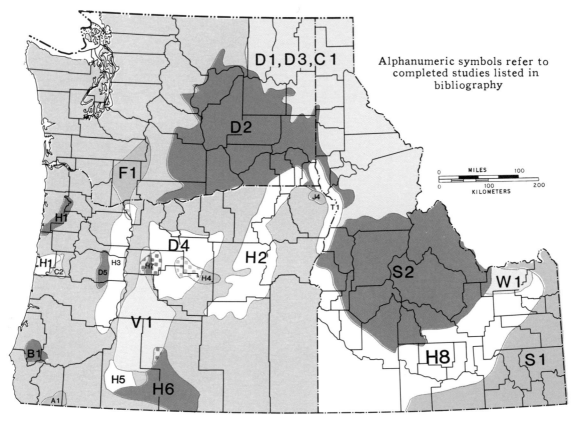

Alphanumeric symbols refer to completed studies listed in bibliography

See Bibliography (page 136) for complete citations.

A1	Atzet 1979.	D5	Dyrness et al. 1974.	H7	Hopkins & Kovalchik 1983.
B1	Bailey 1966.	F1	Franklin 1966.	H8	Hironaka et al. 1983.
C1	Cooper et al. 1983.	H1	Hines 1971.	J4	Johnson 1982.
C2	Corliss & Dyrness 1965.	H2	Hall 1973.	S1	Steele et al. 1983.
D1	Daubenmire 1952.	H3	Hemstrom et al. 1982.	S2	Steele et al. 1981.
D2	Daubenmire 1970.	H4	Hall 1967.	T1	Tisdale 1979.
D3	Daubenmire & Daubenmire 1968.	H5	Hopkins 1979a.	V1	Volland 1976.
D4	Driscoll 1964.	H6	Hopkins 1979b.	W1	Winward 1970.

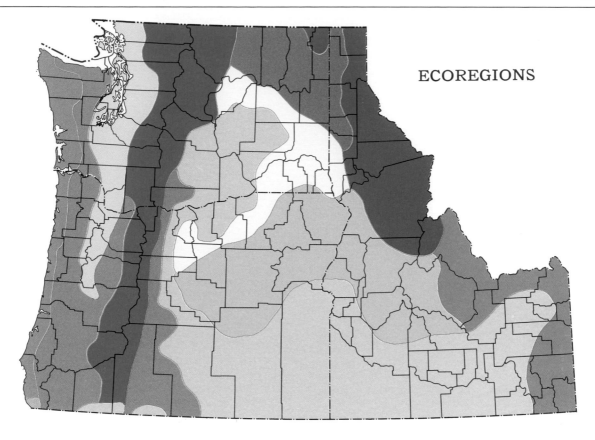

ECOREGIONS

HUMID TEMPERATE DOMAIN

Warm Continental Division

Columbia Forest Province

- Douglas Fir Forest
- Cedar-Hemlock-Douglas Fir Forest

Marine Division

Willamette-Puget Forest Province

Pacific Forest Province

- Redwood Forest
- Sitka Spruce-Cedar-Hemlock Forest
- Cedar-Hemlock-Douglas Fir Forest
- Silver Fir-Douglas Fir Forest

Mediterranean Division

Sierran Forest Province

DRY DOMAIN

Steppe Division

Palouse Grassland Province

Intermountain Sagebrush Province

- Sagebrush-Wheatgrass
- Ponderosa Shrub Forest

Rocky Mountain Forest Province

- Grand Fir-Douglas Fir Forest
- Douglas Fir Forest

Although combining different kinds of physical and biological data into a single system of regionalization is not new, the ecoregion map developed by Bailey (1976 and 1978) establishes a hierarchical system based on

independent data bases. Since macroclimate reflecting broad similarity in zonal heat and moisture availability is regarded as the major control on physical systems, the

(Text continues on page 66.)

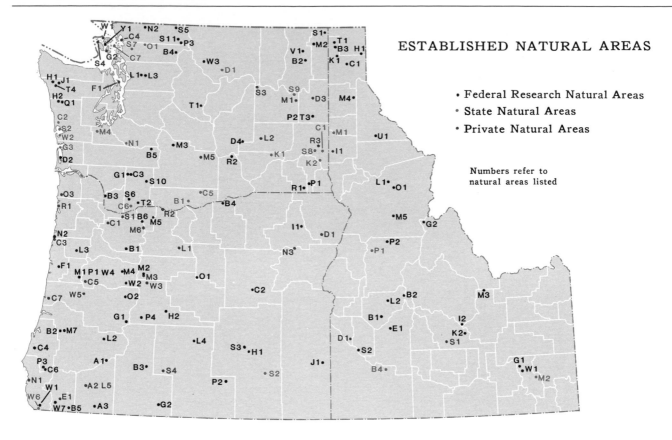

ESTABLISHED NATURAL AREAS

• Federal Research Natural Areas
• State Natural Areas
• Private Natural Areas

Numbers refer to
natural areas listed

Idaho

	Name	Owner-ship	Area Acres	Ha
B1	Bannack Creek	USFS	72	177
B2	Bear Creek	USFS	64	157
B3	Bottle Lake	USFS	42	105
B4	Bruneau Marsh	IDPR	3	8
C1	Canyon Creek	USFS	153	379
D1	Dautrich Memorial Preserve	TNC	140	346
E1	Elk Creek Exclosure	USFS	18	44
G1	Gibson Jack Creek	USFS	362	895
G2	Gunbarrel Creek	USFS	262	648
H1	Hunt Girl Creek	USFS	246	609
I1	Idlers Rest Nature Preserve	TNC	5	13
I2	Iron Bog	USFS	72	177
K1	Kaniksu Marsh	USFS	30	73
K2	Kipuka	NPS	98	243
L1	Lochsa	USFS	210	519
L2	Lowman	USFS	62	154
M1	Mary McCroskey State Park	IDPR	246	607
M2	McCammon Pond	ISU	20	49
M3	Meadow Canyon	USFS	636	1,571
M4	Montford Creek	USFS	48	118
M5	Moose Meadow Creek	USFS	166	411
O1	O'Hara Creek	USFS	1,147	2,834
P1	Ponderosa Peninsula	IDPR	49	122
P2	Pony Meadows	USFS	239	591
S1	Silver Creek Preserve	TNC	210	519
S2	Snake River Birds of Prey	BLM	5,243	12,956
T1	Teepee Creek	USFS	108	267
U1	Upper Fishhook	USFS	53	130
W1	West Fork Mink Creek	USFS	105	259

Washington

	Name	Owner-ship	Area Acres	Ha
B1	Badger Gulch	DNR	33	81
B2	Baird Basin	USFS	26	65
B3	Blackwater Island	FWS	21	52
B4	Boston Glacier	NPS	506	1,251
B5	Butter Creek	USFS/NPS	419	1,035
C1	Campus Prairie	WSU	1	3
C2	Carlisle Bog	DNR	33	81
C3	Cedar Flats	USFS	111	275
C4	Chuckanut Island Preserve	TNC	1	2
C5	Cleveland Shrub-Steppe	DNR	46	113
C6	Columbia Falls	DNR	43	105
C7	Cypress Island Eagle Cliffs	DNR	26	65
D1	Davis Canyon	DNR/BLM	35	87
D2	Diamond Point	FWS	13	32
D3	Dishman Hills Preserve	TNC	53	130
D4	Drumheller Sagebrush Steppe	FWS	76	188
F1	Foulweather Bluff Preserve	TNC	15	38
G1	Goat Marsh	USFS	196	484
G2	Goose and Deadman Islands Preserve	TNC	1	2
G3	Gunpowder Island	DNR	32	80
H1	Hades Creek	NPS	92	227
H2	Higley Creek	NPS	79	194
J1	Jackson Creek	NPS	26	65
K1	Kahlotus Ridgetop	DNR	39	97
K2	Kramer Palouse	WSU	5	11
L1	Lake Twenty-two	USFS	130	320
L2	Lind Shrub-Steppe Preserve	TNC	4	10
L3	Long Creek	USFS	105	259

Washington (Cont.)

	Name	Owner-ship	Area Acres	Ha
M1	Magnuson Butte Preserve	TNC	5	11
M2	Maitlen Creek	USFS	103	254
M3	Meeks Table	USFS	11	28
M4	Mima Mounds	DNR	89	221
M5	Moxee Bog Preserve	TNC	2	6
N1	Newton Creek	UW	7	16
N2	North Fork Nooksack	USFS	230	569
O1	Olivine Bridge	DNR	24	60
P1	Pataha Bunchgrass	USFS	8	21
P2	Pine Creek	FWS	26	65
P3	Pyramid Lake	NPS	19	48
Q1	Quinault	USFS	240	594
R1	Rainbow Creek	USFS	98	243
R2	Rattlesnake Hills	DOE	12,141	30,000
R3	Rose Creek Preserve	TNC	2	5
S1	Salmo	USFS	228	563
S2	Sand and Goose Islands	DNR	17	40
S3	Seaton Canyon Preserve	TNC	31	76
S4	Sentinel Island Preserve	TNC	2	6
S5	Silver Lake	NPS	261	644
S6	Sister Rocks	USFS	35	87
S7	Skagit River Bald Eagle	WDG/TNC	144	356
S8	Smoot Hills	WSU	17	41
S9	Spring Creek Canyon	DNR	39	96
S10	Steamboat Mountain	USFS	230	567
S11	Stetattle Creek	NPS	1,514	3,741
T1	Thompson Clover	USFS	33	81
T2	Thornton T. Munger	USFS	193	478
T3	Turnbull Pine	FWS	32	80
T4	Twin Creek	NPS	16	40
V1	Varline Grove	FWS	26	65
W1	Waldron Island Preserve	TNC	45	110
W2	Whitcomb Flats	DNR	2	4
W3	Wolf Creek	USFS	24	60
Y1	Yellow Island Preserve	TNC	2	5

BLM	Bureau of Land Management, U.S. Department of the Interior
DNR	Department of Natural Resources, State of Washington
DOD	Department of Defense
DOE	U.S. Department of Energy
FWS	Fish and Wildlife Service, U.S. Department of the Interior
IDPR	Idaho Department of Parks and Recreation
ISU	Idaho State University
NPS	National Park Service, U.S. Department of the Interior
SLB	State Land Board, State of Oregon
TNC	The Nature Conservancy
USFS	Forest Service, U.S. Department of Agriculture
UW	University of Washington
WDG	Washington Department of Game
WSU	Washington State University

Oregon

	Name	Owner-ship	Area Acres	Ha
A1	Abbott Creek	USFS	436	1,077
A2	Agate Desert Preserve	TNC	3	7
A3	Ashland	USFS	231	570
B1	Bagby	USFS	92	227
B2	Beatty Creek	BLM	65	160
B3	Blue Jay	USFS	34	85
B4	Boardman	DOD	809	2,000
B5	Brewer Spruce	BLM	34	85
B6	Bull Run	USFS	59	146
C1	Camassia Preserve	TNC	5	11
C2	Canyon Creek	USFS	115	283
C3	Cascade Head Preserve	TNC	46	113
C4	Cherry Creek	BLM	97	239
C5	Cogswell-Foster Preserve	TNC	18	45
C6	Coquille River Falls	USFS	82	202
C7	Cox Island Preserve	TNC	31	76
D1	Downey Lake Preserve	TNC	17	41
E1	Eight Dollar Mountain Preserve	TNC	4	9
F1	Flynn Creek	USFS	110	271
G1	Gold Lake Bog	USFS	76	188
G2	Goodlow Mountain	USFS	206	510
H1	Harney Lake	FWS	4,856	12,000
H2	Horse Ridge	BLM	98	243
I1	Indian Creek	USFS	162	401
J1	Jordan Craters	BLM	5,143	12,709
L1	Lawrence Memorial Grassland Preserve	TNC	64	158
L2	Limpy Rock	USFS	308	760
L3	Little Sink	BLM	13	32
L4	Lost Forest	BLM	1,468	3,628
L5	Lower Table Rock Preserve	TNC	123	304
M1	Maple Knoll	FWS	16	40
M2	Metolius	USFS	216	533
M3	Metolius River Preserve	TNC	5	12
M4	Middle Santiam	USFS	187	463
M5	Mill Creek	USFS	134	330
M6	Multorpor Fen Preserve	TNC	13	33
M7	Myrtle Island	BLM	5	11
N1	Nesika Beach Preserve	TNC	6	15
N2	Neskowin Crest	USFS	195	481
N3	North Powder Thelypodium Preserve	TNC	0.5	1
O1	Ochoco Divide	USFS	314	777
O2	Ollalie Ridge	USFS	118	291
O3	Onion Creek Preserve	TNC	7	17
P1	Pigeon Butte	FWS	11	28
P2	Poker Jim Ridge	FWS	105	259
P3	Port Orford Cedar	USFS	184	454
P4	Pringle Falls	USFS	221	545
R1	Rockaway Old-growth Cedar Swamp Preserve	TNC	8	20
R2	Rowena Plateau Preserve	TNC	28	68
S1	Sandy River Preserve	TNC	67	165
S2	Steens Mountain Summit	SLB	77	191
S3	Stinking Lake	FWS	253	626
S4	Sycan Marsh Preserve	TNC	3,868	9,557
W1	Wheeler Creek	USFS	55	135
W2	Wildcat Mountain	USFS	164	405
W3	Wildhaven Preserve	TNC	26	65
W4	Willamette Floodplain	FWS	39	97
W5	Willow Creek Preserve	TNC	2	5
W6	Winchuck Slope	SLB	32	78
W7	Woodcock Bog	BLM	45	112

Pacific Northwest is first divided into two Domains, Humid Temperate, and Dry. Each domain includes several Divisions based on more specific macroclimatic criteria, e.g., Warm Continental Climate. Each division is in turn divided into several Provinces reflecting bioclimatic and soil criteria as generally expressed at the level of soil orders and vegetation formations, e.g., Douglas-fir Forest.

This hierarchical system of regionalization may be refined at lower levels; for example, provinces are subdivided into Sections reflecting potential vegetation types and sections are broken down into Districts based on land surface forms. Ultimately, the system is capable of defining a Site which is a more or less homogeneous unit of land with respect to local climate, landform, soil, and vegetation for which a management prescription can be effectively prepared.

Natural Areas

The comprehensive system of natural areas in the Pacific Northwest is among the best developed in the United States. A natural area is a physical and biological land unit on which the natural features are maintained in as undisturbed a condition as possible. In some instances special management practices, such as prescribed burning, may be used to retain desired ecosystems. Natural areas are established to protect typical as well as unique ecological systems. From its inception, the progam of dedicating natural areas has had two primary purposes: (1) to preserve a set of significant natural ecosystems representative of the potential range of natural diversity in the region, including aquatic and terrestrial communities and common as well as rare organisms; and (2) to make these ecosystems available for scientific research and educational use so that information about unimpaired ecosystems and natural processes may be employed in managing resources. Natural areas permit us to examine undisturbed systems and compare them with those that have been altered by human activities.

Approaches to the selection of natural areas are common throughout the region. First, a comprehensive listing of needs for natural area types has been developed and refined, representing specific ecological elements, e.g., a plant community, endangered plant or animal, or aquatic system. Second, a systematic inventory of sites is undertaken which lists the ecological elements contained in a given site. Third, an attempt is made to select the best of a number of sites containing one or more ecological elements for a proposed natural area.

Natural area programs in the Pacific Northwest occur under federal, state, and private direction; however, a loose coordination of these efforts exists among these three sectors and between states.

Federal. Federal research natural areas in Oregon and Washington are the responsibility of a committee under the direction of the USDA Forest Service Pacific Northwest Forest and Range Experiment Station. The committee develops uniform criteria for the selection, management, and use of research natural areas. As of 1983, there were 93 established federal research natural areas in the Pacific Northwest, 38 in Oregon, 33 in Washington, and 22 in Idaho.

State. Each state government has its own organization, policies, and procedures for establishing natural areas. In Oregon and Washington, comprehensive legislation has been adopted providing for state natural area systems; in Idaho, a coordinating committee centralizes natural area concerns.

Oregon's Natural Heritage Advisory Council was formed in 1979 and advises the State Land Board which is authorized to dedicate natural heritage conservation areas. The nine-member council has completed the *Oregon Natural Heritage Plan,* is continuing an inventory of these natural areas, and is working toward registration and dedication of natural areas in all jurisdictions within the state. Two state natural heritage conservation areas have been established.

The nine-member Washington Natural Heritage Advisory Council, appointed by the Commissioner of Public Lands, recommends establishment of typical and unique sites for inclusion in a Washington Natural Area Preserve System. The council is supported by a small staff which oversees the program under the Department of Natural Resources. The program has completed the *State of Washington Natural Heritage Plan,* has established eighteen state natural areas, mostly under the ownership of the Department of Natural Resources, and maintains a registry of natural areas.

Though Idaho has no legislation for establishing state natural areas, a number of technical committees and a coordinating committee work with other agencies—including the USDA Forest Service and the Idaho Parks Department—in support of the establishment of natural areas in the state.

The private sector. The Nature Conservancy is a non-profit corporation which purchases significant natural areas. It has established natural areas throughout the region, participated in the development of natural area need plans, and in the inventory of natural areas, mostly on private lands. Three critical activities in its operation are: (1) identification of natural areas; (2) protection of natural areas through acquisition, easement, and agreement; and (3) stewardship and preserve management. The Nature Conservancy has field offices in Oregon and Washington. In 1983, there were 35 preserves owned and managed by the Conservancy in the Pacific Northwest, twenty in Oregon, twelve in Washington, and three in Idaho.

The map of Established Natural Areas on page 64 shows the 152 protected natural areas established for scientific and educational use in the Pacific Northwest.

Soils

Robert E. Frenkel

Differences among soils result from the interaction of several major soil-forming factors: (1) geology—the parent material from which the soil developed; (2) the climate during soil development, especially soil temperature and moisture regimes; (3) the nature of the organic materials in the soil, reflecting the influence of the biota, particularly vegetation; (4) the relief, reflecting local physiography; and (5) the time over which the soil developed.

Soil Taxonomy

Soils may be differentiated and classified in many ways; however, the two major approaches in recent years have been by soil genesis or development (inferential classification) and by diagnostic soil properties (taxonomy). The classification system presented here depends largely on soil properties that can be observed in the field or laboratory. It is commonly referred to as the Soil Taxonomy system and has been adopted by the USDA Soil Conservation Service. Table 18 is included to facilitate comparison between the older genetic system and the more recent comprehensive taxonomic system.

Soil orders. Of the ten soil orders which have world-wide distribution, seven orders, comprising a total of twelve dominant suborders, are shown on the map of

Soil Orders and Sub-Orders on page 68. Soil orders are the highest taxonomic category and are generalized by common properties including horizon development and pattern, color, soil moisture, and degree of oxidation. In this way the distinguishing characteristics selected for the orders tend to give a broad climatic grouping of soils. Soil orders have the suffix *sol*. The formative element of the order name is usually descriptive, e.g., *"Aridisols"* are soils developed in areas with little moisture.

Suborders. Each order is subdivided into suborders primarily on the basis of characteristics which produce classes with the greatest genetic homogeneity. These characteristics include moisture regime, temperature, mineralogy, color, texture, and horizon properties. Altogether, 47 suborders have been identified; the twelve dominant suborders are shown on the map. Suborder nomenclature employs a prefix for that characteristic which is important in defining the suborders and a suffix derived from the appropriate order name; e.g., *"Argids"* are soils in the Aridisol order with argillic or clay horizons.

Great groups. The great group level attempts to consider the whole soil assemblage (similarity of diagnostic horizons), together with similarity of soil moisture and temperature regimes. It is the highest category

(Text continues on page 70.)

Table 18. *Soil Orders in the Soil Taxonomy Compared with Examples of Great Soil Groups in the 1938 Genetic System*

Formative element of soil taxonomy	Derivation of formative element	Examples of Great Soil Groups in the 1938 Genetic System
*Alf*isols	Nonsense syllable from "pedalfer"	Gray-Brown Podzolic soils, Noncalcic Brown soils, and Planosols
*Arid*isols	L. *aridus,* "dry"	Desert, Sierozem, Solonchak, Brown soils, and Reddish Brown soils
*Ent*isols	Nonsense syllable from "recent"	Azonal soils
*Hist*osols	Gr. *histos,* "tissue"	Bog soils
*Incept*isols	L. *inceptum,* "beginning"	Sol Brun Acide, Ando, Brown Forest, and Jumic Grey soils
*Moll*isols	L. *mollis,* "soft"	Chernozem, Chestnut, Brunizem, and Brown Forest soils
*Oxi*sols	F. *oxide,* "oxide"	Laterite soils and Latosols
*Spodo*sols	Gr. *spodos,* "wood ash"	Podzols and Brown Podzolic soils
*Ulti*sols	L. *ultimus,* "last"	Red-Yellow Podzolic soils and Reddish-Brown Lateritic soils
*Verti*sols	L. *verto,* "to turn"	Grumusols

Source: Soil Conservation Service, *Soil Classification, A Comprehensive System,* 1960.

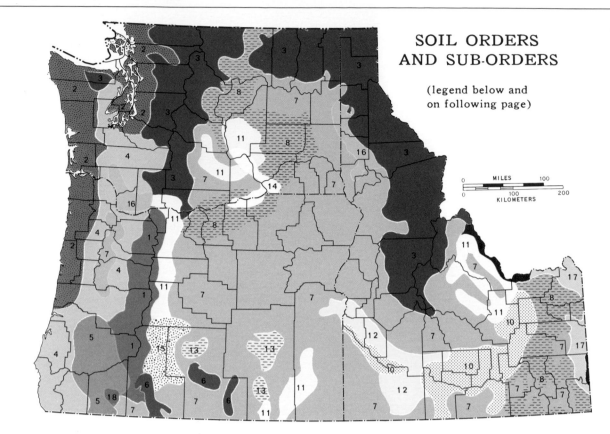

SOIL ORDERS
AND SUB-ORDERS

(legend below and
on following page)

Inceptisols

Inceptisols are soils with weakly differentiated horizons exhibiting some alteration of the parent material, but still containing weatherable materials. The B horizon typically has little clay accumulation. In the Pacific Northwest, these soils generally occur under cool summer climate where parent materials are of a late or post-Pleistocene origin and do not show translocation of clay. The order is present in the Puget Lowland, Coast Range, Cascades, and Idaho mountains. Two suborders are shown:

Umbrepts are soils with surface horizons darkened by high contents of organic matter, having crystalline clay minerals, with relatively high capacity to hold exchangeable cations but with acidic reaction, and are freely drained. They develop in areas of high winter precipitation and moderate winter temperatures in the Coast Range, Oregon Cascades, and Puget Lowland where coniferous forest is the prevailing vegetation.

 Cryumbrepts—in cold regions.

 *Haplumbrepts*—in temperate to warm regions.

Andepts are soils with high contents of volcanic ash and are therefore of low bulk density. They are of recent development, occurring in mountainous areas in Idaho and in the North Cascades under cool summer conditions.

 Cryandepts—in cold regions.

Ultisols

Strong weathering and leaching and a warm (mean annual temperature 46°F), moist (40-120 inches mean annual precipitation), and a summer-dry climate help produce Ultisols. These soils have a clay-rich horizon that is low in bases. Ultisols develop in a variety of parent materials and usually exhibit considerable stability. This order is found in the low hilly regions between the Cascades and Coast Range where they generally support coniferous forest growth, have good drainage, and display increasing acidity and decreasing base saturation with depth. Vegetative nutrient cycling is a key factor in the formation of these soils. Many are reddish. Two suborders are distinguished:

Humults are highly organic Ultisols developing under moist, cool to cold winters, and warm to hot dry summers. Humults show good drainage and are mostly dark colored. They develop on steep slopes, are easily eroded, and are found in southwestern Oregon and the foothills of the Cascades and Coast Range.

4 *Haplohumults*—with subsurface horizon of clay and/or weatherable minerals; in temperate climates.

Xerults are freely drained Ultisols in areas of Mediterranean climate with little organic material in the upper horizons and are seldom saturated with water. They are confined to the hilly regions in the middle portion of the Rogue and Umpqua drainages and support a mixed coniferous-broadleaved evergreen vegetation with xeric elements.

 Haploxerults—with a surface clay-rich horizon either having weatherable minerals or a decreasing clay content with depth, or both.

Mollisols

Soils that have dark-colored, friable, organic-rich surface horizons and which are high in bases, occurring in areas having a cold subhumid and semiarid climate. Mollisols are widespread in the region, especially in areas of steppe and shrub-steppe vegetation. These soils may have clay-enriched horizons, calcic horizons, sodium-rich horizons, or indurate horizons. Most soils are well drained, but wet soils may have soluble salts or high exchangeable sodium, or both. Three suborders are shown:

Aquolls are Mollisols that are seasonally wet with a thick, nearly black surface horizon and gray subsurface horizon. In south-central Oregon in the Warner Valley and Klamath Lake area, horizons have been altered, but no accumulation of calcium or clay has taken place.

Haplaquolls—with horizons in which materials have been altered or removed, but still may contain some calcium carbonate or gypsum.

Xerolls are Mollisols in winter-moist, summer-dry climates. Such soils are continually dry for long periods of time. With irrigation and when adequate natural soil moisture is available, these soils are important for grain and forage. These are the prevailing soils in the steppe and shrub-steppe areas of the region.

Argixerolls—with subsurface clay horizon, either thin or brownish.

Haploxerolls—with subsurface horizon high in bases, but with little clay, calcium carbonate, or gypsum.

Borolls are Mollisols of cool and cold regions exhibiting black surface horizons. In the Pacific Northwest they are confined to the extreme eastern portion of Idaho.

Argiborolls—with subsurface clay horizon, in cool regions.

Aridisols

As suggested by the name, this order occurs in dry areas where the soils are never moist for periods of more than three consecutive months. The soils are low in organic content and the horizons are light in color and have a soft consistency when dry. These soils are found in the rainshadow area of the Cascades and in extensive areas in southern Idaho. Two suborders are shown:

Orthids are Aridisols that display accumulations of calcium carbonate and other salts but do not have clay accumulations in horizons. Such soils are found in scattered localities in the drier areas of the Pacific Northwest.

Calciorthids—with a horizon containing much calcium carbonate or gypsum.

Camborthids—with horizons from which some materials have been removed or altered, but still contain calcium carbonate or gypsum.

Argids are Aridisols distinguished by a horizon in which clay has accumulated. These are mostly found in the Snake River Plain to the south of Boise.

Haplargids—with loamy horizon of clay, without sodium (alkali) accumulation, but may have calcium accumulation below the argillic horizon.

Natrargids—with a clay accumulation horizon and alkali (sodium) accumulation.

Entisols

Soils in this order exhibit little or no horizon development. In the Pacific Northwest these soils develop in sandy parent material and are of very recent origin on gently sloping terrain. They continue to receive parent material. They occur east of the Cascade Range. One suborder is shown on the map:

Psamments are Entisols with loamy fine sand to coarser sand texture developing in areas of shifting to stabilized sand dunes. Sand origin is largely fluvial but with local redeposition by wind.

Torripsamments—moist for less than three consecutive months and developing under cool to warm soil temperatures promoting soluble salt accumulation.

Xeropsamments—freely drained soils developing from weatherable minerals under moist winter, dry summer climates.

Alfisols

Soils in this order are differentiated by clay-enriched horizons, moderate organic matter accumulation, and a gray to brown color. They are usually leached and are acidic occurring where at least three months of growing season are cool and moist. Three areas are dominated by Alfisols: the hilly region north of Portland; the area northeast of Moscow; and the mountains near the eastern boundary of Idaho. Two suborders are shown:

Udalfs are Alfisols with a mesic or warm temperature regime and are almost always moist despite periods of summer dryness. These soils are brownish or reddish. The area north of Portland in which Udalfs prevail has a complex of other soils as well. The Udalf area in Idaho occurs in steep mountainous terrain.

Hapludalfs—with subsurface clay horizon below a thin eluvial horizon. These are good farming soils.

Boralfs are found in cool and cold regions and may be water-saturated in winter. A bleached eluvial horizon often grades into a horizon containing clay or alkali. They occur in the mountains of eastern Idaho.

Cryoboralfs—in cold regions; with sandy upper layers, grayish color, and subsurface clay horizon.

Vertisols

Relegated to this order are clayey soils that have wide, deep cracks which form during the dry season. They occur in areas with marked dry-wet periods. One suborder is present:

Xererts are Vertisols that have wide deep cracks that open and close once a year, remaining open for more than two months in summer and closing for more than two months in winter. In the Pacific Northwest, one area in the vicinity of Medford is characterized by this suborder.

Chromoxererts—with a brownish surface horizon.

evaluating the whole soil. The Soil Conservation Service recognizes 203 great groups and these are named by affixing a prefix of one or more formative elements to the suborder name. Therefore, a great group will have a three- or more syllable name ending in the suborder name; e.g., *Durargid* for an indurate, clay-layered Aridisol.

Families and series. There are also soil subgroups designated by two names, which group subdominant soil properties; soil families differentiated on the basis of properties important for utilization, especially for plant growth; and soil series, each a collection of soil individuals with essentially uniform differentiating characteristics. Soil series are given place names suggesting the fusion of the heirarchical soil taxonomy outlined above with real soils observed as soil individuals. Soil series are mapped and described in considerable detail and provide the resource manager with important information. It should however be noted that mapped soil series represent dominant groupings of soil individuals, while the actual region mapped will almost certainly include a minority of other soil individuals.

Type and phase. The comprehensive soil taxonomy also identifies soil type, which represents a lower category based on texture of the plow layer and soil phase, of which texture is just one significant property distinguishing a variety of soil species.

Soil Survey Status

The map of Soil Survey Status above shows the status of soil surveys in the Pacific Northwest as of 1982. Soil surveys for agricultural, engineering, and planning purposes are made cooperatively by federal and state government personnel, usually with the USDA Soil Conservation Service in charge and the agricultural experiment stations attached to land-grant universities as chief contributors. Other agencies—including the Bureau of Land Management, Bureau of Indian Affairs, Bureau of Reclamation (irrigation suitability studies), Forest Service, and state forestry departments—may enter into cooperative agreements. This joint effort, initiated in 1899, is referred to as the National Cooperative Soil Survey.

Modern soil surveys are extensive documents describing the geography of the region's soils, normally on a county basis, initiated on a priority basis depending on the presence of productive agricultural lands. Soil maps of a scale of 1:20,000 based on air photos and soil series descriptions are qualified by pedological notes. The surveys include sections on use and management of soils for a variety of purposes.

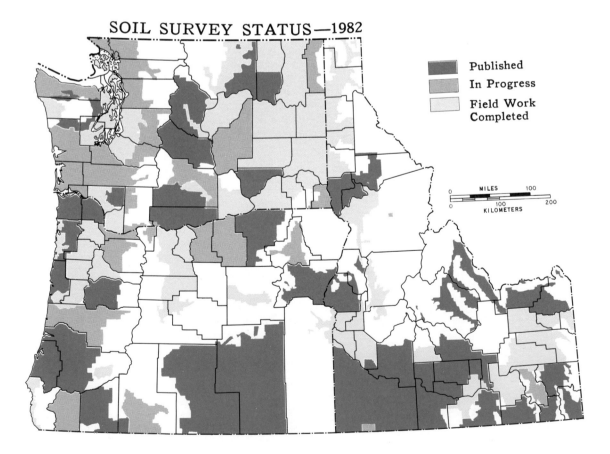

SOIL SURVEY STATUS—1982

Published
In Progress
Field Work Completed

Water Resources
Keith W. Muckleston

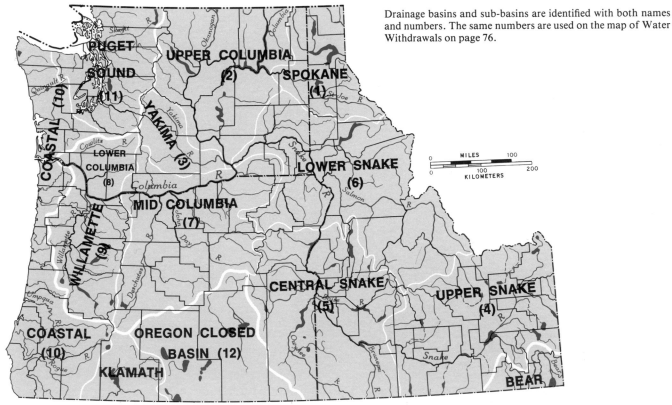

DRAINAGE BASINS AND SUB-BASINS

Drainage basins and sub-basins are identified with both names and numbers. The same numbers are used on the map of Water Withdrawals on page 76.

The Pacific Northwest is richly endowed with fresh water of relatively good quality. The volume of runoff from the region exceeds that of any other water region in the conterminous United States, surpassing most regions manyfold. In terms of per capita runoff, the relative position of the region is even more favorable. The utility of such a bountiful supply is diminished, however, by marked variations in spatial and temporal patterns of supply.

Unless otherwise indicated, the data in this section refer to the Columbia-North Pacific Region used by the Pacific Northwest River Basins Commission (PNRBC). This includes the Columbia drainage in the United States, coastal streams in Washington and Oregon, and the closed basin of south-central Oregon.

Supply

The map of Drainage Basins and Sub-Basins above shows the major sub-basins within the Pacific Northwest. The most significant source of fresh water is the Columbia River system. Rising in the Rocky Mountains of the United States and Canada, this system provides drainage for approximately 75% of the region and accounts for about 55% of the total runoff. When runoff from Canada is included, the Columbia system discharges approximately 65% of the total.

East of the Cascade Range the Columbia Basin is divided into seven sub-basins, where much of the land is subhumid to arid, and traversed by rivers that originate in various mountain ranges lying both within and to the north and northeast of the region. The Rocky Mountains provide much of the flow. Thus, the Lower Snake sub-basin contributes much more runoff than the Central Snake sub-basin.

There are three additional sub-basins east of the Cascade Range that are not part of the Columbia system. A number of streams in Oregon with internal drainage are designated as the Oregon Closed Basin, and portions of the Klamath and Bear rivers also drain small parts of the region. The Klamath rises in Oregon, flows through northern California, and discharges into the Pacific Ocean. Waters of the Bear River rise in Utah and Wyoming before crossing southeastern Idaho, finally discharging into Utah's Great Salt Lake.

Of the four humid sub-basins west of the Cascade Range, two—the Willamette and Lower Columbia—are part of the Columbia River system, while the streams of the coastal and Puget Sound sub-basins discharge into the Pacific Ocean.

The map below shows Major Surface Waters and Runoff. The runoff value for an area is derived by subtracting evaporation and transpiration from the amount of precipitation received. The values on the map refer to the mean annual depths of water in inches entering streams and rivers as surface flow from locations along the various isolines. The various depths of runoff from areas between the isolines may be inferred.

Based on runoff characteristics, the Pacific Northwest may be divided into two subregions. West of the Cascade Mountains runoff is generally high, reflecting relatively heavy precipitation and moderate levels of

Table 19.   Discharge of Selected Rivers in the Pacific Northwest

	Millions of acre-feet
Columbia River at mouth	180.1
Columbia River at The Dalles	133.7
Snake River at mouth	36.8
Willamette River at mouth	23.8
Skagit River at mouth	12.1
Rogue River at mouth	8.2

Notes: Acre-feet are given to the nearest .1 maf. For the Columbia system, the average annual runoff is based on a 50-year period, 1897-1946 (water years). For the Rogue and Skagit rivers, regulated values are for base period 1929-1958 with estimated 1970 conditions of development.

Sources: *Water Resources,* Appendix V, Vol. 1, p. 18, and Vol. 2, p. 782.

evapotranspiration. Indeed, the yield of runoff west of the Cascades is unrivaled in the conterminous United States. Yields of more than 80 inches (200 centimeters) are common in the Coast and Cascades ranges, while some of the windward slopes of the Olympic Mountains contribute more than 160 inches of runoff. Streams west of the Cascades produce about two-thirds of the total runoff from the Pacific Northwest although they drain less than one-fourth of the region.

By contrast, the much larger subregion east of the Cascade Range generates markedly lower levels of runoff per square mile. Lands in much of this subregion contribute less than 10 inches of runoff, and most of the

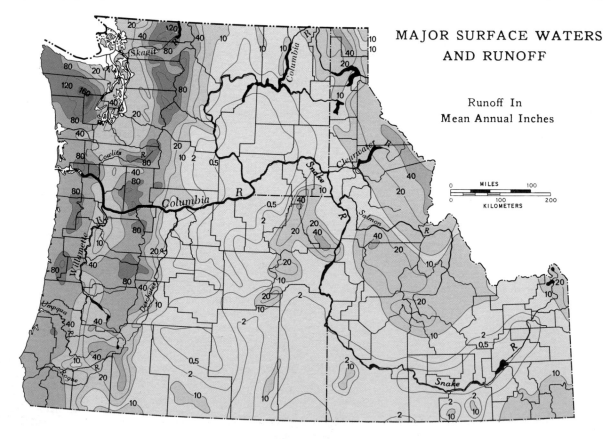

MAJOR SURFACE WATERS
AND RUNOFF

Runoff In
Mean Annual Inches

surface waters originate in relatively small mountainous areas. The position of mountains can be identified on the map by locating areas of relatively high runoff (20 inches or more). For example, the Blue Mountains in northeastern Oregon and southeastern Washington, the Wallowa Mountains in northeastern Oregon, and the Bitterroot and Coeur d'Alene Mountains along the northeastern border of Idaho stand out as islands of relatively high runoff.

The map of Major Aquifers on this page indicates that over one-half of the Pacific Northwest is underlain by aquifers with moderate to large potential yields of groundwater. The potential value of this source is great because it generally coincides with areas of heavy water use. The coastal areas are notably lacking in potentially productive aquifers. At present aquifers in the Snake River Plain account for most of the groundwater use in the region, although extensive withdrawals are also made in some parts of the Puget Sound and Willamette sub-basins.

The map of Surface Water Yearly Flow Cycle below illustrates that the patterns of temporal distribution of surface runoff vary considerably within the region. The hydrographs show average monthly discharges as a percentage of the yearly average. If the runoff remained constant throughout the year, 8.33% would be discharged each month.

Until recent decades the temporal patterns of runoff largely reflected natural phenomena within a river basin including: the mean elevation of the drainage basin; its

location in either marine or continental subregions of the Pacific Northwest; the type and extent of natural vegetation within the drainage basin; and the structure of aquifer units underlying the basin. Although the combined effects of natural phenomena remain dominant in most river basins within the region, anthropogenic influences have become more important in some basins during recent decades of increasingly intensive water use. Principal anthropogenic influences include stream flow depletions from extensive irrigation withdrawals and the construction and operation of large storage reservoirs, the major purpose of which is to reduce temporal variations of runoff.

MAJOR AQUIFERS

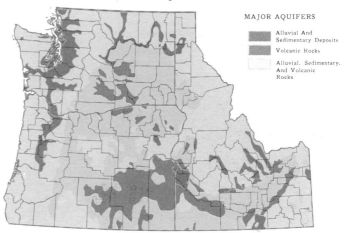

SURFACE WATER YEARLY FLOW CYCLE

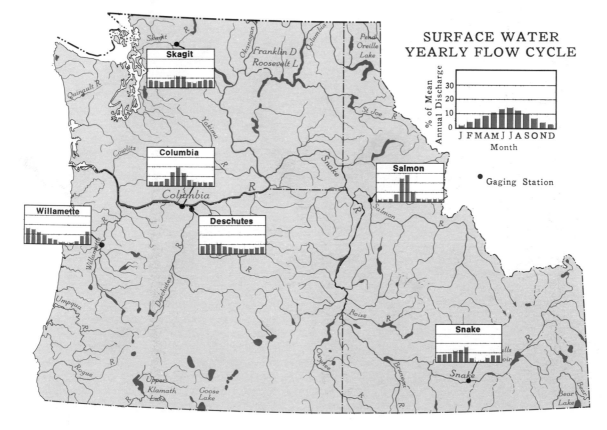

Columbia River. The hydrograph of the Columbia River at The Dalles, Oregon reflects average discharge conditions for a 35-year period from 1930-1965. It shows that a disproportionately high percentage of discharge takes place during the late spring and early summer. This pattern results because most of the precipitation above The Dalles falls on the various ranges of the Rocky Mountains stretching from northwestern Wyoming through Idaho and western Montana and far into British Columbia. Although most of this precipitation takes place in the late autumn and winter, water is retained in the mountainous headwater areas of the Columbia in the form of snow and ice, being released months later as melt water.

Since 1965 this hydrograph has been somewhat modified by the provision of large volumes of upstream storage. Thus the mean flows of May, June, and July, although still noticeably higher than those of other months, are reduced while, conversely, the mean discharge levels in the late fall and winter are increased by the release of stored water.

Salmon River. The hydrograph for the Salmon River illustrates the mean monthly discharge for a 55-year period of record from 1910-1965. In this case the combined discharge of May and June constitutes approximately one-half of the yearly total. The July discharge is somewhat less than that of the Columbia River because the more southerly location of the Salmon drainage basin results in an earlier period of maximum runoff. Very little storage or irrigation development in the Salmon River basin means that the monthly pattern of discharge in the 1980s remains essentially as shown.

Snake River. The hydrograph of the Snake River at Milner, Idaho reflects the headwater conditions in the Middle Rockies as well as anthropogenic modifications. The relatively heavy spring runoff is characteristic of a snowmelt regime, but occurs earlier than those in the Salmon and Columbia river drainages because of the

more southerly location. Heavy irrigation use above Milner (see the map of Water Withdrawals on page 76) further reduces the already modest summer flows.

Deschutes River. The moderate temporal variation of runoff in the Deschutes Basin reflects the fact that much of it is underlain with porous basalts. These basaltic and andesitic volcanic rocks of Quarternary and late Tertiary age absorb potentially high runoff and later release it when discharge would otherwise fall to much lower levels. Provision of storage and irrigation development have not notably altered the hydrograph.

Willamette River. The temporal flow regime of the Willamette River is representative of many rivers west of the Cascades in both Washington and Oregon. Runoff reflects the temporal distribution of precipitation because relatively little is retained as ice and snow. The Willamette hydrograph is compiled from a 55-year period of record (1909-1966) and the temporal distribution of present flows has been modified somewhat by the completion of many flood control reservoirs since the end of World War II. While the high mean flows of the winter months have remained practically unchanged and those of March and April have been reduced somewhat, the low mean flows of July, August, and September have been increased appreciably.

Skagit River. This hydrograph is atypical of rivers west of the Cascades. Higher mean flows occur in June and July because much of the runoff originates at high elevations in the North Cascades of Washington and British Columbia. Since completion of Ross Dam by Seattle City Light in 1949, considerable reservoir storage space reduces summer high flows while increasing flows during the winter when energy demands are highest.

Water Use

Water uses may be divided into two major categories: offstream uses which divert water out of its channel before use, and instream uses which utilize water within stream banks.

Offstream uses include rural domestic, stock watering, irrigation, public water supply (municipal and light industrial), and industrial, including cooling water for thermal electric generating plants. The map of Water Withdrawals on page 76 illustrates the spatial variation of the three most important offstream uses—irrigation, industries, and municipalities.

Irrigation is clearly the dominant offstream use in the Pacific Northwest, accounting for approximately ten times the combined volumes of water withdrawn by municipal and industrial systems. In seven of the twelve sub-basins for which data are shown, irrigation withdrawals represent more than 95% of the total. In the Upper Snake sub-basin alone, irrigation withdrawals approximate five times those by municipal and industrial users in the entire Pacific Northwest. Irrigation withdrawals are even more significant in the more humid western sub-basins of the region where population and water-using industries are concentrated. Here normally dry summers require supplemental irrigation for many types of crops. In the Willamette, Puget Sound, and Coastal sub-basins irrigation withdrawals account for approximately 49%, 13%, and 57% of the total offstream uses, respectively.

Municipal withdrawals are relatively significant in the populous Puget Sound, Willamette, and Clark Fork-Kootenai-Spokane sub-basins, accounting for about 33%, 28%, and 32% of the total withdrawals, respectively.

Industrial withdrawals are the heaviest in the Puget Sound sub-basin but have the greatest relative significance (87% of the total) in the Lower Columbia sub-basin. The distribution of industrial withdrawals is significantly affected by the location of the pulp and paper industry. This industry, which requires over one-half of the total industrial withdrawals in the Pacific Northwest, is concentrated in the Lower Columbia, Puget Sound, and Willamette sub-basins. Food processing is usually the most significant industrial use of water east of the Cascades, but primary metals are significant in the Clark Fork-Kootenai-Spokane and Mid-Columbia sub-basins. Unlike other regions of the United States, cooling water for the thermal electric industry is not yet significant.

Instream uses comprise the other major division of water use. Included in this type of use are generation of hydroelectric energy, navigation, fish and wildlife habitat, waste carriage and assimilation, recreation, preservation of wild and scenic rivers, and aesthetic appreciation. Unlike other regions of the western United States, water

When the third powerhouse (foreground) was completed in the 1970s the generating capacity at Grand Coulee Dam increased approximately three times. In the background are the siphons, the canal leading to Banks Lake, and the lake—key features in the water supply systems of the Columbia Basin Irrigation Project.

utilization in the Pacific Northwest is characterized by a heavy dependence on instream uses, especially for the generation of hydroelectric energy of which the Pacific Northwest is the nation's leading producer. In the middle 1970s more than one billion acre-feet were utilized yearly by hydroelectric plants in the Pacific Northwest. This volume is much greater than the total runoff of the region because the same water is used repeatedly at successive powerhouses along several river systems. For example, the main stem of the Columbia River within the United States includes eleven large dams with hydroelectric generating facilities. For more detail on hydroelectric energy see the chapter on energy resources and distribution, page 80.

Navigation. This is another major instream use. Large expenditures by the federal government have been made to enhance inland water navigation on the Columbia System. From the Bonneville locks at river mile 145 to the Port of Lewiston in Idaho, a chain of eight reservoirs stretches 320 miles (515 kilometers), which not only allows slack water navigational conditions for inland water carriers but also guarantees a navigation channel of 15 feet (4.5 meters) depth. Navigation locks at the eight dams lift barge tows from 8 feet above mean sea level at the Bonneville lock to 738 feet on the reservoir reaching Lewiston, Idaho. Seven of the eight dams are equipped with large single lift locks, the dimensions

of which are 86 by 675 feet. Bonneville Dam, the first of the eight to be constructed, presently has a somewhat smaller lock of 76 by 500 feet. Thus the lock that carries the greatest volume of freight has the least capacity and will eventually cause a bottleneck if the volume of inland water transport continues to increase. In the mid-1980s Congress was seriously considering the enlargement of Bonneville lock so that it would equal the dimensions of the other seven locks above it.

If congressional action extends commercial navigation up the Columbia to Wenatchee, the existing PUD dams will be retrofitted with navigation locks matching those on the Columbia-Snake system. Such an extension does not, however, appear probable for at least the remainder of this century.

Earlier concern for navigation may alter hydrologic conditions even though navigation is no longer significant. The situation on the Willamette is a case in point. Although there is no longer commercial navigation on the river above Willamette Falls, releases of water from flood control reservoirs continue to be made in accordance with a 1938 Act which directs that releases be adequate to maintain a flow of 6,000 cubic feet/second (168 cubic meters/second) for navigation at Salem. During the normal low months of July-September these releases contribute significantly to improved water quality in the Willamette.

WATER WITHDRAWALS

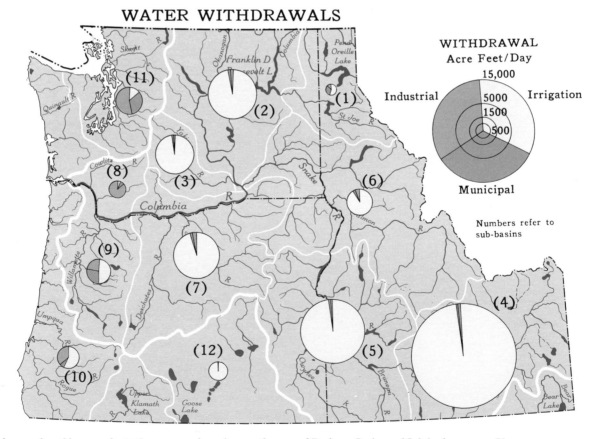

The numbers used on this map refer to the names and numbers on the map of Drainage Basins and Sub-basins on page 71.

Fish and wildlife habitat. Another significant flow use is the maintenance of fish and wildlife habitat. Water resource developments in the region have affected aquatic life markedly. Although enhancement of habitat sometimes results, the consequences have more frequently been negative. Until the 1970s inadequate consideration of biological factors during project design and/or operation resulted in severe losses. Animal communities, especially fur bearers, have in general been negatively impacted by the development of water resources. On the other hand, one large irrigation project (the Columbia Basin Project) has greatly enhanced the habitat for migratory waterfowl by creating many lakes and extensive marshes in a semiarid area.

Valuable anadromous fisheries (salmon and steelhead) have been adversely affected by the development of water resources. This is particularly evident in the Columbia-Snake system. The once bountiful natural runs that were thought to be inexhaustible have declined sharply and a few have even disappeared. Remaining runs are the focus of controversy among competing interests: between sports, commercial, and Indian fishermen; between the states of the Pacific Northwest; and, more recently, between the U.S. and Canada.

Hatchery programs have mitigated some of the losses. Indeed hatchery fish now (far) outnumber wild stocks. Hatchery programs are less successful above the confluence of the Columbia and Snake rivers, however, because of the cumulative effects of losses at dams below the hatcheries. If anadromous fisheries are to be substantially increased over the low levels of the mid-1980s, some reduction in the future output of hydropower, irrigated agriculture, and perhaps other water-related goods and services probably will be necessary.

Recreation. Another instream use of water is by recreationists. Many outdoor recreational activities are water oriented. The region has a disproportionately large per capita supply of surface waters suitable for outdoor recreation and all types of recreational uses of water in the Pacific Northwest have grown rapidly over the last four decades. Recreation is treated separately in a chapter beginning on page 124.

Wastes. One of the principal instream uses of water is to carry away, dilute, and assimilate wastes. When the ratio of wastes to the volume of receiving waters is small, assimilation of organic wastes and adequate dilution of many other waste products takes place. In such instances water quality is not seriously impaired, and this was the case in the early settlement period of the region. During the 20th century, however, the rapid growth of population and economic productivity in the Pacific Northwest have caused the volume and variety of wastes deposited in the region's waters to increase markedly. This has overtaxed the capacity of some of the receiving waters to assimilate and/or dilute wastes. The result is poor water quality (pollution) in some of the region's surface waters.

Improved treatment by industries—especially in chemical recovery—has been chiefly responsible for decreased levels of biochemical oxygen demand in the region, thus freeing up oxygen for fish and other aquatic life. However, there is an apparent widespread increase in the presence of organic and inorganic toxins from broader nonpoint sources of pollution, including over 20 million acre feet of irrigation return flows. In addition, water quality problems exist downstream from densely populated areas, including excessive counts of coliform bacteria and low levels of dissolved oxygen. Although the region has few problems associated with siltation, erosion of the loess-mantled Palouse Hills creates undesirable levels of turbidity and turbine scour at some of the generating plants on the lower Snake River.

Thermal pollution is considered a serious problem in some river reaches because anadromous salmonid fish such as salmon and steelhead have a low tolerance to thermal pollution. Temperatures exceeding 68°F and nitrogen gas supersaturation are serious in reaches of the lower Snake River, while concern is widely expressed about water temperatures in the Yakima sub-basin. Both problems result from dam construction.

Flood hazards may be considered with instream conditions. Despite considerable flood storage and some levee construction and channel improvements, much riverine land remains susceptible to inundation. Unregulated flows on some tributaries of the Columbia and in the Puget Sound and Coastal sub-basins contribute to continued losses. Another contributing factor to mounting potential and real flood damage is the continued conversion of flood-prone lands to more intensive uses.

Water Management Techniques

During recent decades, significant growth of population and economic activity have caused a marked increase in the existing and potential conflicts between water-using interests in the region. The principal need is to reach agreement on the use and control of the Columbia River system by states and other water-using interests within the basin. Until such an agreement is reached and implemented, the techniques discussed below will have limited effectiveness.

The map of Water Management Techniques on page 78 indicates some of the ways in which water and related lands are utilized. With various combinations of capital, technology, administration and/or entrepreneurship, water can be transformed into a variety of water-related services. Some of these diverse services include residential use, inland water transport, flood-hazard mitigation, recreation, electrical energy, and waste carriage and assimilation.

Structural techniques. Water management techniques may be categorized as either structural or nonstructural. The structural approach utilizes a variety of tools—dams, levees, pumps, turbogenerators, sprinklers, etc.—to create water-related services. This approach usually modifies the spatial and temporal distribution of water as well as its quality. As the map indicates, the structural approach is dominant in the Pacific Northwest.

WATER MANAGEMENT TECHNIQUES
Columbia-North Pacific Region

Dams
Existing or under construction

] Army Corps of Engineers
] Bureau of Reclamation
] Non-Federal public
] Non-Federal private
] Other

]⚫ Natural lake with storage control

Other Management Techniques

🐟 Soil Conservation Service project areas
〰️ Existing Wild and Scenic river
〰️ Study Wild and Scenic river

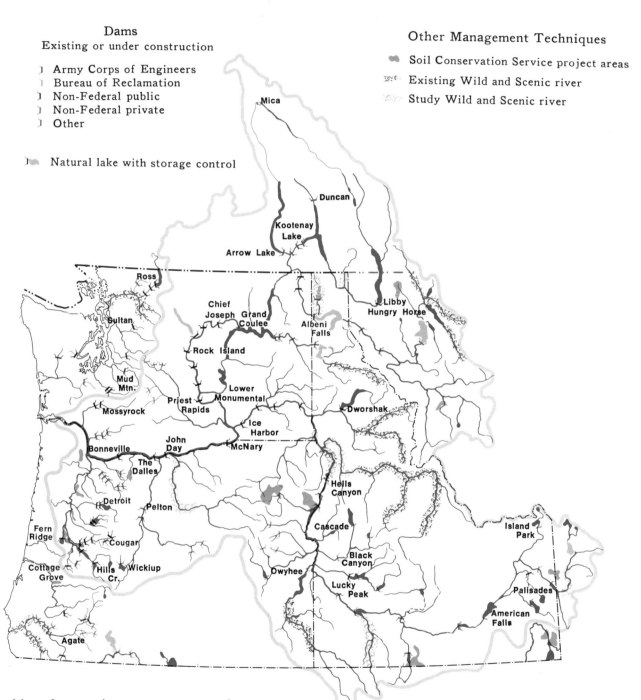

Provision of storage is a common structural management technique. The normal runoff patterns are modified by reservoirs that store water during normal high water periods and release it during the low flow season.

The Columbia system has approximately 44 million acre-feet of storage assigned to flood control; this is also important for energy production. Storage in the Columbia system is used to reduce flood peaks in the late spring and early summer by impounding water then, and to increase low flows in the fall and winter through releases of the stored water. Storage would reduce record peak flows by 45% along the lower Columbia, where the greatest potential flood hazards exist.

The storage releases in the late fall and winter are very beneficial because the regional demand for electric energy is greatest then. Most of the hydroelectric generating capacity is installed at run-of-river dams where cold season output of energy is increased markedly from releases of water stored upstream. Thus the firm energy—that which can be assured year around—is increased by upstream storage. For example, ten large run-of-river generating plants lie on the main stem of the Columbia below Grand Coulee with its large storage reservoir. The further up the system the storage is provided, the greater the increases in firm energy production, because more generating facilities can use the released water.

More than twenty million acre-feet of storage capacity are provided by three Canadian reservoirs operated under provision of the Columbia River Treaty. This treaty was negotiated because attempts to provide adequate amounts of additional upstream storage in Idaho and Montana were meeting with increasing resistance from economic interests and environmental groups. In return for providing upstream storage, Canada receives payments for the resulting flood-hazard mitigation in the United States and shares the benefits from increased generation at hydroelectric plants in this country.

In the Upper and Central Snake and Yakima subbasins storage is used principally for irrigation. High flows in the spring and early summer are stored and then released throughout the growing season for irrigation projects downstream. Storage may also be provided principally for flood damage mitigation. In accordance with flow regimes west of the Cascades, reservoirs on the Willamette system are drawn down during the autumn in preparation for the flood season, November through March. In the spring the reservoirs are allowed to fill, providing water for recreation, irrigation, and low flow augmentation during the summer months.

Another structural approach indicated on the map is land treatment carried out by the Soil Conservation Service. Contour plowing and manipulation of vegetation in small watersheds are sometimes combined with small dams and reservoirs.

Nonstructural techniques. A growing awareness that water resources are finite and that additional acceptable storage is limited has led to increasing efforts to implement nonstructural approaches to water management. Nonstructural approaches modify human behavior rather than the distribution of water. Since this type of approach manages demand (for example, through pricing, zoning, and setting water quality standards) rather than increasing the supply of some water-related service, it is less readily acceptable than the traditional, structural approach which usually does not require the public to modify accustomed patterns of resource consumption. The nonstructural approach may be used to complement structures or it may also be the principal means of achieving a desired goal. Floodplain zoning, which is designed to keep people away from floodwaters, is used increasingly to complement dams and levees, which are designed to keep floodwaters away from people.

Implementation of the National Wild and Scenic River Act illustrates reliance on a nonstructural approach to achieve a water-related goal, in this case the preservation of selected rivers in their natural state. The Pacific Northwest has a disproportionately large number of rivers in this program. Most are in rugged and remote parts of the region. While existing rivers are permanently in the system, study rivers may not be included if they do not meet the standards of naturalness or are determined to be more beneficial for society in a developed state. During the years of study required to determine the suitability for inclusion within the Wild and Scenic System, dam construction or installation of other facilities is not allowed to alter the existing state of a study river.

Like any water management technique—structural or nonstructural—the Wild and Scenic Rivers Program requires trade-offs. Superior aesthetic/leisure-time experiences, white-water recreation, and scientific benefits are gained at the expense of such traditional benefits as slack water recreation, hydroelectric generation, and provision of upstream storage for several downstream uses. For example, over twenty million acre-feet of storage are foregone at major potential storage sites in existing and study river areas.

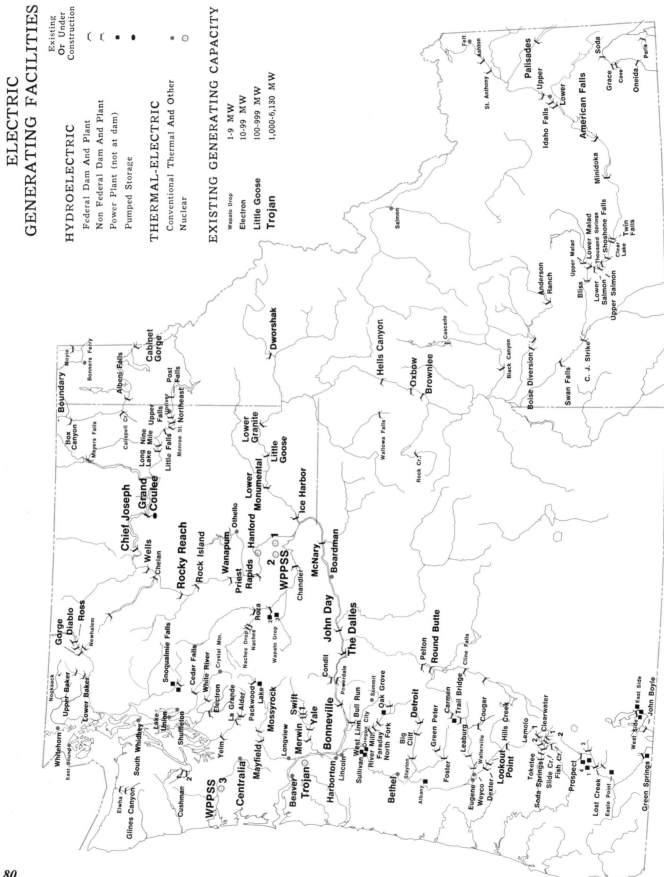

ELECTRIC
GENERATING FACILITIES

Existing
Or Under
Construction

HYDROELECTRIC

Federal Dam And Plant
Non Federal Dam And Plant
Power Plant (not at dam)
Pumped Storage

THERMAL-ELECTRIC

Conventional Thermal And Other
Nuclear

EXISTING GENERATING CAPACITY

Wapato Drop   1-9 MW
Electron   10-99 MW
Little Goose   100-999 MW
Trojan   1,000-6,130 MW

Energy Resources and Distribution

Steven R. Kale

Energy consumption and supply in the Pacific Northwest is undergoing a period of transition. Long dependent on inexpensive hydroelectric energy, the region is now experiencing rapidly increasing electricity rates. Moreover, recent evidence suggests that projections made during the 1970s seriously overstated the region's future requirements for electricity. Adjustments by consumers and producers to rising costs and to other impacts of past decisions will play a large part in the future development of energy in the region.

Consumption

Hydroelectricity accounts for nearly half of the energy consumed in the Pacific Northwest, compared to only 4% for the nation as a whole. While just over 3% of the nation's population lives in the region, 40% of the national consumption of hydroelectricity occurs in the Pacific Northwest.

Petroleum and nuclear energy are consumed in approximately the same proportions in the Pacific Northwest as in the nation, but natural gas and coal are much less important regionally than nationally. Natural gas is the source of about 10% of the region's and 25% of the nation's energy consumption, whereas coal contributes 20% of national consumption but only 4% of the region's.

ENERGY CONSUMPTION—1980

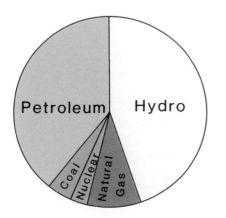

In terms of end-use, almost 40% of the Pacific Northwest's energy is consumed by the industrial sector. Transportation consumes another 26%, residential 21%, and commercial 15%. These percentages are nearly identical to national averages.

Supply

Electricity is the most important source of energy in the Pacific Northwest. In 1982, hydroelectricity contributed 91% of total generation, and the region was the nation's leading producer of electricity from hydro sources. Conventional steam (mostly from coal) accounted for 4% of the regional total, and another 5% was attributable to nuclear in 1982.

Much of the region's electricity is derived from hydro generating facilities in the Columbia River Basin. Dams built by the U.S. Bureau of Reclamation, the Army Corps of Engineers, and others back up water used at successive powerhouses on the Columbia River and its tributaries. Of the eleven dams and generating facilities on the main stem of the Columbia, the largest is Grand Coulee. Generating capacity at Grand Coulee is just over 6,000 megawatts, which exceeds the total capacity in eighteen states and is over five times as much as at the Trojan nuclear facility in Oregon. Hydro facilities are also located along streams outside the Columbia River system in western and southwestern Oregon, western and northwestern Washington, and southeastern Idaho.

Nearly all the conventional and nuclear steam generating capacity of the region is located in Oregon and Washington. Deposits of coal are found at several locations in the region, and a large generating facility in southwestern Washington near Centralia is fueled by nearby deposits extracted from an open-pit mine. A large coal-fired plant in north-central Oregon near Boardman is fueled by coal obtained from mines in Wyoming. Additionally, the region imports electricity from several coal-fired plants in Montana and Wyoming.

Nuclear generation occurs at the Trojan plant on the Oregon side of the lower Columbia River, and at several plants on the Hanford Atomic Energy Reservation near Richland, Washington. Electricity is also available from another nuclear facility on the Hanford Reservation:

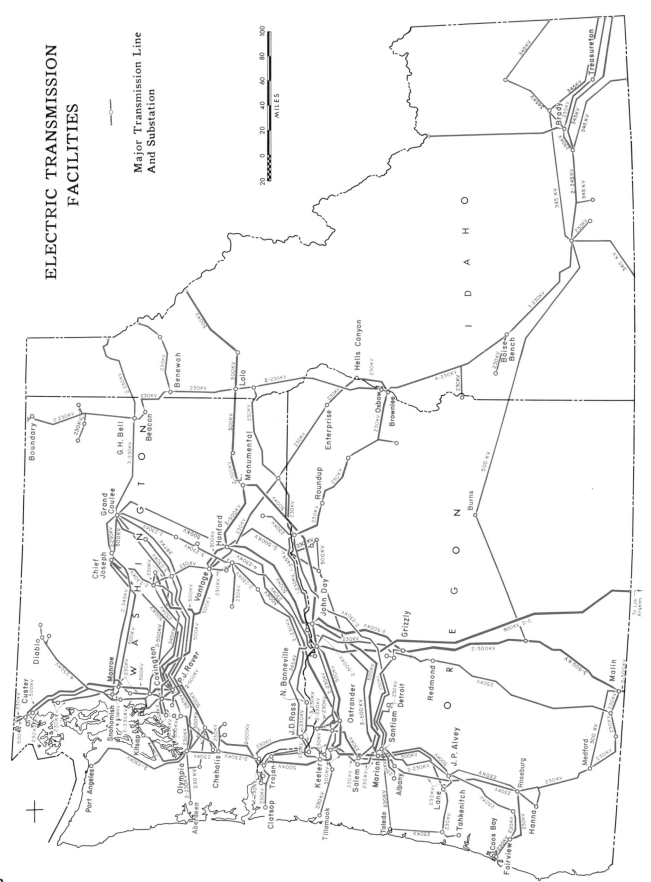

ELECTRIC TRANSMISSION FACILITIES

Major Transmission Line
And Substation

Plant Number Two of the Washington Public Power Supply System (WPPSS). Construction on four other nuclear plants—two near Satsop, Washington and two on the Hanford Reservation—was also started by the WPPSS in the 1970s. Because of regional oversupply of electricity and other reasons, further construction on these plants was delayed or terminated in the early 1980s. Resolution of problems associated with the financing of the WPPSS plants is an important economic issue to utilities and ratepayers in the Pacific Northwest and to holders of bonds for these plants.

Real electricity demands are met primarily from hydro facilities when supplies of water are adequate. Additional peak generating capacity is available from higher-priced oil- and gas-fired facilities in the region and from utilities in California.

Electricity generated at dams operated by the federal government is marketed by the Bonneville Power Administration. The BPA wholesales electricity to utility districts and cooperatives and, when supplies are available, to investor-owned utilities and large industrial (direct-service) customers, mostly companies in the aluminum industry. The availability of this energy to direct-service customers depends largely on the depth of snowpack, the amount of upstream storage, and the amount of demand by residential and commercial customers. Steep increases in the price of electricity during the early 1980s have led to an increasingly uncertain future for the region's aluminum industry.

Electricity is moved from generating stations to markets by transmission lines. The transmission line network is most developed near generating facilities and major population centers. When electricity beyond the needs of the region is available, some of it is sent by extra-high-voltage transmission lines to out-of-region buyers, primarily in California.

The region's future electricity supply will be at least partly based upon the actions of the Northwest Power Planning Council. Authorized in 1980 by the U.S. Congress, the Council is legislatively directed to encourage conservation and the development of renewable resources in its member states—Idaho, Oregon, Washington, and western Montana. In April 1983 the Council issued the Northwest Conservation and Electric Power Plan, which is intended to assure that the region has enough power for the fastest projected growth in demand, that the cheapest power will be acquired first, and that the most efficient use will be made of the region's existing power supplies. The Council has set priorities for the development of electricity sources up to the year 2002 in the following order: conservation (considered a power resource in the plan), hydropower (mostly from small dams), industrial cogeneration, oil- or gas-fired generation from combustion turbines, and thermal plants. Conservation is projected to be the largest contributor to future supplies of electricity, but there are no provisions in the plan for the development of renewable resources other than hydropower. The Council is emphasizing

PIPELINES AND REFINERIES

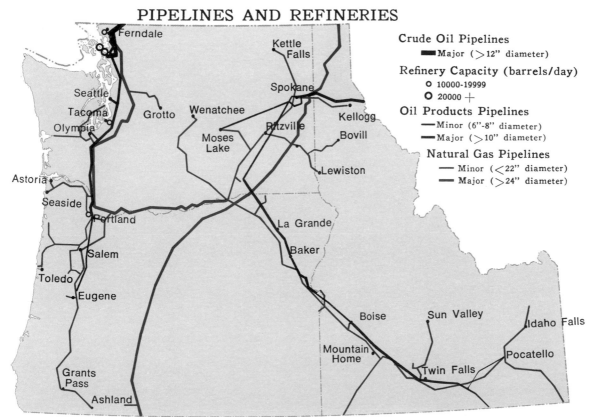

NATURAL GAS AND COAL

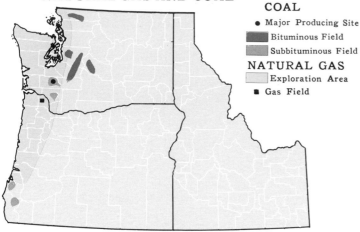

COAL
- Major Producing Site
- Bituminous Field
- Subbituminous Field

NATURAL GAS
- Exploration Area
- Gas Field

SOLAR POWER RESOURCE

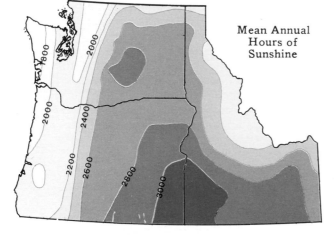

Mean Annual
Hours of
Sunshine

coal-fired rather than nuclear thermal plants because coal plants can be built in a shorter time and in smaller units.

Petroleum and natural gas. Since petroleum is not produced in the Pacific Northwest, supplies are imported. Pipelines transport crude oil from Alberta and British Columbia, and major refineries are located in the vicinity of Anacortes, Washington. Petroleum products are distributed by pipeline from the Anacortes refineries to customers throughout western Washington and Oregon. Portland, Spokane, and Boise are major distribution points for channeling refined products to consumers. Petroleum products are also imported into the region from source areas to the south via Salt Lake City, Utah.

Another petroleum-related issue is the Northern Tier Pipeline. Intended to carry Alaskan oil to the Midwest, the pipeline was to have stretched from Port Angeles, Washington to central Minnesota. In April 1982, Governor John Spellman of Washington vetoed construction of the pipeline because of concern about environmental risks to the Puget Sound. One year later, the Northern Tier Pipeline Company abandoned plans to continue seeking permits for the project.

Most of the region's natural gas is also imported by pipeline, primarily from Alberta and British Columbia. Lesser quantities are obtained from the Southwest. To help meet seasonal demands, underground and liquified natural gas storage facilities are available at several locations in the region. Natural gas fields were tapped near Mist, Oregon in 1979, but only a very small fraction of the state's needs are met by this source.

Renewable energy sources. Renewable sources of energy used in the Pacific Northwest are hydro, biomass (mostly wood), solar, and wind. Although not strictly renewable, geothermal energy also is available in the region. As noted earlier, hydro is the region's most important source of energy.

Solar panels on a house in Eugene, Oregon.

Approximately 10% of the demand for energy in the Pacific Northwest is attributable to biomass. Industrial mill-residue use and residential wood burning each account for about half of the biomass consumed. It is estimated that 10% of the households in the region use wood as the main heating fuel, and that another 34% rely upon wood for secondary heat. Recent increases in residential wood burning have led to severe air pollution problems in some parts of the region, and in 1983 the Oregon Legislature passed a law requiring woodstoves sold after July 1, 1986 to meet emission standards. Other biomass facilities in the Pacific Northwest are fueled by agricultural residues, food waste, and sewage.

Solar energy is used for active and passive space heating as well as for active hot-water heating. Available evidence suggests that solar is used more west of the Cascades where much of the region's population resides. In terms of solar radiation, however, the potential is greater east of the Cascades. By 1981, an estimated 6,750 active solar systems, 2% of the nation's total, had been installed in the region.

Wind potential is greatest in the Columbia River gorge, along the coast, and in certain mountainous parts of the region. Electricity is generated by the wind in several locations, and three large experimental generators are located at the edge of the Columbia River gorge near Goldendale, Washington. Additionally, the Northwest's first commercial wind farm was built along the Pacific Coast near Bandon, Oregon in 1983.

Known and potential geothermal resources underlie portions of the entire region. There are several direct-use facilities, including major ones in the Klamath Falls area of southern Oregon, and in Boise, Idaho. A 1983 report by the Oregon Department of Geology and Mineral Industries reveals that the Oregon Cascades may have enough geothermal potential to generate twenty times as much electricity as Columbia River hydroelectric plants.

GEOTHERMAL RESOURCES AND FACILITIES

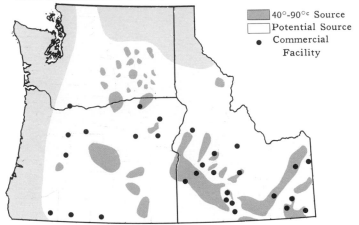

- 40°-90°c Source
- Potential Source
- • Commercial Facility

ANNUAL AVERAGE WIND POWER

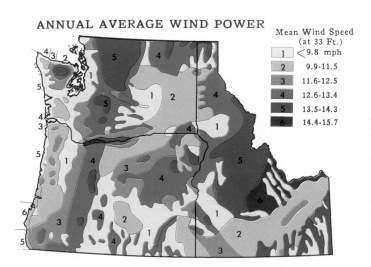

Mean Wind Speed (at 33 Ft.)

1	<9.8 mph
2	9.9-11.5
3	11.6-12.5
4	12.6-13.4
5	13.5-14.3
6	14.4-15.7

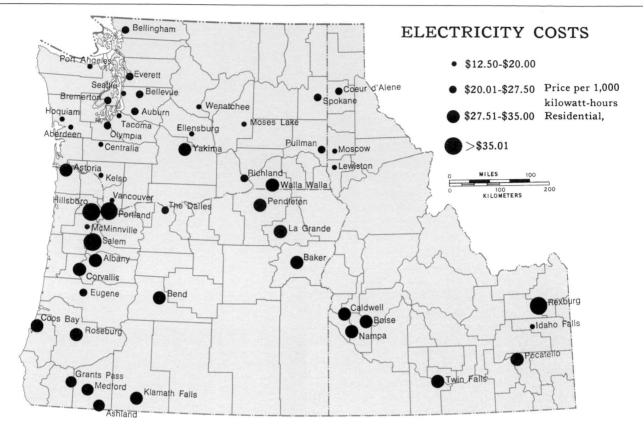

ELECTRICITY COSTS

- • $12.50-$20.00
- ● $20.01-$27.50 Price per 1,000 kilowatt-hours
- ⬤ $27.51-$35.00 Residential,
- ⬤ >$35.01

MILES 100
KILOMETERS 200

Cost

Energy costs in the Pacific Northwest vary by location and according to type of fuel used. Consumer price data indicate that fuel and other utilities are slightly higher than the national average in the Portland metropolitan area, but are lower in the Seattle-Everett area. Electricity and coal costs tend to be lower in the Northwest than in much of the rest of the nation, but natural gas rates are somewhat higher. Depending upon the location of the consumer, petroleum rates tend to be slightly above or slightly below the national average.

Average bills for commercial, industrial, and residential electricity in each of the three states are among the six lowest for all fifty states, though costs vary from community to community.

With rates about one-third the national average, Washington has the lowest-priced electricity in the nation. This low cost results because of the high proportion (90%) of electricity generated at publicly owned (mostly hydro) generating facilities. The proportions of electricity generated at publicly owned facilities is approximately 60% in Oregon and 30% in Idaho and, while rates are higher in these two states than in Washington, they are still low in comparison to rates outside the Pacific Northwest.

Natural gas costs are somewhat higher in the region than in much of the rest of the United States. Only Hawaii and several states in the East have higher rates. In 1982, average natural gas prices were 19% higher than the national average in Idaho, 30% higher in Washington, and 33% higher in Oregon.

Coal is used mainly for the generation of electricity. In Oregon during 1982, coal was obtained from Wyoming mines for $28.50 per ton. In-state mines supplied generating facilities in Washington for $22.50 per ton. These costs were lower than the $34.90 national average.

Agriculture

Philip L. Jackson

Agriculture in the Pacific Northwest is diverse, reflecting differences in climate, topography, soils, and water supply. As in many other aspects of life in the region, a major contrast is between the areas east and west of the Cascade Range. A wide range of agriculture is possible in the region, including wheat and dry pea production in the Palouse, cattle and sheep grazing in the open spaces of eastern Oregon and southern Idaho, production of vegetables and grass seeds in the Willamette Valley, dairying in the Puget Lowland and in Oregon's coastal zone. High value specialty crops such as berries, vegetables, and grapes are grown on relatively small tracts, while cattle and sheep are grazed and forage crops are grown on extensive acreages.

Trends in agriculture have been difficult to pinpoint because of changes in the definition of "farm" by the Census of Agriculture. From 1974-1978, however, the definition has remained unchanged: "Any place from which $1,000 or more of agricultural products were sold during the census year." According to this definition, 19,000 new farms were enumerated in this period, an increase of about 24%. Recent trends also seem to indicate an expansion of agricultural acreage. Land in farms increased by about 2%, croplands by 5%, and irrigated lands by more than 24% from 1974-1978. While some farmlands have been replaced by residential, commercial, and other uses in urban areas, the census indicates an overall increase in the total number of farms and in farm acreage. It should be noted, however, that this increase has not been uniform either by location or by size, and that there is a trend away from the small family farm and towards larger farms in the Pacific Northwest as in the nation as a whole. The value of farmland and buildings has increased dramatically since 1974, with very large increases in total farm values over $500,000 in all three Pacific Northwest states. In terms of farm sales, just over 11% of the farms produce over 72% of the region's sales. The maps on pages 87-92 indicate the distribution of farms in the Pacific Northwest and the regional variation of average farm size and value per acre. Farms classed as corporations, including family corporations, have increased significantly in the Pacific Northwest.

Presently, about 32% of the land area of the Pacific Northwest is in farms.

Livestock grazing is the most extensive agricultural land use in the Pacific Northwest, utilizing 59% of total farm land, approximately 72.7 million acres (29 million hectares) of private and public land. Stock ranches for sheep and cattle production are generally of large size, over 500 acres, and are often situated near federal forest or range land which is often leased for grazing. Ranches of over 10,000 acres are fairly common in eastern Oregon and in north-central Washington where acreage requirements per grazing animal are high—often between 25 and 70 acres per animal unit—due to limited precipitation.

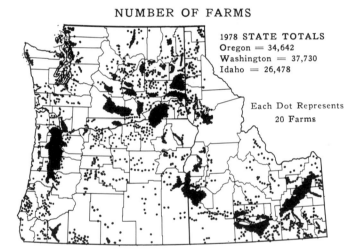

NUMBER OF FARMS

1978 STATE TOTALS
Oregon = 34,642
Washington = 37,730
Idaho = 26,478

Each Dot Represents
20 Farms

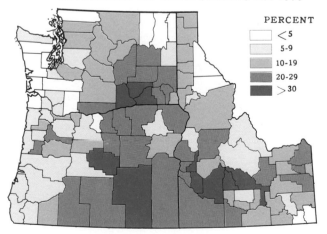

PERCENT OF LAND IN FARMS
OPERATED BY CORPORATIONS: 1978

PERCENT
< 5
5-9
10-19
20-29
> 30

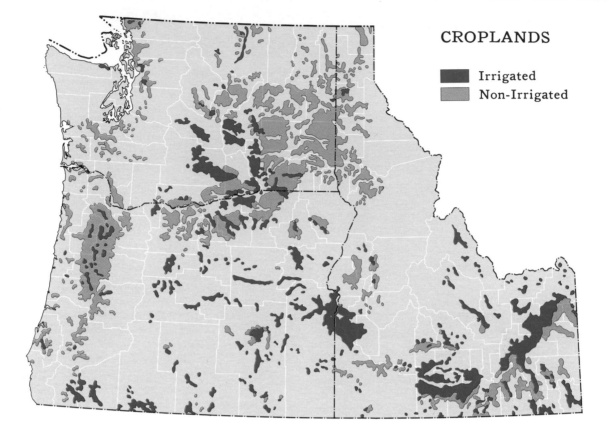

CROPLANDS

■ Irrigated
▨ Non-Irrigated

Table 20. *Number of Farms[a] in Pacific Northwest States, 1954-1978*

	1954	1964		1974		1978	
	number	number	% change	number	% change	number	% change
Oregon	38,740	29,661	−23.4	23,680	−20.2	34,642	+ 29.4
Washington	65,175	45,574	−30.1	29,410	−35.5	37,730	+ 28.2
Idaho	54,441	39,757	−27.0	26,753	−32.7	26,478	+ 11.8

Source: 1978 Census of Agriculture.

[a] Not fully comparable due to changes in census definitions.

AVERAGE FARM SIZE

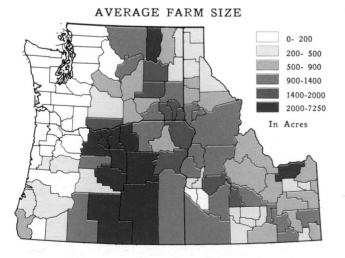

	0- 200
	200- 500
	500- 900
	900-1400
	1400-2000
	2000-7250

In Acres

VALUE OF FARMLAND PER ACRE

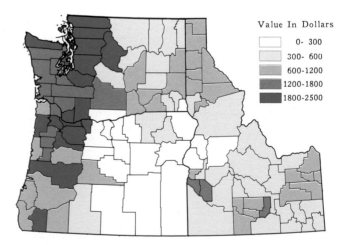

Value In Dollars

	0- 300
	300- 600
	600-1200
	1200-1800
	1800-2500

IRRIGATED LAND AS A PERCENT OF LAND IN FARMS: 1978

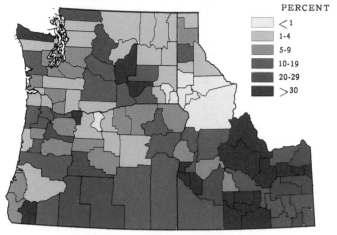

PERCENT

	<1
	1-4
	5-9
	10-19
	20-29
	>30

Cropland represents only 41% of total farm land, though crop acreages have continued to expand in recent years as irrigation of arid lands has been made possible by extensive use of pumped groundwater and center pivot irrigation technology. Nearly 30% of cropland is irrigated, and future cropland development is dependent on the potential for irrigation.

Wheat, hay, and barley comprise nearly 80% of the cropland harvested, and cattle, calves, and wheat are the leading agricultural commodities by value in the Pacific Northwest. Over fifty additional crops are grown in significant quantities in the region, and several are important in national totals. Hops, peppermint, dry peas, snap beans, fall Irish potatoes, grass seeds, apples, winter pears, sweet cherries, bush berries, and filbert nuts are but a few of the crops of special note. Increased wine consumption has encouraged the planting of varietal grape vineyards in both Oregon and Washington in recent years, and production continues to grow.

VALUE OF AGRICULTURAL PRODUCTS SOLD 1978

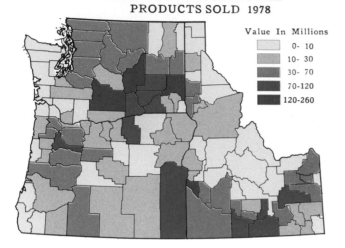

Value In Millions

- 0- 10
- 10- 30
- 30- 70
- 70-120
- 120-260

AVERAGE VALUE PER FARM OF AGRICULTURAL PRODUCTS SOLD: 1978

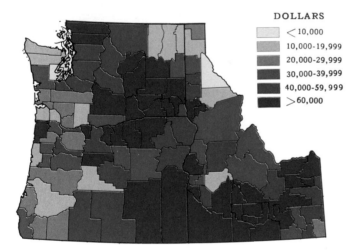

DOLLARS

- < 10,000
- 10,000-19,999
- 20,000-29,999
- 30,000-39,999
- 40,000-59,999
- > 60,000

Orchard crops. The Pacific Northwest has earned an international reputation for high quality orchard crops. Major centers of orchard acreages include the Wenatchee, Yakima, and Okanogan valleys of Washington, The Dalles, Hood River, Rogue, and Willamette valleys of Oregon, and the Payette area and Emmet Valley of Idaho.

Filbert nut orchards are found almost exclusively in Oregon, with major acreage in the northern Willamette Valley. Commercial apple, pear, and cherry orchards developed in the Yakima Valley of Washington after about 1905 with the introduction of rail service and irrigation projects. Because of highly favored growing conditions and innovative marketing, the Yakima area was developed for the fresh fruit export market. Heavy production of high quality fruit of good size, shape, and color is made possible by hot, clear, dry summer days, cool nights, and ample irrigation water. The Okanogan orchard district also produces apples, pears, and cherries. Orchards are situated on river terraces and along linear lakes in order to reduce frost hazard by promoting late spring blooming. Production of apples, pears, and cherries is also favored in The Dalles and Hood River Valley where spring dormancy is extended, summer days are hot and dry, and nights are cool. The Rogue Valley is primarily a pear growing area. Moderate winters and hot, dry summers favor ripening of many pear varieties. Bartlett pears are packed and shipped throughout the United States, and the Comice pear, grown nearly exclusively in the Rogue Valley, is a high-value specialty crop.

The Willamette Valley of Oregon represents one of the largest concentrations of diversified cropland in the Pacific Northwest. A wide range of cropping is possible. Agricultural production includes orchard crops, vegetables, grains, hay, livestock, poultry, and many specialty crops. One specialty crop that has gained international importance in recent years is grass seed. Known as the "grass seed capital of the world," the Willamette Valley produces an average of 250 million pounds of rye grass

Table 21.   Land in Farms and Farm Land Use in Idaho, 1954-1978

	1954	1964		1974		1978	
	acres	acres	% change	acres	% change	acres	% change
Land in farms	14,364,471	15,301,500	+ 6.5	14,274,258	− 6.7	14,869,911	+ 4.2
Total cropland	5,475,520	5,877,675	+ 7.3	6,247,750	+ 6.3	6,631,994	+ 6.2
Harvested cropland	3,727,616	3,934,650	+ 5.5	4,531,164	+15.1	4,877,569	+ 7.7
Pastured cropland	545,073	695,875	+27.7	873,607	+25.5	765,918	− 12.3
Other cropland	1,202,831	1,247,150	+ 3.7	842,934	− 32.4	988,507	+17.3
Woodland	1,427,618	1,393,415	− 2.4	818,549	− 41.3	891,162	+ 8.9
Other land	7,461,333	8,030,055	+ 7.6	7,208,004	− 10.2	7,346,755	+ 1.9
Irrigated land	2,324,571	2,801,550	+20.5	2,859,047	+ 2.0	3,508,254	+22.7

Source: 1978 Census of Agriculture.

AVERAGE VALUE PER ACRE OF
AGRICULTURAL PRODUCTS SOLD: 1978

LAND IN FARMS

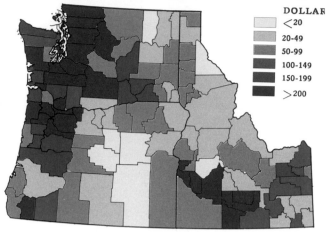

DOLLAR
<20
20-49
50-99
100-149
150-199
>200

Percent of County Land Area
0- 10
10- 25
25- 50
50- 75
75-100

seed on 190,000 acres. This represents 99% of the national rye grass production. Wet winters and poorly drained soils initially promoted grass seed as an alternative crop. Production success has since turned thousands of acres of pasture land into profitable grass seed farms.

The Snake River Plain in Idaho and eastern Oregon is known for potato production. "Famous Potatoes," Idaho's unofficial state motto, announces the pride Idaho

takes in the economically important crop. Centers of Idaho's potato production are the Idaho Falls, Twin Falls, and Boise-Payette districts. Fall Irish potatoes are more commonly grown in the Pacific Northwest. Potato acreages have continued to increase in recent years as groundwater irrigation has provided water supplies in addition to the Snake River irrigation projects.

The maps on pages 92-97 show the distribution patterns of the region's principal crops and livestock by county.

Table 22.   Land in Farms and Farm Land Use in Washington, 1954-1978

	1954	1964		1974		1978	
	acres	acres	% change	acres	% change	acres	% change
Land in farms	17,641,429	19,052,500	+ 8.0	16,661,902	– 12.5	17,002,288	+ 2.0
Total cropland	7,693,274	8,064,135	+ 4.8	7,945,063	– 1.5	8,410,749	+ 5.9
Harvested cropland	4,342,833	4,423,450	+ 1.9	4,946,306	+11.9	5,073,078	+ 2.6
Pastured cropland	620,606	783,635	+26.2	688,343	– 12.2	614,240	– 10.8
Other cropland	2,729,835	2,857,050	+ 4.7	2,310,414	– 19.1	2,723,431	+17.9
Woodland	3,709,784	3,750,115	+ 1.1	2,733,151	– 27.1	2,683,874	– 1.8
Other land	6,238,371	7,241,295	+16.1	5,983,688	– 17.4	5,907,665	– 1.3
Irrigated land	778,135	1,149,850	+47.8	1,309,018	+13.8	1,681,268	+28.4

Source: 1978 Census of Agriculture.

Table 23.   Land in Farms and Farm Land Use in Oregon, 1954-1978

	1954	1964		1974		1978	
	acres	acres	% change	acres	% change	acres	% change
Land in farms	21,047,340	20,509,500	– 2.5	18,241,445	– 11.1	18,414,484	+ 1.0
Total cropland	5,249,888	5,281,915	+ 0.6	5,074,988	– 3.9	5,247,487	+ 3.4
Harvested cropland	3,265,385	3,050,250	– 6.6	3,213,399	+ 5.3	3,280,005	I 2.1
Pastured cropland	807,142	926,415	+14.8	815,197	– 12.0	814,484	– 0.1
Other cropland	1,177,361	1,305,250	+10.9	1,046,392	– 19.8	1,152,998	+10.2
Woodland	4,637,964	3,193,595	– 31.1	1,730,245	– 45.8	1,786,919	+ 3.3
Other land	11,159,488	12,033,685	+ 7.8	11,436,212	– 5.0	11,380,078	– 0.5
Irrigated land	1,490,366	1,607,650	+ 7.9	1,561,438	– 2.9	1,920,318	+23.0

Source: 1978 Census of Agriculture.

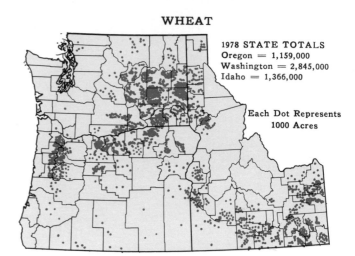

WHEAT

1978 STATE TOTALS
Oregon = 1,159,000
Washington = 2,845,000
Idaho = 1,366,000

Each Dot Represents
1000 Acres

Table 24. Pacific Northwest Farms by Value of Land and Buildings

	Oregon	Washington	Idaho
$ 39,999 and under	4,160	4,150	3,464
$ 40,000 to $ 99,999	10,699	11,025	6,033
$100,000 to $149,999	5,304	5,600	3,157
$150,000 to $199,000	3,585	3,561	2,628
$200,000 to $499,999	6,967	7,833	6,810
$500,000 and over	3,928	5,560	4,387

Source: 1978 Census of Agriculture.

BARLEY FOR GRAIN
—Farms With Sales of $2500 And Over—

1978 STATE TOTALS
Oregon = 217,000
Washington, 375,000
Idaho = 1,015,000

Each Dot Represents
1000 Acres

CHANGE IN NUMBER OF FARMS 1974-1978

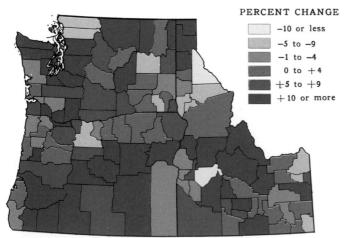

PERCENT CHANGE

	−10 or less
	−5 to −9
	−1 to −4
	0 to +4
	+5 to +9
	+10 or more

FIELD CORN FOR ALL PURPOSES

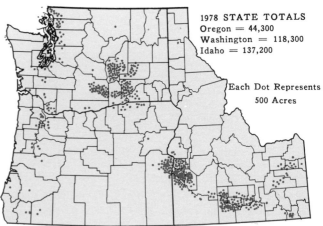

1978 STATE TOTALS
Oregon = 44,300
Washington = 118,300
Idaho = 137,200

Each Dot Represents
500 Acres

Table 25. Value of Farm Sales in Pacific Northwest States, 1964-1978

Income	1964			1974			1978		
	number of farms	% of farms	% of total sales	number of farms	% of farms	% of total sales	number of farms	% of farms	% of total sales
$100,000 and over	721	0.6	28.5	9,163	11.5	68.3	10,969	11.1	72.4
$ 40,000 to $99,999	6,136	5.5	23.5	11,805	14.7	17.3	12,680	12.8	16.1
$ 20,000 to $39,999	11,544	10.1	20.8	9,688	12.1	6.8	9,569	9.7	5.5
$ 10,000 to $19,999	15,488	13.6	14.3	9,103	11.4	3.2	9,647	9.8	2.7
$ 9,999 and under	80,003	70.1	10.9	39,870	50.0	2.6	55,759	56.4	3.1
Abnormal farms	163	0.1	2.0	214	0.3	1.8	224	0.2	0.2
Totals	114,055	100.0	100.0	79,843	100.0	100.0	98,848	100.0	100.0

Source: 1978 Census of Agriculture.

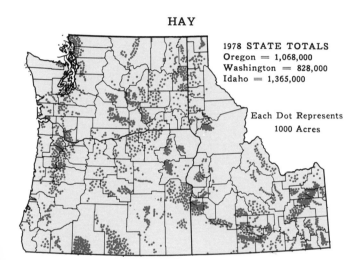

HAY

1978 STATE TOTALS
Oregon = 1,068,000
Washington = 828,000
Idaho = 1,365,000

Each Dot Represents
1000 Acres

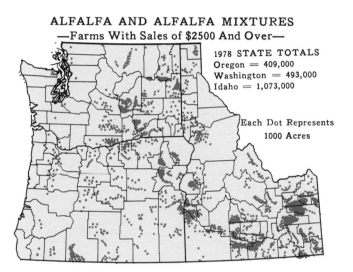

ALFALFA AND ALFALFA MIXTURES
—Farms With Sales of $2500 And Over—

1978 STATE TOTALS
Oregon = 409,000
Washington = 493,000
Idaho = 1,073,000

Each Dot Represents
1000 Acres

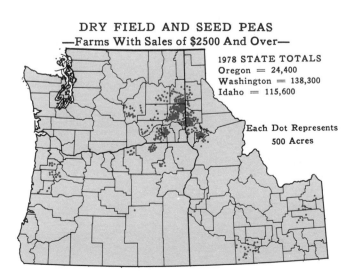

DRY FIELD AND SEED PEAS
—Farms With Sales of $2500 And Over—

1978 STATE TOTALS
Oregon = 24,400
Washington = 138,300
Idaho = 115,600

Each Dot Represents
500 Acres

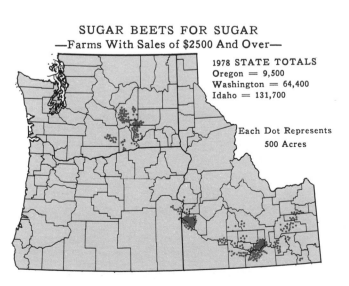

SUGAR BEETS FOR SUGAR
—Farms With Sales of $2500 And Over—

1978 STATE TOTALS
Oregon = 9,500
Washington = 64,400
Idaho = 131,700

Each Dot Represents
500 Acres

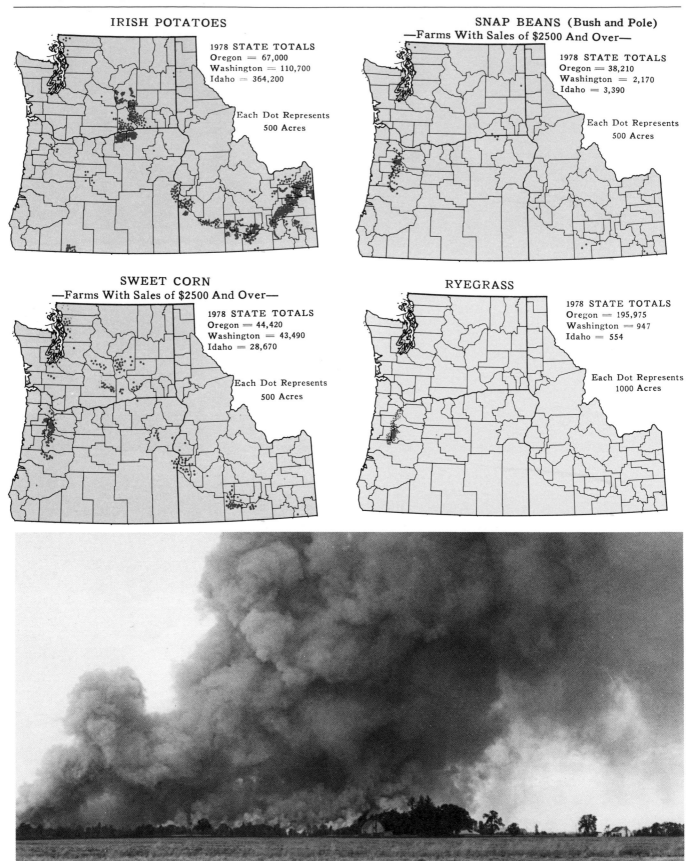

IRISH POTATOES

1978 STATE TOTALS
Oregon = 67,000
Washington = 110,700
Idaho = 364,200

Each Dot Represents
500 Acres

SNAP BEANS (Bush and Pole)
—Farms With Sales of $2500 And Over—

1978 STATE TOTALS
Oregon = 38,210
Washington = 2,170
Idaho = 3,390

Each Dot Represents
500 Acres

SWEET CORN
—Farms With Sales of $2500 And Over—

1978 STATE TOTALS
Oregon = 44,420
Washington = 43,490
Idaho = 28,670

Each Dot Represents
500 Acres

RYEGRASS

1978 STATE TOTALS
Oregon = 195,975
Washington = 947
Idaho = 554

Each Dot Represents
1000 Acres

Every year thousands of acres of straw are burned in the Willamette Valley by ryegrass seed growers.

APPLES
—Farms With Sales of $2500 And Over—

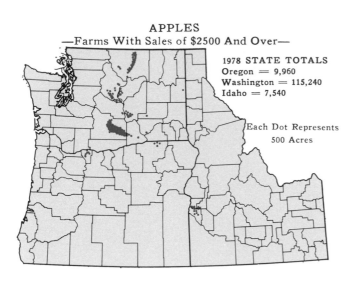

1978 STATE TOTALS
Oregon = 9,960
Washington = 115,240
Idaho = 7,540

Each Dot Represents
500 Acres

PEARS
—Farms With Sales of $2500 And Over—

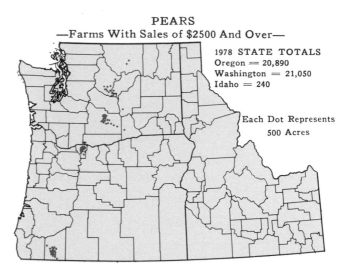

1978 STATE TOTALS
Oregon = 20,890
Washington = 21,050
Idaho = 240

Each Dot Represents
500 Acres

CHERRIES (Tart and Sweet)
—Farms With Sales of $2500 And Over—

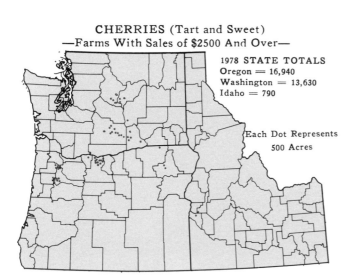

1978 STATE TOTALS
Oregon = 16,940
Washington = 13,630
Idaho = 790

Each Dot Represents
500 Acres

FILBERTS AND HAZELNUTS

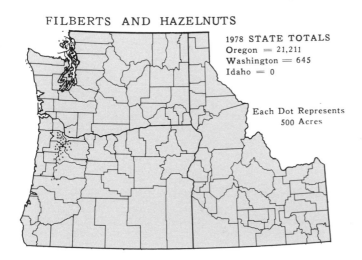

1978 STATE TOTALS
Oregon = 21,211
Washington = 645
Idaho = 0

Each Dot Represents
500 Acres

MINT

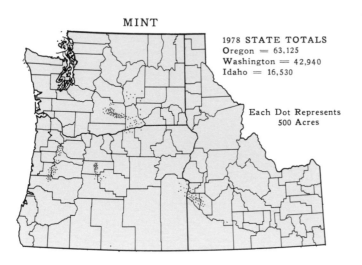

1978 STATE TOTALS
Oregon = 63,125
Washington = 42,940
Idaho = 16,530

Each Dot Represents
500 Acres

GRAPES
—Farms With Sales of $2500 And Over—

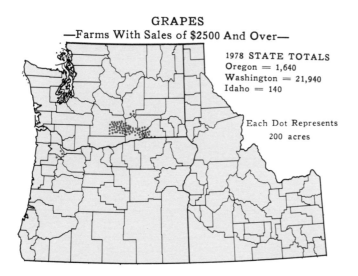

1978 STATE TOTALS
Oregon = 1,640
Washington = 21,940
Idaho = 140

Each Dot Represents
200 acres

Table 26. Value of Commodity Groups, 1978

	Oregon	Washington	Idaho
		$000's	
Grains	171,122	454,755	362,983
Field seeds, hay, forage	116,914	90,403	89,248
Vegetables, sweet corn & melons	82,584	81,407	24,482
Fruits, nuts & berries	115,680	398,038	15,170
Poultry & poultry products	58,532	73,725	10,920
Dairy products	109,114	260,888	143,869
Cattle & calves	360,095	421,870	615,518
Sheep, lambs & wool	31,467	4,445	32,271
Hogs & pigs	15,299	10,441	11,720
Other livestock & livestock products	14,689	21,747	27,328
Nursery & greenhouse products	85,590	63,784	8,235

CATTLE AND CALVES

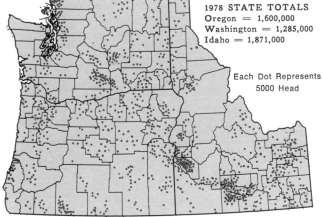

1978 STATE TOTALS
Oregon = 1,600,000
Washington = 1,285,000
Idaho = 1,871,000

Each Dot Represents
5000 Head

HOGS AND PIGS

1978 STATE TOTALS
Oregon = 120,600
Washington = 89,400
Idaho = 105,100

Each Dot Represents
1000 Head

SHEEP AND LAMBS

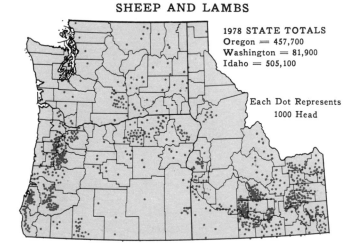

1978 STATE TOTALS
Oregon = 457,700
Washington = 81,900
Idaho = 505,100

Each Dot Represents
1000 Head

BROILERS AND OTHER MEAT TYPE CHICKENS

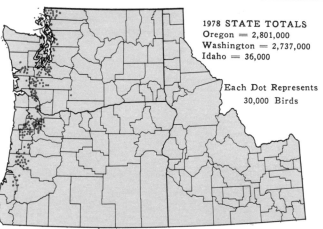

1978 STATE TOTALS
Oregon = 2,801,000
Washington = 2,737,000
Idaho = 36,000

Each Dot Represents
30,000 Birds

MILK COWS

1978 STATE TOTALS
Oregon = 94,200
Washington = 195,800
Idaho = 138,200

Each Dot Represents
500 Head

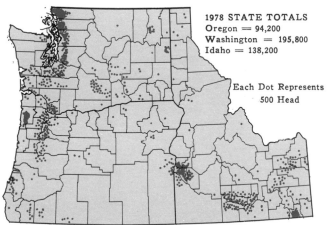

Commercial Timberland Resources and Industries

J. Granville Jensen

Commercial timberlands are lands naturally capable of growing a minimum of 20 cubic feet per acre per year (0.22 cubic meters/hectare/year) and not withdrawn from commercial harvest such as in parks and wilderness. Commercial timberlands cover 36% of the Pacific Northwest land area, and support the employment of about 200,000 people in primary forest industries, a major component of the region's economy. They are also of national importance, accounting for 12% of the nation's commercial timberlands and for 36% of all softwood growing stock. Pacific Northwest forest industries produce about half of the nation's softwood lumber and plywood.

The location of commercial timberlands and commercially valuable forest types within the region is closely related to terrain and climate. The area west of the Cascade Mountains, with its mild, wet winters, is a superior environment for timber growth and is 68% commercial timberland. Dominated by stands of Douglas-fir, this area is known as the Douglas-fir subregion. In the zone fronting the Pacific Ocean, where summer drought is less severe, important stands of Sitka spruce and western hemlock occur in association with western red cedar and red alder, the region's principal hardwood. Higher elevations support true firs, mountain hemlock, and other subalpine species of commercial significance.

East of the Cascades, the semi-arid environment is less favorable for tree growing except at the more humid higher elevations. Consequently, commercial timberlands cover only 30% of eastern Washington, 25% of eastern Oregon, 15% of southern Idaho, but 65% of mountainous northern Idaho. Pine species, especially ponderosa,

GENERALIZED COMMERCIAL FOREST TYPES

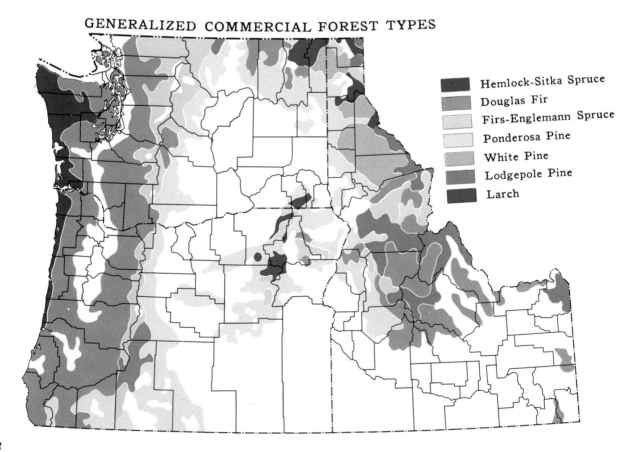

- Hemlock-Sitka Spruce
- Douglas Fir
- Firs-Englemann Spruce
- Ponderosa Pine
- White Pine
- Lodgepole Pine
- Larch

lodgepole, and western white pine, generally dominate, although major stands of Douglas-fir, true firs, Englemann spruce, and western larch also occur. (The maps on page 59 show the natural distribution of tree species in the region.)

Ownership

Forest lands of the Pacific Northwest were recognized early as having national resource significance and therefore large areas were incorporated into the National Forest system. In consequence, 63% of the timberland and 70% of all growing stock timber was in public ownership in 1977. This fact has fundamental implications for resource use and for the regional economy. The USDA Forest Service, holding 47% of the commercial timberland, manages 52% of the growing stock and the Bureau of Land Management controls 5% of the timberland, mostly in western Oregon. Industry ownership, mostly in the more productive Douglas-fir subregion, accounts for only 19% of commercial timberland. Farm and other private ownership, although comprising 18% of the timberland, accounts for only 12% of the growing stock.

Conversion of commercial timberland to such uses as homesteads, parks, and wilderness totaled 4.5 million acres (1.8 million hectares) from 1952-1977. National Forests lost two million acres of timberland, 1.5 million

were converted to farmland, and 700,000 acres of other private forest holdings were converted to other uses, while industry ownership increased by 700,000 acres.

Productivity

Natural productivity of the region's timberland is notably high, with major contrasts between subregions. Thus the Douglas-fir subregion, with 60% of its commercial timberlands producing more than 120 cubic feet per acre annually, is one of the world's best tree growing environments. The Douglas-fir subregion, comprising only 5% of the nation's land, accounts for 29% of the nation's timberland in this highest productivity class. In contrast, the pine subregion has 67% of its commercial timberlands in the lowest two productivity classes and only 13% in the highest class.

Forest industry owned timberlands are noted for highly productive lands, as revealed by the fact that 72% of industry lands are in the two highest productivity classes. Only half of other private timberlands are in these classes. Eighty percent of these privately owned high quality timberlands are in the Douglas-fir subregion. In contrast, public agencies, including the Forest Service, manage most of the region's low productivity timberlands (53% in the two lowest classes) especially in the pine subregion.

COMMERCIAL TIMBERLAND AND TIMBER BY OWNERSHIP
—1977—

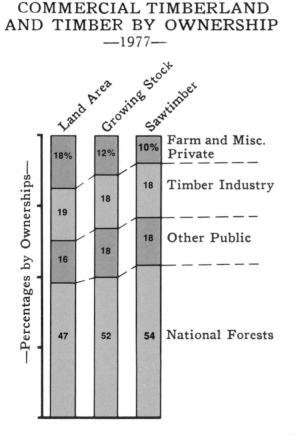

Table 27. Area of Commercial Timberlands by Ownership
(Thousand Acres)

	Total of All Land	Commercial Timberland[a]	National Forests	Bureau of Land Management	Indian	State	Other Public	Forest Industries	Farm	Other Private
Douglas-fir subregion	34,659	23,439	6,787	1,998	194	2,110	347	7,746	1,511	3,016
Western Washington	15,694	9,788	2,200	2	187	1,358	244	3,581	434	1,782
Western Oregon	18,965	13,651	4,587	1,996	7	752	103	3,895	1,077	1,234
Pine subregion	121,829	32,235	19,166	636	1,806	1,655	142	3,312	3,184	2,334
Eastern Washington	26,762	8,134	2,967	45	1,359	726	106	738	1,383	810
Eastern Oregon	42,391	10,560	7,046	182	377	68	9	1,627	1,024	227
Northern Idaho	----------[b]	----------	----------	----------	----------	----------	----------	----------	----------	----------
Southern Idaho	52,676	13,541	9,153	409	70	861	27	947	777	1,297
Total Pacific Northwest	156,488	55,674	25,953	2,634	2,000	3,765	489	10,788	4,695	5,350
(1952 Total Comparisons)	----------	(60,351)	(27,937)	(3,029)	(2,836)	(3,759)	(617)	(10,000)	(6,189)	(6,050)
Total United States	2,254,792	482,486	88,718	5,803	6,062	23,415	11,723	68,782	115,777	162,205

Source: Table 3.4 in *Forest Resource Report No. 23,* U.S.D.A. Forest Service 1982.

[a] Forest lands capable of producing at least 20 cubic feet of industrial wood per acre per year and not withdrawn from commercial harvest.

[b] Data not available.

Harvest and Growth

Timber harvested from Pacific Northwest forests in the years 1975-1981 ranged from 12 to 17 billion board feet (30 million cubic meters) annually. This harvest, which was about 97% softwood of which 50% was Douglas-fir, accounted for about 40% of the nation's annual softwood sawtimber production. Oregon produced an average of 6 to 8 billion board feet, Washington 5 to 7 billion board feet, and Idaho about 1.3 to 1.9 billion board feet per year. Two-thirds of the harvest is from counties west of the Cascade Mountains, of which five counties—Douglas, Lane, and Linn in Oregon, and Cowlitz and Lewis in Washington—each harvest over 500 million board feet annually. The pine subregion east of the Cascades accounts for about a third of the annual harvest, mostly from mountainous northern Idaho (especially Clearwater County), from the eastern slopes of the Cascades, and from other highlands in eastern Washington and Oregon. The six above-mentioned counties produce a third of the region's total harvest.

Significant differences exist in relationships between timberland areas, standing timber resources, and annual growth and harvest. The outstanding fact is that timberlands owned by forest industries tend to be intensively managed in order to produce high annual growth, and supply a disproportionately large share of the region's annual harvest. In the Douglas-fir subregion, industry-owned timberlands in 1976 accounted for 52% of the harvest from only 32% of the land, 24% of the standing timber volume, and 39% of the annual growth. Comparable relationships are found in the pine subregion. In contrast, National Forests, which manage for multiple uses, have on average a much lower annual growth rate and supply a disproportionately smaller share of the total harvest from a larger volume of standing timber.

COMMERCIAL TIMBERLAND PRODUCTIVITY
—Percentage of Land, 1977—

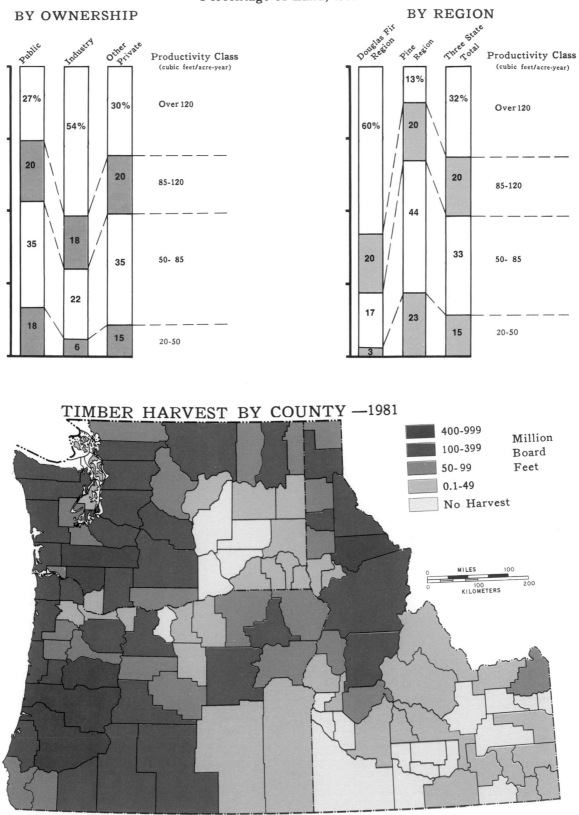

BY OWNERSHIP

Public	Industry	Other Private	Productivity Class (cubic feet/acre-year)
27%	54%	30%	Over 120
20		20	85-120
35	18	35	50- 85
	22		
18	6	15	20-50

BY REGION

Douglas Fir Region	Pine Region	Three State Total	Productivity Class (cubic feet/acre-year)
60%	13%	32%	Over 120
	20	20	85-120
20	44	33	50- 85
17	23	15	20-50
3			

TIMBER HARVEST BY COUNTY —1981

400-999
100-399   Million
50- 99   Board
0.1-49   Feet
No Harvest

MILES 100
KILOMETERS 100 200

Location of Primary Forest Industries

Location of primary forest industries correlates closely with timber harvest areas due to the high cost of transporting bulky raw materials. Hence, mills west of the Cascades process about 70% of the total wood harvest. Moreover, timber utilization differs considerably from area to area. Western Washington mills are primarily oriented to pulp and paper production and account for about 60% of Pacific Northwest pulpwood consumption. In contrast, the western Oregon industry is oriented more to production of lumber and of veneer for plywood, but pulp and paper production is also important. In the pine subregion sawmilling is predominant.

Small sawmills are common throughout the forest areas of the Pacific Northwest. Nearly two-thirds of the lumber, however, is produced by some 200 sawmills in western Oregon (44%) and about 150 mills in western Washington (21%). Sawmills in Lane and Douglas counties of western Oregon alone account for about 15% of the regional total. Idaho sawmills produce about 15% of the region's total lumber output, eastern Oregon 13%, and eastern Washington 7%. About half of Pacific Northwest lumber production is Douglas-fir, about 29% pine, and 15% hemlock.

Sawmills are generally located close to timber harvest areas and to roads and rail lines, since most logs are transported by truck and most lumber is shipped by rail or truck. Although a few large integrated processing plants are able to fully utilize all types of logs, the current trend is to sort logs in the woods and to route

TIMBERLAND, GROWING STOCK VOLUME, GROWTH AND HARVEST—1977
Percent By Ownership

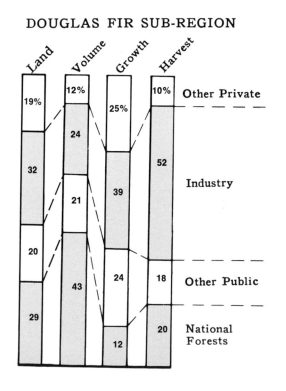

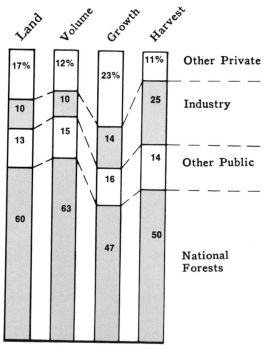

them to appropriate mills for veneer, lumber, or pulp. Most sawmill waste wood is now being chipped and sent by truck or rail to pulpmills.

The distribution of Pacific Northwest pulpmills indicates the importance of available water supply and access to transport facilities. Although the region's pulp industry started in western Oregon, by 1982 more than half of the pulpmill capacity was concentrated in the lowlands of western Washington bordering Puget Sound and along the lower Columbia River. Pulpmills along the Oregon coast, in the Willamette Valley, and along the lower Columbia River account for 44% of the region's pulping capacity. Idaho, with only one mill at the confluence of the Snake and Clearwater rivers, accounts for about 5%. In total, the 38 pulpmills of the Pacific Northwest produce 12-15% of the nation's woodpulp.

About half of the nation's softwood plywood is produced by about 115 mills in the Pacific Northwest. Plywood mill locations are strongly related to availability of veneer-size logs. Consequently southwestern Oregon mills dominate, with about 70% of the plywood capacity.

ROUNDWOOD CONSUMPTION BY MILL TYPE

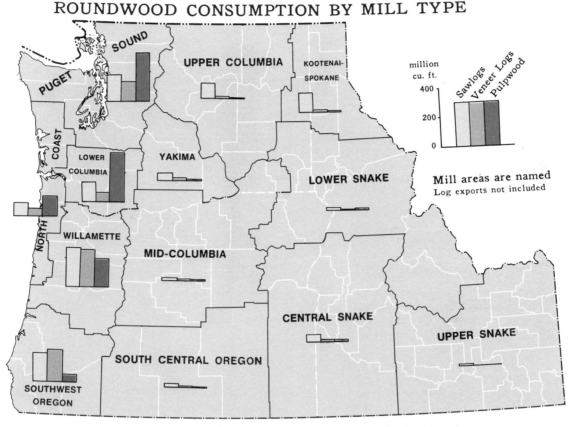

Table 28.   *Volume of Timber Growing Stock by Principal Species*
(Million Cubic Feet)

	Total Soft-woods	Douglas-fir	Western Hemlock	True Firs	Ponderosa and Jeffrey Pine	Lodge-pole Pine	Western Red Cedar	Sitka and Englemann Spruce	Western Larch	Western White Pine	Hard-woods
Douglas-fir subregion	93,685	51,290	23,184	9,911	672	398	4,583	1,202[b]	36	547	10,326[d]
Western Washington	41,082	15,303	15,689	5,736	32	137	3,335	585	10	107	5,532
Western Oregon	52,603	35,987	7,495	4,175	640	261	1,248	617	26	440	4,794
Pine subregion	70,512	17,509	2,262	13,907	15,042	9,250	2,243	3,297[c]	3,124	2,254	418
Eastern Washington	16,718	5,690	553	2,576	3,704	1,415	230	612	612	243	171
Eastern Oregon	22,132	3,262	570	4,464	8,257	3,835	7	565	904	98	25
Northern Idaho	----------[a]	----------	----------	----------	----------	----------	----------	----------	----------	----------	----------
Southern Idaho	31,662	8,557	1,139	6,867	3,081	4,000	2,006	2,120	1,608	1,913	222
Total Pacific Northwest	164,197	68,799	25,446	23,818	15,714	9,648	6,826	4,499	3,160	2,801	10,744
Total United States	455,779	93,502	----------	----------	----------	----------	----------	----------	----------	----------	255,189

Source: Table 3.17 in *Forest Resource Report No. 23,* U.S.D.A. Forest Service 1982.

[a] Data not available.
[b] Sitka Spruce.
[c] Engelmann and other Spruce.
[d] Mostly Red Alder (6,782).

PULP MILLS —1982

CAPACITY
—tons per day—

● 1,000-2,499
● 500-999
· 250-499
· 100-249

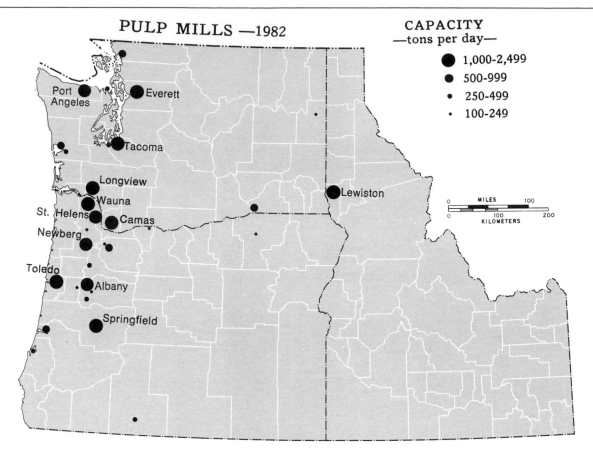

Port Angeles
Everett
Tacoma
Longview
Wauna
St. Helens
Camas
Newberg
Toledo
Albany
Springfield
Lewiston

MILES 100
KILOMETERS 200

SOFTWOOD PLYWOOD MILLS

CAPACITY
(million sq. ft. per year)

● 400-799
● 200-399
· 100-199
· 50-99
· 10-49

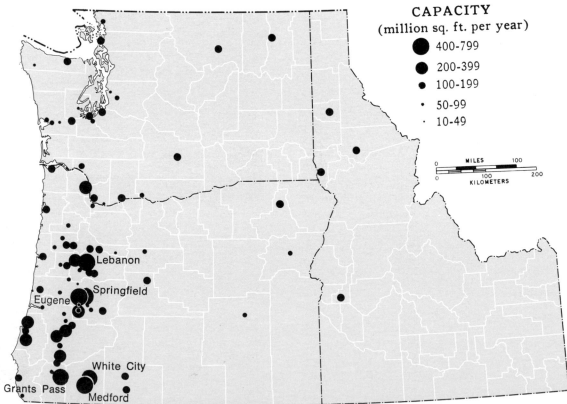

Lebanon
Springfield
Eugene
White City
Grants Pass
Medford

MILES 100
KILOMETERS 200

Commercial Fisheries

J. Granville Jensen

Commercial fisheries resources of the Pacific Northwest are generous in variety and in quantity, and support an important regional industry despite problems with El Nino, declining catches, conflicts with fishers of other nations, and Indian Treaty rights. Food fish landings at Oregon and Washington ports average about 325 million pounds (147 million kilograms) annually, about 9% of the nation's total, valued at about $150 million in 1981. Fulltime fishermen number about 10,000 in Washington and about 5,000 in Oregon. In addition, fish handling and processing facilities seasonally employ from 4,000-6,000 people.

Major Harvest

Salmon species constitute the most economically important fish landed at Pacific Northwest ports, accounting for 15-20% of all landings and about 40% of value. However, total catch varies greatly from year to year, as does the mix of species landed, due to environmental factors coupled with conservation regulations aimed at preserving and improving stocks. Washington ports receive about three-fourths of all salmon landings in the region.

Tuna landings, which were very large in the 1970s, by 1981 had declined to only about 3% of total landings due to lack of appropriate canning facilities in the region. The tuna fishing areas are mostly off the Oregon coast and southward, with fishing in Mexican waters within the 200 mile zone now restricted.

Groundfish landings, including cod, halibut, ocean perch, sole, and hake increased greatly to become the largest tonnage accounting for half of all landings by the late 1970s. At least three-fourths of all groundfish are landed at six major ports (see below). The halibut harvest is mainly from Alaskan waters with landings at Washington ports, notably Seattle.

In 1981, shellfish accounted for 23% of landings and 28% of value. Oyster cultivation is mostly in Washington waters, notably Willapa Bay (53%), Puget Sound areas (32%), and Grays Harbor (8%). About 5% of shrimp landings are made at Newport and Coos Bay on the Oregon coast. Shrimp landings assumed major importance in the 1970s, with major fishing efforts off the coast of southern Oregon and extending from California to Alaska. Scallops were landed mainly at Coos Bay (54%) and Astoria (35%) in Oregon.

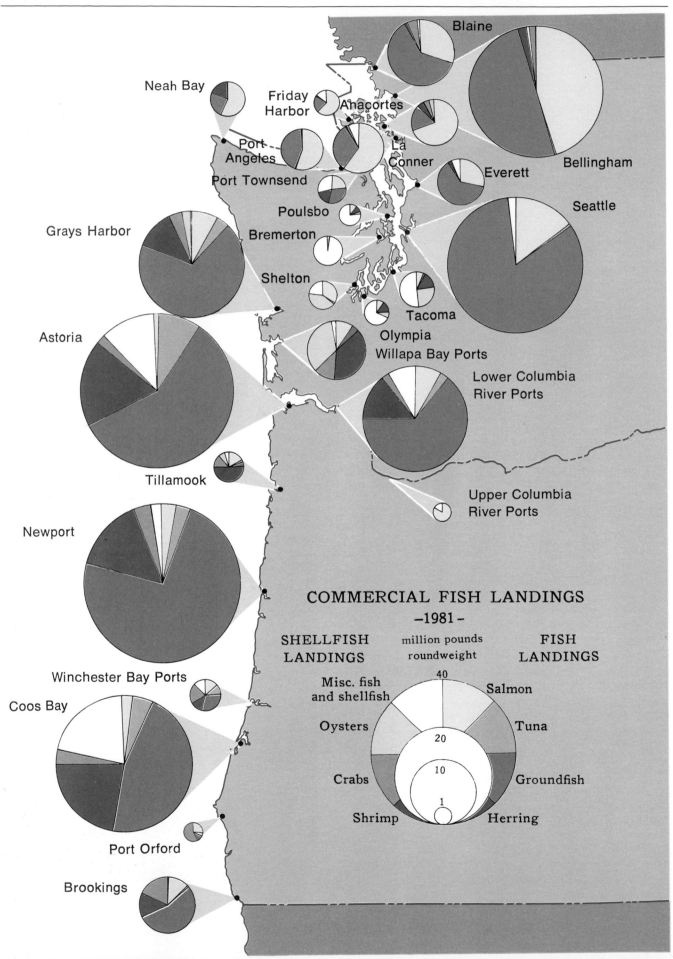

Neah Bay

Friday
Harbor

Blaine

Ancortes

La
Conner

Bellingham

Port
Angeles

Everett

Port Townsend

Seattle

Poulsbo

Bremerton

Grays Harbor

Shelton

Tacoma

Olympia

Astoria

Willapa Bay Ports

Lower Columbia
River Ports

Tillamook

Upper Columbia
River Ports

Newport

COMMERCIAL FISH LANDINGS
−1981−

SHELLFISH
LANDINGS

million pounds
roundweight

FISH
LANDINGS

Misc. fish
and shellfish

Salmon

Oysters

Tuna

Winchester Bay Ports

Coos Bay

Crabs

Groundfish

Shrimp

Herring

Port Orford

Brookings

WASHINGTON FOOD FISH LANDINGS

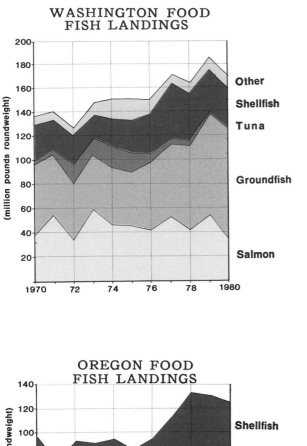

OREGON FOOD FISH LANDINGS

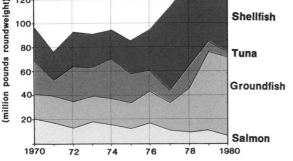

Major Ports

Although many ports receive landings which support processing and distribution facilities, six major ports accounted for 68% of all landings in 1981. Bellingham (11%) is the major salmon landing port and is also important for groundfish. Seattle (11%) mainly receives groundfish but is also a major salmon port. Grays Harbor ports, notably Westport, are famed for landings of crabs, oysters, and shrimp, although groundfish provide the largest tonnage. In Oregon, Astoria (14%) is still the leading tuna port despite recent declines which have left groundfish, scallops, and shrimp to dominate the landings. Newport (14%) receives mainly groundfish followed by shrimp, crabs, and salmon. Coos Bay-Charleston is a major shellfish port, handling large quantities of shrimp, crab, and scallops as well as smaller landings of groundfish.

Conservation Management

Conservation management of the region's fisheries has long been a major concern of state and federal agencies. Problems facing commercial fisheries include limiting harvests to achieve optimal long-term yields, control of water pollution, the negative impact of dams on anadromous species, the conflict with Indian Treaty rights and sports fishing, competition from foreign vessels, and increasing transportation costs to limited markets.

The Fisheries Conservation and Management Act of 1976 established the Fisheries Conservation Zone, extending from 3-200 miles (5-320 kilometers) offshore. Within the zone federal agencies have exclusive management authority and U.S. fishermen have preferential fishing rights. Fishing by foreign vessels within the zone is only by permit, and their allowed catch is limited to the remainder of the estimated optimal yield. The Act also created two councils involving Oregon and Washington—the Pacific Fishery Management Council and the North Pacific Fishery Management Council—to develop specific management plans and to establish definitive optimal yields.

Minerals and Mining

Thomas J. Maresh

A variety of mineral resources is found throughout the Pacific Northwest, although the region does not rank as a major national producer. In 1981, for example, Idaho, Washington, and Oregon ranked 18th, 30th, and 36th, respectively, among the states in value of mineral production. The region accounts for about 3% of the total national value of mineral production. Moreover, the mineral industries are not major employers, accounting for less than 2% of the labor force in all three states.

The local importance of the mineral resource base and mineral industries is greater, however, than the above figures suggest. The map of Average Value of Mineral Production below indicates areas in which value of output is substantial, and it should be remembered that mine products are commonly processed, generating further employment and income in the region. Most importantly, however, mineral resources provide a base for other productive activities, such as the use of sand, gravel, and stone in building construction.

Although the mix of minerals contributing to the value of mineral production varies among the three states in the region, all have been showing an increase in total value of production.

Mineral Production in Oregon

Total value of mineral production in Oregon closely parallels production of sand, gravel, and stone, reflecting trends in the building industry and highway and dam construction. Lime, cement, clays, gemstones, nickel, pumice, silver, copper, diatomite, emery, gold, lead, and talc are among the other commodities produced.

Mineral resource potential is widespread, but much of the current mineral production occurs in the more

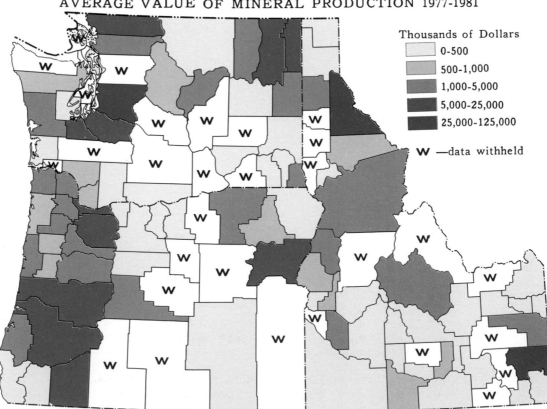

AVERAGE VALUE OF MINERAL PRODUCTION 1977-1981

Thousands of Dollars

0-500
500-1,000
1,000-5,000
5,000-25,000
25,000-125,000

W —data withheld

Table 29. *Value of Mineral Production in the Pacific Northwest, 1980-1982 Average*
(Thousand dollars)

	Washington	Oregon	Idaho	Total
Cement	90,112	W	W	90,112
Clay	1,399	256	767	2,422
Copper	W	W	6,673	6,673
Gem stones	183	583	85	851
Gold	W	708[a]	W	708
Lead	W	W	33,531[a]	33,531
Phosphate rock			103,279	103,279
Sand and gravel	47,653	39,767	12,801	100,221
Silver	709[b]	48[a]	194,515	195,272
Stone	27,781	46,095	6,549	80,425
Zinc			22,876[c]	22,876
Other	32,986	48,220	40,579	121,785
Total	200,823	135,677	421,655	758,155

W = Withheld.
[a] 1980 and 1982 only.
[b] 1981 only.
[c] 1980 only.

populous areas of the state, where there is demand for construction materials. Important metallurgical research facilities are operated by the Bureau of Mines in Albany, and aluminum, silicon, iron, and rare metals are processed at several processing plants located in the state.

VALUE OF MINERAL PRODUCTION IN OREGON

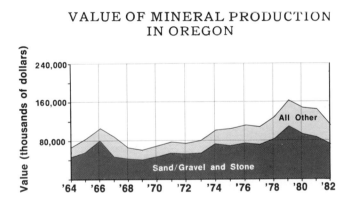

VALUE OF MINERAL PRODUCTION IN IDAHO

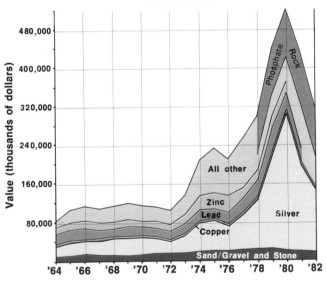

Mineral Production in Idaho

Idaho is the region's major producer by total value of metals and lead and is among the leading states in the nation in the production of silver, lead, phosphate rock, antimony, and zinc. Levels of production have varied in recent years, reflecting labor strikes and price fluctuations. The rich Coeur d'Alene mining district has produced more silver than any other district in the world.

Phosphate rock production is important in southeastern Idaho. Copper, gold, sand, gravel, stone, clay, tungsten, vanadium, and a number of other minerals are also produced. Mining thus provides a major source of income in Idaho.

Mineral Production in Washington

As in Oregon, construction materials, such as sand, gravel, stone, and cement are the major mineral commodities produced. Annual production reflects changes in the general economy and in the level of building activity. Minerals produced in lesser quantities include clays, gem stones, peat, copper, gold, gypsum, lead, lime, olivine, talc, tungsten, silver, and diatomite. King County, a major producer of construction materials, leads in value of mineral production.

Washington is an important metals processor of aluminum, copper, magnesium, and other metals. Both ores produced locally and imported ores are processed in the state.

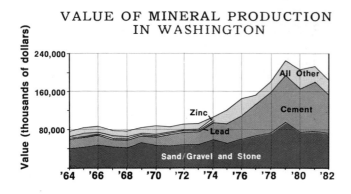

VALUE OF MINERAL PRODUCTION
IN WASHINGTON

Industrial Minerals

The major industrial minerals of the region—sand, gravel, and stone—are produced at sites distributed throughout the region. These sites are too numerous to be shown in detail; only major producing areas are indicated on the map of Industrial Minerals. Transportation costs constitute an important share of delivered costs, with the result that most consumption takes place within 25 miles (40 kilometers) of the point of production. Land use restrictions and urban expansion have, in some localities, prohibited development of sand and gravel resources. Selected sites of resource potential, production, and processing for a variety of nonmetals are shown on the map. Noteworthy are the deposits of phosphate rock in southeastern Idaho, which provide 10% of the U.S. output.

Ferrous Metals, Bauxite, and Titanium Potential

Although the Pacific Northwest has the potential for producing iron as well as a number of ferroalloys, only nickel is produced in significant quantities. Hanna Mining Company operates the nation's only domestic nickel mine, in Douglas County, Oregon. Recent annual output has been approximately 15,000 tons (approximately 13 million kilograms), although production was suspended in 1982-1983 in response to market fluctuations. Antimony is produced as a by-product of silver ores, vanadium is recovered from phosphate rock, and small amounts of tungsten have been mined in Idaho in recent years.

Bauxite and titanium deposits are known to exist in the Pacific Northwest, but are not presently developed. The bauxite deposits of the Willamette Valley have been tested for possible use in the aluminum industry, but they are not yet competitive with sources outside the region. Development in the near future has been speculated.

The map at the top of page 111 shows sites of Uranium and Mercury Potential. Midnite Mine, on the Spokane Indian Reservation in Washington, continues to produce uranium ore. Mercury has not been produced in recent years, as a result of continuing low prices.

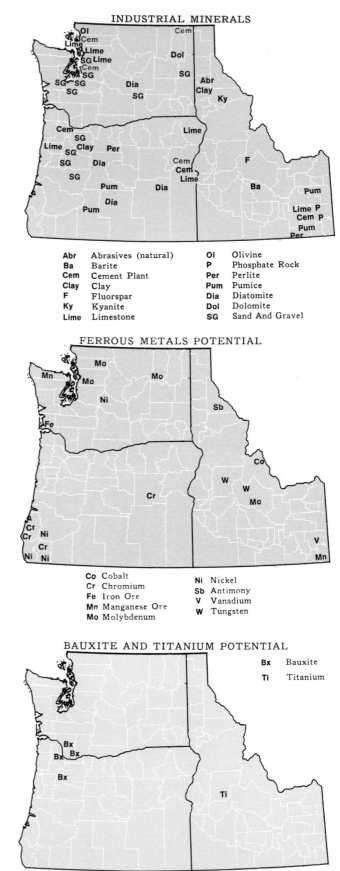

INDUSTRIAL MINERALS

Abr	Abrasives (natural)
Ba	Barite
Cem	Cement Plant
Clay	Clay
F	Fluorspar
Ky	Kyanite
Lime	Limestone
Ol	Olivine
P	Phosphate Rock
Per	Perlite
Pum	Pumice
Dia	Diatomite
Dol	Dolomite
SG	Sand And Gravel

FERROUS METALS POTENTIAL

Co	Cobalt
Cr	Chromium
Fe	Iron Ore
Mn	Manganese Ore
Mo	Molybdenum
Ni	Nickel
Sb	Antimony
V	Vanadium
W	Tungsten

BAUXITE AND TITANIUM POTENTIAL

Bx	Bauxite
Ti	Titanium

MERCURY AND URANIUM POTENTIAL

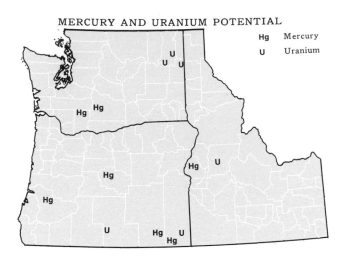

Hg   Mercury

U   Uranium

COPPER, LEAD, AND ZINC POTENTIAL

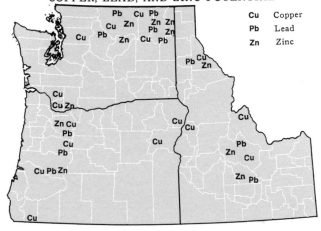

Cu   Copper

Pb   Lead

Zn   Zinc

GOLD AND SILVER POTENTIAL

Au   Gold

Ag   Silver

Copper, Lead, and Zinc Potential

The Pacific Northwest is an important producer of lead and zinc, most of which is produced in Shoshone County, Idaho, where the Coeur d'Alene mining district has produced, since the 1860s, approximately 7 million tons of lead and 2.6 million tons of zinc. Idaho ranks second in the nation in lead production and fifth in zinc, accounting for about 5% of the U.S. output of both metals. Zinc and lead are produced in Washington in Pend Oreille, Ferry, and Steven counties. Most of the copper produced in the Pacific Northwest comes from complex ores in association with such metals as zinc, lead, gold, and silver.

Gold and Silver Potential

The Pacific Northwest is the nation's major producer of silver, with Idaho alone accounting for over 40% of total U.S. production. The Sunshine Mine in the Coeur d'Alene district is renowned as a silver producer; Galena, Coeur, and Lucky Friday mines are also noteworthy. The Delamar and Lucky Friday mines were the leading gold producers in the region, with Idaho ranking seventh among the states. Lesser amounts of gold and silver are produced in Washington, mainly in the Republic district in Ferry County.

While recent instability in the economy has caused fluctuations in mineral production, the outlook is for continued general increases in production in the Pacific Northwest. This will reflect both the expansion of existing operations and development of new sites. Yet many obstacles face the minerals industries, including land use restrictions, restrictions on entry for exploration and development on public lands, classification of lands as wilderness, environmental regulations on surface disruption and processing facilities, and increasing energy costs.

Acknowledgment is given to the U.S. Bureau of Mines for assistance in compiling the data and maps on mineral resources. Unfortunately, many restrictions, designed to protect the privacy of individual firms, limit the data which may be obtained on individual mineral commodities or on production in individual counties. In such cases, estimates have been made by the author when reasonable to do so.

Maps portray both sites of production and areas of anticipated potential.

Manufacturing

Thomas J. Maresh

Although experiencing a recent decline in response to the general slow-down in the economy, the long-term trend in manufacturing employment continues upward in the Pacific Northwest. In 1980 manufacturing employment was 583,000. Value added by manufacturing in the region was $23,821,000. As can be seen on the map of Total Manufacturing Employment by County on the opposite page, there are important spatial variations in the pattern of manufacturing employment in the region. The graph of Manufacturing Employment by Major Industrial Sectors, 1981 on page 115 shows significant variation in composition.

This factor is significant in explaining the growth rate of manufacturing shown in the graph of Manufacturing Employment in the Pacific Northwest below, and is important in terms of the economic stability of an area. Decline or growth in the demand for forest products as a result of changes in the level of the building industry, for example, will be felt more sharply in some areas than others. Similarly, changes in the demand for aircraft can have a significant although localized impact on employment. As can be seen in Manufacturing Employment by Major Industrial Sectors, the three largest sectors in all three states account for more than half of the manufacturing employment, and in each instance two of the three largest sectors include lumber and wood products and food and kindred products.

Whereas all three states have exhibited long-term increases in manufacturing employment, relative changes differ. Washington, the leading manufacturer in the region, accounted for approximately two-thirds of the region's manufacturing employment at the turn of the century and now accounts for 51%. Oregon's share has increased from 31% to 39%, and Idaho's from 3% to 10%.

Manufacturing is predominantly an urban activity, with agglomerations of manufacturing facilities most pronounced in the major metropolitan areas. More than 60% of manufacturing employment is found in the region's thirteen Standard Metropolitan Statistical Areas.

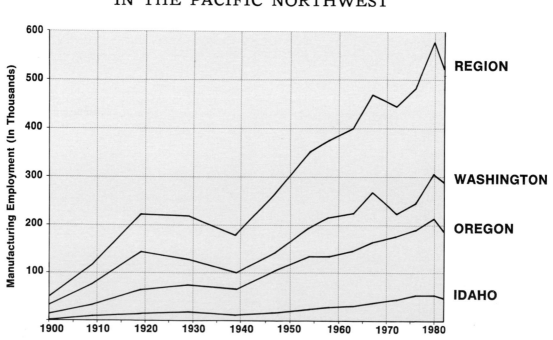

MANUFACTURING EMPLOYMENT
IN THE PACIFIC NORTHWEST

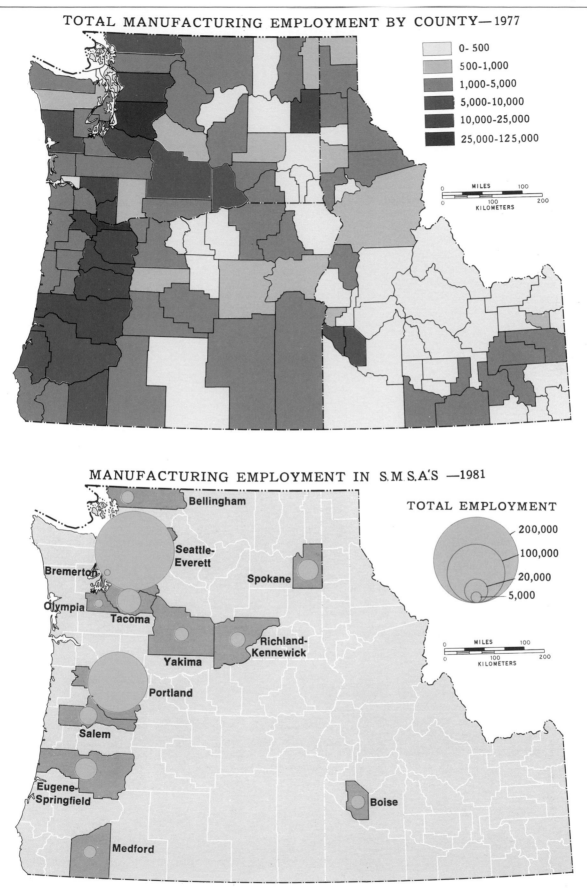

TOTAL MANUFACTURING EMPLOYMENT BY COUNTY—1977

	0- 500
	500-1,000
	1,000-5,000
	5,000-10,000
	10,000-25,000
	25,000-125,000

MANUFACTURING EMPLOYMENT IN S.M.S.A'S —1981

TOTAL EMPLOYMENT

200,000
100,000
20,000
5,000

MANUFACTURING EMPLOYMENT IN
S.M.S.A.'S BY SECTOR —1981

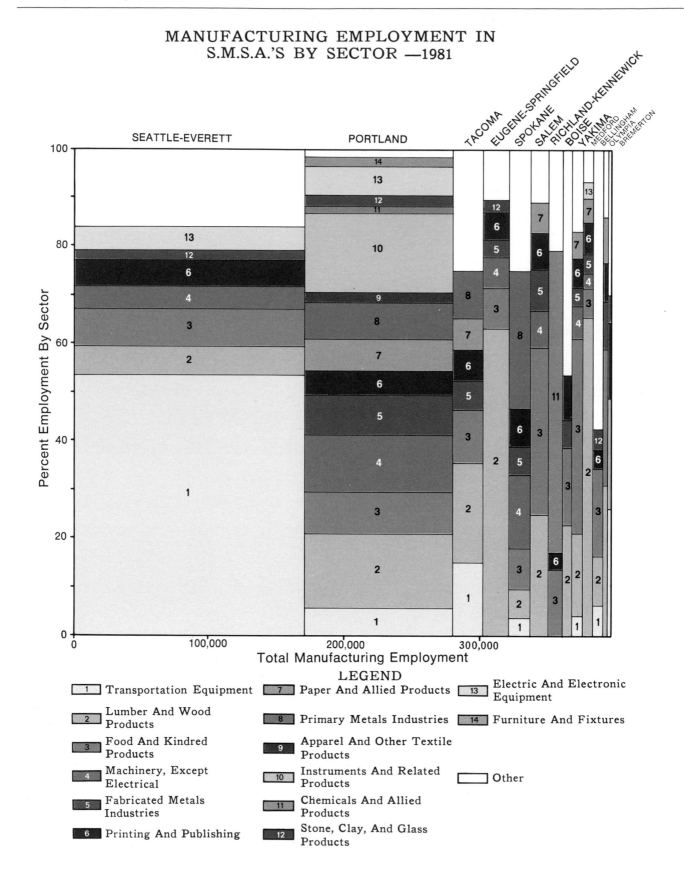

Percent Employment By Sector

Total Manufacturing Employment

SEATTLE-EVERETT   PORTLAND   TACOMA EUGENE-SPRINGFIELD SPOKANE SALEM RICHLAND-KENNEWICK BOISE YAKIMA MEDFORD BELLINGHAM OLYMPIA BREMERTON

LEGEND

1 Transportation Equipment	7 Paper And Allied Products	13 Electric And Electronic Equipment
2 Lumber And Wood Products	8 Primary Metals Industries	14 Furniture And Fixtures
3 Food And Kindred Products	9 Apparel And Other Textile Products	
4 Machinery, Except Electrical	10 Instruments And Related Products	Other
5 Fabricated Metals Industries	11 Chemicals And Allied Products	
6 Printing And Publishing	12 Stone, Clay, And Glass Products	

MANUFACTURING EMPLOYMENT BY
MAJOR INDUSTRIAL SECTORS -1981

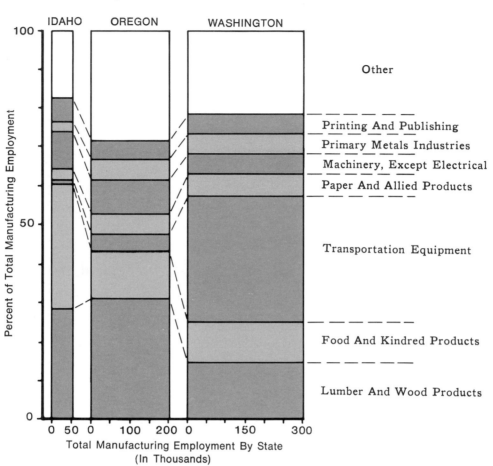

IDAHO OREGON WASHINGTON

Percent of Total Manufacturing Employment

100

50

0

0 50 0 100 200 0 150 300

Total Manufacturing Employment By State
(In Thousands)

Other

Printing And Publishing
Primary Metals Industries
Machinery, Except Electrical
Paper And Allied Products

Transportation Equipment

Food And Kindred Products

Lumber And Wood Products

The mix of manufacturing is extremely varied among these metropolitan areas. Portland's manufacturing structure is relatively diversified, in contrast to the relatively specialized situation in Seattle and Eugene. Specialization in one or two sectors may result in rapid expansion if these are growth sectors, but may also result in high unemployment and local economic problems when they are depressed. Efforts are being made in the region to diversify the industrial base and to disperse new industrial activity throughout the region.

The graph of Manufacturing Employment in S.M.S.A.'s by Sector on page 114 shows that food and kindred products and lumber and wood products are important in virtually all metropolitan areas in the region. Transportation equipment, primary metal industries, and other sectors are significant locally.

Aluminum plant at Troutdale, Oregon.

Primary Metals Industries

The primary metals industries are involved in the processing of both imported and locally produced metals. Among the larger firms are copper, lead, and zinc smelters, iron and steel mills, and aluminum smelters and rolling mills. Seven aluminum plants in Washington, processing alumina from Jamaica and Australia, produce 23% of the primary aluminum in the U.S. Two plants in Oregon, with a combined annual capacity of 220,000 tons, contribute approximately 4% of the national total.

Included among the smaller firms are several ferroalloy plants and foundry and casting operations. Employment is predominantly in the more densely populated areas of western Washington and Oregon. Plants processing local ores provide some employment in more remote sites.

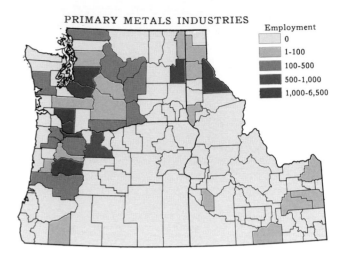

PRIMARY METALS INDUSTRIES

Employment
- 0
- 1-100
- 100-500
- 500-1,000
- 1,000-6,500

Steel and Ferroalloy Plants

Steel production in the Pacific Northwest is concentrated in Seattle and Portland. Plants are relatively small, producing mainly construction steel for the regional market. Production of steel in the area is done in electric furnaces, with most firms processing scrap metal. However, in Portland, iron ore slurry imported from Peru is concentrated into pellets and then processed into steel.

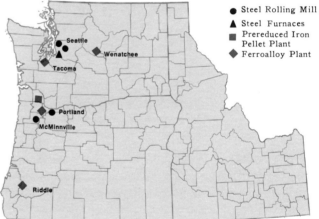

STEEL AND FERROALLOY PLANTS

- ● Steel Rolling Mill
- ▲ Steel Furnaces
- ■ Prereduced Iron Pellet Plant
- ◆ Ferroalloy Plant

Seattle, Wenatchee, Tacoma, Portland, McMinnville, Riddle

Nonferrous Plants

The process of reducing alumina to aluminum requires the input of large quantities of electricity, a factor which has attracted smelters to sources of low-cost electricity. The location of approximately one-third of the nation's reduction capacity in the Pacific Northwest is in large part explained by the relatively low-cost power advantage the region has enjoyed in the past. This attraction has now diminished because of the increasing cost of electricity in the region.

Recent economic conditions have also led to closures, on at least a temporary basis, of the copper smelter and refinery operated by American Smelting and Refining Company in Tacoma and the zinc smelter and lead smelter and refinery operated by the Bunker Hill Company in the Coeur d'Alene district of Idaho.

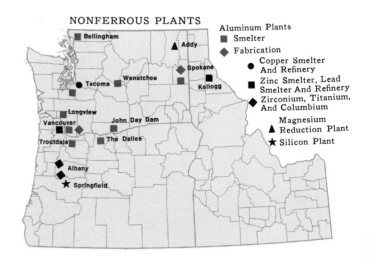

NONFERROUS PLANTS

Aluminum Plants
- ■ Smelter
- ◆ Fabrication
- ● Copper Smelter And Refinery
- ● Zinc Smelter, Lead Smelter And Refinery
- ◆ Zirconium, Titanium, And Columbium
- ▲ Magnesium Reduction Plant
- ★ Silicon Plant

Bellingham, Addy, Spokane, Wenatchee, Kellogg, Tacoma, Longview, Vancouver, John Day Dam, Troutdale, The Dalles, Albany, Springfield

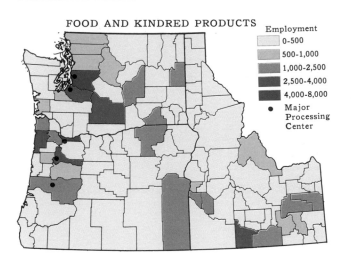

FOOD AND KINDRED PRODUCTS

Employment
- 0-500
- 500-1,000
- 1,000-2,500
- 2,500-4,000
- 4,000-8,000
- ● Major Processing Center

Food and Kindred Products

This category includes such activities as meat packing, dairy processing, canning and freezing, flour production, fish canning, and sugar beet processing. Although food processing is, in general, widespread through the Pacific Northwest, certain activities are localized. Dairy processing facilities and meat packing plants tend to be located near populated market areas. Activities such as sugar beet processing and fish canning are located with access to the producing areas.

Over 13% of the region's manufacturing employment is involved in food processing. Particularly important are processing of fruits and vegetables, dairy products, and meat products.

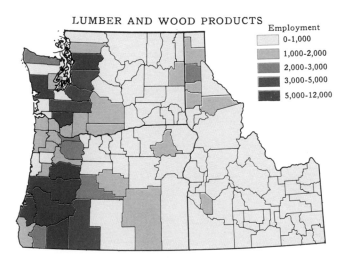

LUMBER AND WOOD PRODUCTS

Employment
- 0-1,000
- 1,000-2,000
- 2,000-3,000
- 3,000-5,000
- 5,000-12,000

Lumber and Wood Products

Employment in lumber and wood products industries accounts for approximately 30% of the manufacturing employees in the region. This sector, although widespread in the Pacific Northwest, is particularly important in western Washington and Oregon. Sawmills, planing mills, veneer and plywood plants, in addition to logging operations, are major employers. Recent studies suggest that, in the future, employment in lumber and wood products industries will decline in the Pacific Northwest.

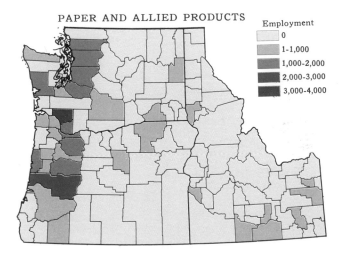

PAPER AND ALLIED PRODUCTS

Employment
- 0
- 1-1,000
- 1,000-2,000
- 2,000-3,000
- 3,000-4,000

Paper and Allied Products

Paper mills and pulp mills account for the greatest share of the employment in this sector. These activities are based on the softwood resources of the region. Accordingly, plants producing paper and allied products are largely concentrated in western Washington and Oregon. Although they directly support only approximately 4% of the total employment in the Pacific Northwest, they are highly significant in a number of local economies.

Transportation Equipment

This is the leading sector of manufacturing employment in Washington and contributes significantly to the manufacturing base of Seattle, Portland, Boise, and Tacoma. Aircraft, ship, and boat building and repairing, motor vehicle equipment, trailer coaches, recreation vehicles, and railroad equipment are among the more important products in this sector. Dominant is the Boeing Corporation, with its aircraft operations in Washington. Recent years have seen an increase in smaller firms producing trailers, campers, and other recreational vehicles and equipment.

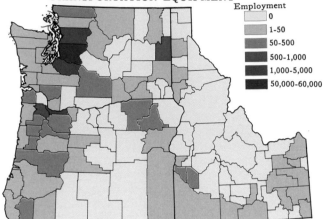

Chemicals and Allied Products

This category includes establishments manufacturing and processing fertilizers, industrial chemicals, soaps and detergents, and paints and varnishes. East of the Cascades agricultural chemicals are relatively important in such areas as Yakima County, the Tri-cities area, Lewiston, and southeastern Idaho. These locations reflect both agricultural markets and the presence of phosphate deposits in southern Idaho. The broader mix of chemicals produced west of the Cascades is a consequence of a larger, more varied market. Numerous chemicals are produced for industrial consumers, such as wood products firms.

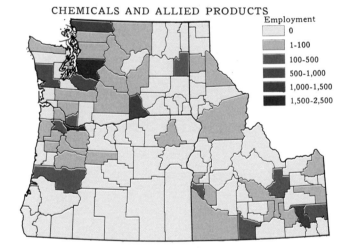

Printing and Publishing

In contrast to other manufacturing sectors, printing and publishing is widely distributed throughout the region. The major activities are newspaper publishing and commercial printing. In general, they are distributed in relation to population distribution. Thus, this sector of manufacturing, which is composed of many firms, most with fewer than ten employees, is significant in even the smallest communities of the region. Similarly, machine shops, small bakeries, and other local manufacturers contribute to the local economies and, collectively, are important to the region.

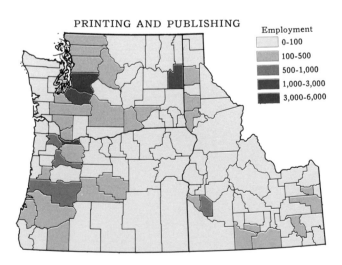

Trade and Services

Ray M. Northam

Trade and service industries include retail trade, wholesale trade, personal services, and professional services. Collectively, these industries account for about 65% of the region's work force. These industries, usually located in urban centers, dispense goods and services to the population of the urban center itself, as well as to a trade area or hinterland that will vary in areal extent depending upon the nature of the goods or services being distributed. Retail trade areas tend to include areas peripheral to the distribution center for the most part, while wholesale trade areas tend to be larger. Personal service and professional service areas tend to be quite restricted in areal extent, with the exceptions of large corporate or governmental facilities that distribute services statewide or regionwide.

Some specific components of the larger business centers serve nonlocal demands beyond the borders of the Pacific Northwest. The consulting services of Boeing Company in Seattle, Tektronix in Portland, for example, satisfy demands that are overwhelmingly national or international in scope, yet both cities also serve as regional distribution points for other types of goods and services.

Business centers are divided into three levels—national, regional, and local by: (1) the volume of sales of goods and services dispensed; (2) the hinterland population served; and (3) the areal extent of the distribution of good and services from a particular business center (see map of Business Centers and Trade Areas below).

Retail Trade

Cities vary in terms of retail trade employment and in the role of retail trade in the employment mix of the city. Employment in retail trade in urban centers with populations of 10,000 or greater in the Pacific North-

BUSINESS CENTERS AND TRADE AREAS

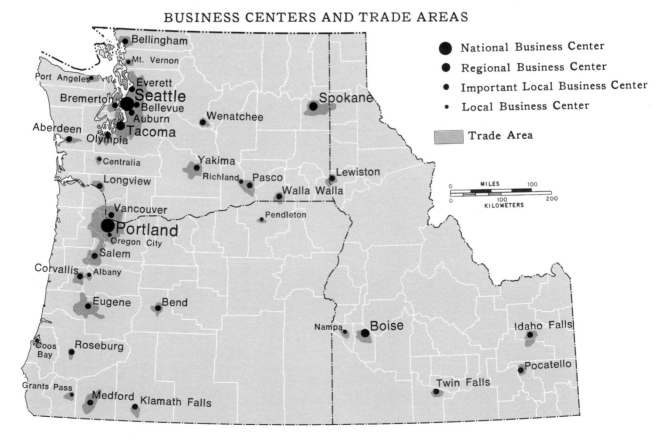

● National Business Center
● Regional Business Center
● Important Local Business Center
• Local Business Center

Trade Area

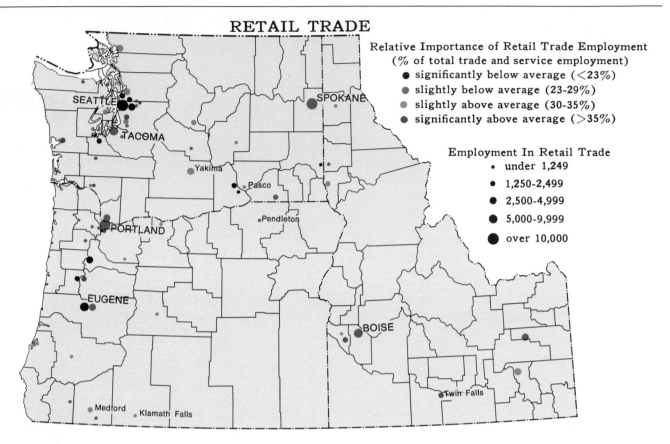

RETAIL TRADE

Relative Importance of Retail Trade Employment
(% of total trade and service employment)
- ● significantly below average (<23%)
- ● slightly below average (23-29%)
- ● slightly above average (30-35%)
- ● significantly above average (>35%)

Employment In Retail Trade
- · under 1,249
- ● 1,250-2,499
- ● 2,500-4,999
- ● 5,000-9,999
- ● over 10,000

west tends to increase as a function of larger population. In larger cities, there tend to be more retail establishments, a greater number of retail functions, and greater duplication of retail outlets. Smaller cities, by contrast, usually have fewer retail trade establishments and less than a complete mix of retail offerings. Major centers of retail trade employment in the region are Seattle, Portland, Spokane, Boise, Eugene, and Tacoma.

Perhaps more interesting than the absolute number of people employed in retail trade in a city is the relationship between this absolute number and the average retail trade employment for all cities over 10,000 in the Pacific

Northwest. Many cities with a large retail workforce nevertheless have a below-average percentage of the work force engaged in retail trade. This could indicate either a lower propensity to spend by residents of larger cities or, more likely, alternative shopping opportunities provided by outlying suburban and satellite shopping centers. To a considerable degree, this is the case for Seattle, Portland, Eugene, Spokane, Boise, and Salem. Also, a number of cities with lower employment in retail trade—e.g. Corvallis, Bellevue, Edmonds, Pasco, and Olympia—experience leakage of consumer dollars to competing commercial centers.

Table 30. *Retail Trade in Standard Metropolitan Statistical Areas (S.M.S.A.s)*

	Total		Convenience goods		Shopping goods[a]		Others	
	No. retail establish-ments	Sales $000's	No. retail establish-ments	Sales $000's	No. retail establish-ments	Sales $000's	No. retail establish-ments	Sales $000's
Seattle-Everett	10,795	3,243,012	4,051	1,188,919	2,559	879,797	4,185	1,174,296
Portland-Vancouver	8,190	2,515,231	3,054	907,214	1,845	633,104	3,291	975,513
Tacoma	2,872	793,551	1,020	263,900	635	217,661	1,217	311,990
Spokane	2,220	689,982	802	N.A.[b]	491	209,733	927	N.A.
Eugene	1,906	538,220	691	177,815	418	136,987	797	233,418
Salem	1,593	420,546	560	148,081	346	N.A.	687	N.A.
Yakima	1,410	322,125	536	N.A.	279	N.A.	595	120,954
Boise	1,183	320,233	414	N.A.	266	N.A.	503	138,397
Richland-Kennewick	809	203,160	280	74,650	193	N.A.	336	N.A.

Source: Census of Retail Trade, 1972.

[a] Includes general merchandise, apparel, and furniture and appliances.

[b] N.A. Data not available due to Census of Business disclosure rule.

By contrast, there are a number of smaller and often more isolated cities that have relatively low absolute employment in retail trade, but in which such employment is greater than the average for the region. Such strength in retail trade often derives from the fact that these cities are fairly distant from other retail trade centers and provide goods and services for a large population in outlying areas. The provision of goods and services to such an extensive hinterland contributes to the economic base of the smaller retail trade center relatively more than it would to a city with larger retail trade employment. Examples are such centers as Centralia-Chehalis, Longview-Kelso, Medford, Klamath Falls, Twin Falls, and Pocatello.

The maps of Retail Trade, Wholesale Trade, Personal Services, and Professional Services on pages 120, 122, and 123, refer to average employment in cities with populations of 10,000 or more.

Wholesale Trade

The wholesale trade industry accounts for approximately 4% of the labor force of the Pacific Northwest, as compared to about 20% in the retail trade industry. In this context, wholesale trade is not a major employment sector in the region, but serves a vital role in the distribution of a myriad of commodities to localized outlets. Food and beverages, machinery and machinery parts, hardware, large and small appliances, medical and educational materials, fertilizers and chemicals, petroleum products, and printed materials are major types of goods distributed by wholesalers in the region.

Wholesale trade employment is relatively high in major urban centers, especially Portland, Seattle, and Spokane. These cities serve as subregional wholesale trade centers and usually serve tributary areas within one day driving time by truck. Portland is the wholesale trade center for the Willamette Valley, Tacoma serves the southern Puget Sound Lowland area, Seattle provides wholesale items for the central and northern Puget Sound area, and Spokane distributes wholesale goods to much of the intermontane area. Boise receives wholesale goods from Salt Lake City to a considerable degree, resulting in disproportionately low wholesale trade employment.

The largest urban centers tend to have above-average employment in wholesale trade, as do relatively free-standing centers beyond the daily truck service range of a larger wholesale trade center, while medium-size urban centers such as Tacoma, Salem, and Eugene tend to have below-average. Small urban centers that are relatively important wholesale trade centers exist in two spatial settings: (1) suburban and/or satellite centers within metropolitan areas; and (2) smaller free-standing centers that serve large hinterlands containing numerous rural centers of still smaller sizes. Examples of the first case include Renton, Bothell, and Bellevue in the Seattle metropolitan area, and Hillsboro, Milwaukie, and Oregon City in the Portland metropolitan area. Examples of smaller free-standing wholesale trade centers include Pasco, Yakima, and Moses Lake in Washington; Medford in Oregon; and Twin Falls and Pocatello in Idaho.

Personal Services

Approximately 13% of total employment in the Pacific Northwest is involved in the personal service industries. This sector includes many engaged in the private sector, ranging from barbers and beauticians to workers in large insurance and consulting establishments. In the public sector, this group is represented largely by persons employed by various levels of government, especially local and state governments.

Centers where personal service employment is especially noteworthy include the large cities of Seattle, Portland, Tacoma, Spokane, Boise, and Salem, and the smaller cities of Pasco, Olympia, Idaho Falls, and Pocatello. Cities that have significant above-average employment in this sector as a percentage of total local employment include Olympia, Bremerton, Pasco, Richland, and Idaho Falls. Cities in which personal service employment is slightly less significant in the employment mix are more numerous and widely distributed within the region. These include Seattle, Tacoma, Spokane, Vancouver, Walla Walla, and Renton in Washington; Salem, Oregon City, and Milwaukie in Oregon; and Lewiston in Idaho. Centers noticeably lacking in employment of this type are the university cities of Eugene and Corvallis, since personal services employment in these centers is overshadowed by employment in other sectors of the local economies.

WHOLESALE TRADE

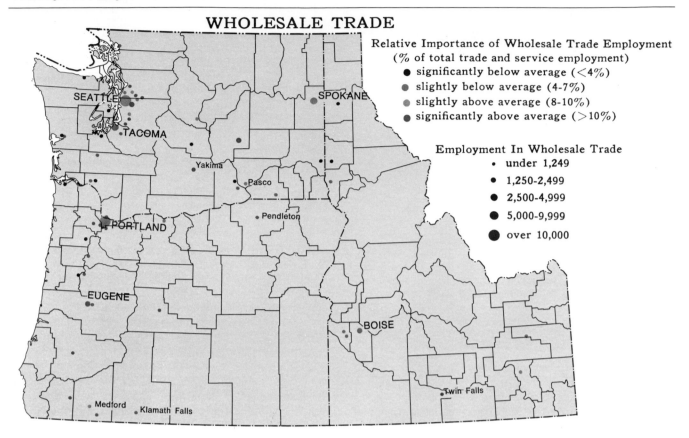

Relative Importance of Wholesale Trade Employment
(% of total trade and service employment)
● significantly below average (<4%)
● slightly below average (4-7%)
● slightly above average (8-10%)
● significantly above average (>10%)

Employment In Wholesale Trade
· under 1,249
● 1,250-2,499
● 2,500-4,999
● 5,000-9,999
● over 10,000

Professional Services

Professional services account for approximately 30% of the labor force of the Pacific Northwest. Included in this total are the many persons employed in teaching in public and private schools, those employed in higher education, the medical doctors, the many lawyers, thousands employed in administrative capacities, and other professionals such as engineers, architects, and accountants. Since some of these occupations are not as commonly encountered in smaller urban centers, the numbers so employed are concentrated in larger cities or in smaller, free-standing cities.

Seattle, Tacoma, Portland, Spokane, and Eugene have the greatest employment in professional services, with Corvallis, Salem, and Renton also having significant employment of this type. Above-average employment in professional services is characteristic of smaller, more isolated cities that have an institution of higher education. Examples include Bellingham, Vancouver, Ellensburg, and Pullman in Washington, Moscow, Idaho, and Corvallis, Eugene, and Ashland, in Oregon. College and university employment contributes significantly to total employment in these cities. Several cities are considerably below average in professional service employment, including Olympia, Pasco-Kennewick, Twin Falls, and Idaho Falls. Cities that are slightly below average in professional service employment include Longview-Kelso, Yakima, Walla Walla, Lewiston, Boise, Pocatello, Medford, and all cities in the coastal zone with populations exceeding 10,000.

PERSONAL SERVICES

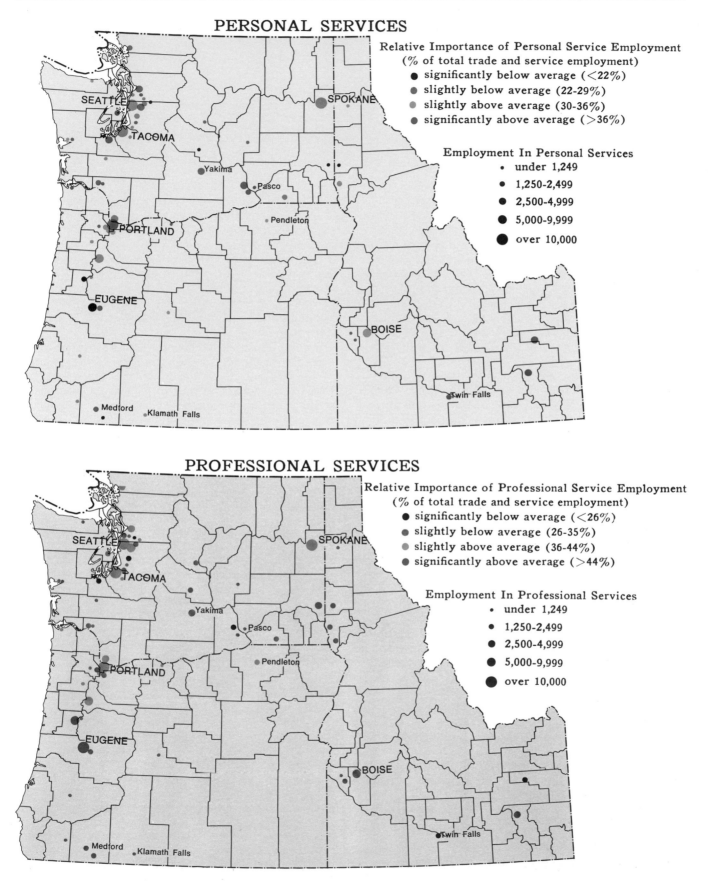

Relative Importance of Personal Service Employment
(% of total trade and service employment)
- significantly below average (<22%)
- slightly below average (22-29%)
- slightly above average (30-36%)
- significantly above average (>36%)

Employment In Personal Services
- under 1,249
- 1,250-2,499
- 2,500-4,999
- 5,000-9,999
- over 10,000

SEATTLE · TACOMA · SPOKANE · Yakima · Pasco · Pendleton · PORTLAND · EUGENE · BOISE · Twin Falls · Medford · Klamath Falls

PROFESSIONAL SERVICES

Relative Importance of Professional Service Employment
(% of total trade and service employment)
- significantly below average (<26%)
- slightly below average (26-35%)
- slightly above average (36-44%)
- significantly above average (>44%)

Employment In Professional Services
- under 1,249
- 1,250-2,499
- 2,500-4,999
- 5,000-9,999
- over 10,000

SEATTLE · TACOMA · SPOKANE · Yakima · Pasco · Pendleton · PORTLAND · EUGENE · BOISE · Twin Falls · Medford · Klamath Falls

Recreation Resources and Activities

Mary Lee Nolan

The Pacific Northwest offers a wide variety and abundance of outdoor recreation opportunities. This wealth of opportunities contributes significantly to the quality of life of Northwest residents and forms the basis for the important economic contributions of tourism throughout the region.

Diversity in the landscape is a principal contributing factor. Contained in a relatively small area are beaches and rugged headlands, forested hills and snowcapped peaks, placid estuaries and turbulent mountain streams, and lush green valleys and high desert plateaus. Resources necessary for specific activities are available— mountains to climb, untrammeled wilderness to hike, beaches to comb, forests and fields to hunt, and lakes and streams to fish. While these resources provide activity opportunities with little development other than provisions for access, other recreation pursuits depend on the provision of additional facilities. Recreation possibilities are expanded, for example, by lifts and cleared runs on mountainsides for skiers, by launch ramps and marinas to accommodate boaters on lakes, rivers, and estuaries, and by developed campgrounds in scenic surroundings.

The history of the region is also attractive to recreational travelers. Sites related to the Indian cultures of the coasts, the river valleys, and the inland plains; points of discovery and early European settlement; the route of the Oregon Trail; and sites that recall the colorful days of early logging, mining, and ranching, are all potential tourist attractions.

Management of the diverse natural and cultural recreation resources in the Pacific Northwest is shared by federal, state, and local government agencies along with private non-profit or commercial operations. Public lands, mostly under federal management, make up the bulk of the total area available for recreation. The existence of large contiguous areas in public ownership have made it possible to develop extensive trail systems and designate Scenic Rivers and Wilderness Areas with greater ease than in other parts of the U.S. The abundance of recreation opportunities on public lands has in some cases reduced the potential for commercial recreation development. However, the presence of readily available access to public areas has stimulated the growth of tourism as residents of more restricted states flock to the Pacific Northwest for outdoor recreation opportunities. Their presence has enabled private enterprise to invest profitably in the services required by tourists and to develop resorts and highly specialized recreation facilities that could not exist in isolation from the diversity of opportunities available in the Northwest.

The importance of recreation to the region's economy is evident in estimates of expenditures by out-of-state tourists. The combined annual income from tourism for the region is more than four billion dollars, and in all three states tourism ranks as the third largest sector of the economy.

In addition to economic contributions, the region's recreation resources are important to Northwesterners as part of a high quality environment. The region has exhibited an active concern with basic environmental quality, such as pure air and clean water, reflected in state programs. In addition, land-use planning to ensure development compatible with resources is emphasized, with Oregon one of the nation's leading states in this respect.

Several of the most outstanding scenic and historic resources in the Pacific Northwest are administered by the National Park System. In addition to large areas of major significance entitled national parks, the National Park System includes other parks with a variety of designations such as national monuments, national historic sites, and national recreation areas. These well-publicized attractions are important in drawing tourists to the Pacific Northwest and also provide a travel and recreational focus for residents of the region. Many of the parks are primarily important for their natural beauty, whereas others preserve and interpret places of national historic importance. National recreation areas are usually found in association with natural landscapes which have been dramatically modified by human activity, such as reservoirs behind dams.

Parks Emphasizing Natural Features

Crater Lake National Park, Oregon. About 6,000 years ago, fiery eruptions led to the collapse of Mount Mazama's peak. The near-circular deep blue lake which now lies in the caldera is dramatically encircled by steep slopes of multicolored volcanic materials. The park covers more than 160,000 acres (65,000 hectares) in the southern Oregon Cascades.

Mount Rainier National Park, Washington. This giant volcano rises 14,410 feet (440 meters) above sea level. Its peak is covered with glaciers and the lower slopes with flowered subalpine meadows and dense forests. The entire mountain is included in this park of more than 235,000 acres.

North Cascades National Park, Washington. The heavily glaciated, jagged peaks of the North Cascades loom above an alpine region of meadows, forests, fast-running streams, and spectacular waterfalls. The park's 504,785 acres are rich in wildlife.

Olympic National Park, Washington. Only trails penetrate this mountain wilderness in the heart of the Olympic range. Heavy rainfall on the Pacific slopes of these mountains results in temperate rainforest vegetation. The park's 901,216 acres also include 50 miles (80 kilometers) of coastal headlands and beaches.

Craters of the Moon National Monument, Idaho. The volcanic landscape in this 53,545-acre park includes cinder cones, jagged lava flows, and lava caves.

John Day Fossil Beds National Monument, Oregon. A vividly eroded landscape exposes plant and animal fossils spanning most of the Cenozoic from the Eocene epoch to the late Pleistocene. This priceless record of ancient North American life is preserved in three separate park units covering 14,402 acres.

Oregon Caves National Monument, Oregon. This fascinating labyrinth of underground passages developed in the Siskiyou Mountains of southwestern Oregon as groundwater dissolved the marble and limestone bedrock over eons of time. The park contains 465 acres.

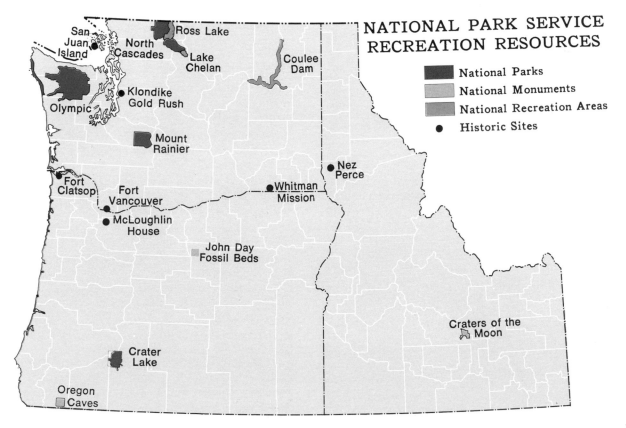

NATIONAL PARK SERVICE RECREATION RESOURCES

National Parks
National Monuments
National Recreation Areas
● Historic Sites

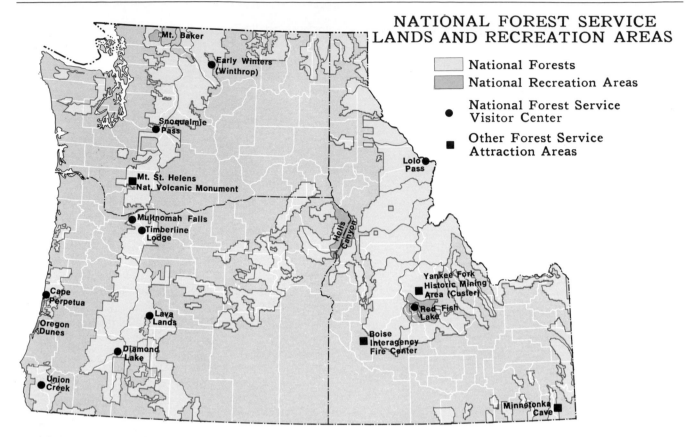

NATIONAL FOREST SERVICE
LANDS AND RECREATION AREAS

National Forests

National Recreation Areas

● National Forest Service
Visitor Center

■ Other Forest Service
Attraction Areas

Mount St. Helens National Volcanic Monument, Oregon. The approximately 110,000 acres devastated by the May 18, 1980 eruption of this volcano are preserved for scientific research and compatible uses.

Historical Parks

Fort Clatsop National Memorial, Oregon. A replica of the log fort where the Lewis and Clark expedition spent the winter of 1805-1806 is the principal attraction.

Fort Vancouver National Historic Site, Washington. Fort Vancouver on the Columbia River was the western headquarters of the Hudson's Bay Company. From 1825-1860 it was the center of fur-trading and political activity in the Pacific Northwest. Vancouver Barracks, a U.S. military post established in 1848, took over the fort in 1860, and it remained an active military reservation until 1949.

Klondike Gold Rush National Historic Park, Washington. This park in downtown Seattle commemorates the city's historic role as the major embarkation point for the Alaskan gold fields.

McLoughlin House National Historic Site, Oregon. Dr. John McLoughlin, who lived in this house from 1847-1857, was in charge of strategic Fort Vancouver through most of the second quarter of the 19th century. In this role, he was important in the development of the Pacific Northwest and gave substantial aid to early settlers from the U.S. The site is owned and administered by the McLoughlin Memorial Association in affiliation with the National Park Service.

Nez Percé National Historical Park, Idaho. The scattered sites in central western Idaho which make up this park are dedicated to the commemoration, interpretation, and preservation of important features of history and culture in the Nez Percé Indian country.

San Juan Island National Historical Park, Washington. British and American military campsites are included in a park which commemorates the peaceful relations between the United States, Great Britain, and Canada since an 1872 boundary dispute in the islands.

Whitman Mission National Historic Site, Washington. Marcus and Narcissa Whitman established a mission at this site in 1836. Until they were killed by Indians in 1847, the Whitmans provided aid to Oregon-bound pioneers. The site, which includes a monument to the couple, contains 98 acres.

Coulee Dam National Recreational Area, Washington. This 100,059-acre park centers on the 130-mile-long Franklin D. Roosevelt Lake which was created by the construction of Grand Coulee Dam, a part of the Columbia River Basin project.

Lake Chelan National Recreation Area, Washington. Glacially carved Lake Chelan in the beautiful Stehekin Valley is the principal feature of this recreation area which adjoins North Cascades National Park.

Ross Lake National Recreation Area, Washington. This reservoir in the Skagit River drainage, surrounded by mountains, lies between the north and south units of North Cascades National Park.

Wilderness Recreation

During recent years recreational activities such as backpacking, mountain climbing, and river running have become increasingly popular. The demand for recreation in a wilderness setting has reached such proportions that managers are faced with serious problems of environmental degradation caused by overuse of fragile ecosystems. Increasing numbers of people seek the wilderness experience, often interpreted as the opportunity for solitary communion with nature; but, unfortunately, the more people who seek this experience the more difficult it is to achieve, especially in the most popular and therefore most crowded wilderness areas.

In the Pacific Northwest, unlike many parts of the U.S., there is a relatively extensive amount of wild land and numerous areas have been proclaimed as formal wilderness. According to the 1964 National Wilderness Act, wilderness is defined as an area where "the earth and its community of life are untrammeled by man, where man himself is a visitor who does not remain." To qualify for inclusion in the wilderness system, an area must be large (usually at least 5,000 acres), generally unaffected by human activity including permanent

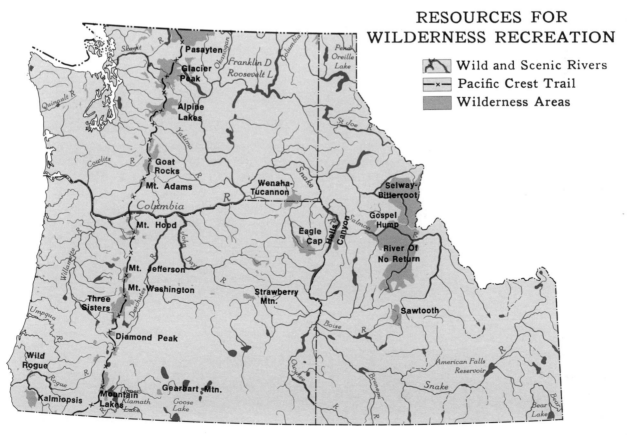

RESOURCES FOR
WILDERNESS RECREATION

⌒ Wild and Scenic Rivers
-×- Pacific Crest Trail
▓ Wilderness Areas

CAMPGROUNDS

• Private
• Public

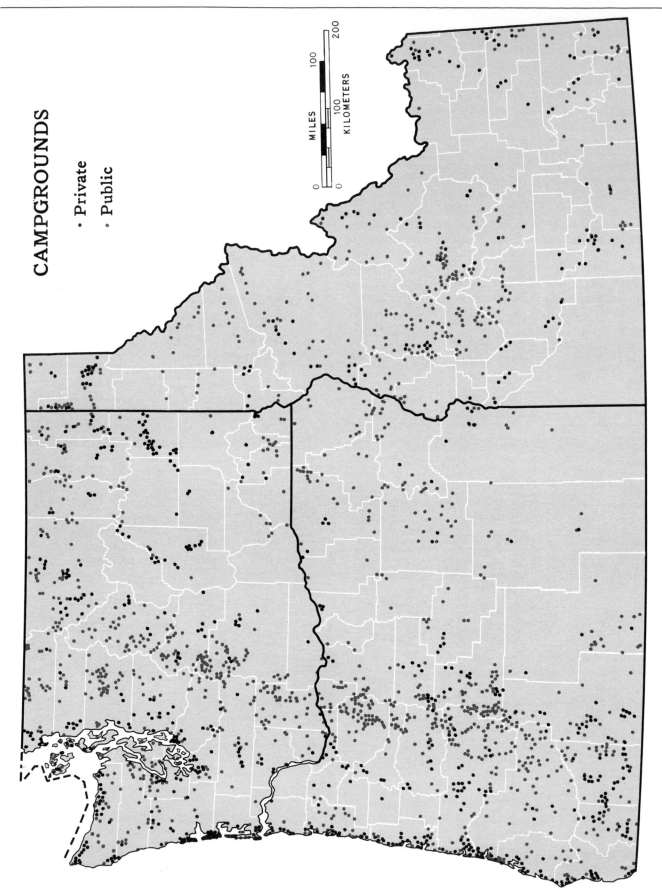

improvements and places of human habitation, and characterized by outstanding opportunities for primitive recreation and solitude. Many wilderness areas also contain important geological and ecological features considered to have educational, scenic, historic, or scientific value. Wilderness areas must be on federal lands but can be administered by any one or a combination of several agencies—the National Park Service, the U.S. Forest Service, and the Bureau of Land Management.

Float trips and rapid running are possible on many of the region's rivers, and certain particularly remote and/or scenic stretches of free-flowing rivers have been established as Wild and Scenic Rivers in accordance with 1968 legislation. These sections of rivers and their shorelines are to be maintained in a natural condition.

Trails such as the Pacific Crest Trail are ordinarily followed on foot or on horseback. Numerous shorter hiking and horseback trails exist in the region, especially on federal lands.

Recreation Activities

The most popular recreation activities among residents of the Pacific Northwest include pleasure walking, picnicking, swimming, camping, bicycling, sightseeing, fishing, various kinds of boating, and outdoor games. State parks provide a setting for many of these activities. These parks range from small wayside areas with a few picnic tables to larger parks with campgrounds, nature trails, interpretive centers, and other facilities.

The importance of camping as a popular recreation activity is shown by the number of developed campsites in the region. As indicated by the map of Campgrounds opposite, campgrounds are not evenly distributed. They tend to be clustered in particularly scenic areas which offer a variety of recreational activities to the camper and, to a lesser extent, along major highway routes where they serve the needs of that part of the traveling public which prefers camping to staying in hotels and motels. The majority of Pacific Northwest campgrounds are managed by the U.S. Forest Service. Other federal agencies which maintain campgrounds include the Bureau of Land Management, the Army Corps of Engineers, and the National Park Service. Many of the state parks have campgrounds as do some city and county parks. Privately owned campgrounds play a role by providing campers with special kinds of facilities and offering camping opportunities in areas where few public campgrounds have been developed, as along much of the Washington coast.

Camping is typical of those recreational activities usually associated with fairly extensive periods of leisure time such as long weekends and vacations, and camping trips often involve more travel than many other forms of recreation. For example, a study of Idaho residents indicates that the average distance traveled for camping trips, and for trips for the purposes of outdoor photography and visiting historic sites, is well over 100 miles.

The recent increase in popularity of downhill and cross-country skiing along with other winter activities such as snowmobiling, snowshoeing, and snowcamping has extended the recreation-tourism season into the winter months in the region's snowclad mountainous areas. Some of the more popular sites are indicated on the map of Selected Winter Sports Areas on page 130.

Some recreational attractions of the region, although of relatively minor interest for local participants, do bring people from afar. Rockhounding, for example, is engaged in by far fewer people than camping, swimming, or pleasure walking, but for those who enjoy collecting lapidary materials, the region is rich in opportunity as suggested by the map of Lapidary Material Sites on page 131. Sites yielding agates, jaspers, and semi-precious stones such as garnets attract collectors from all over North America and as far away as New Zealand.

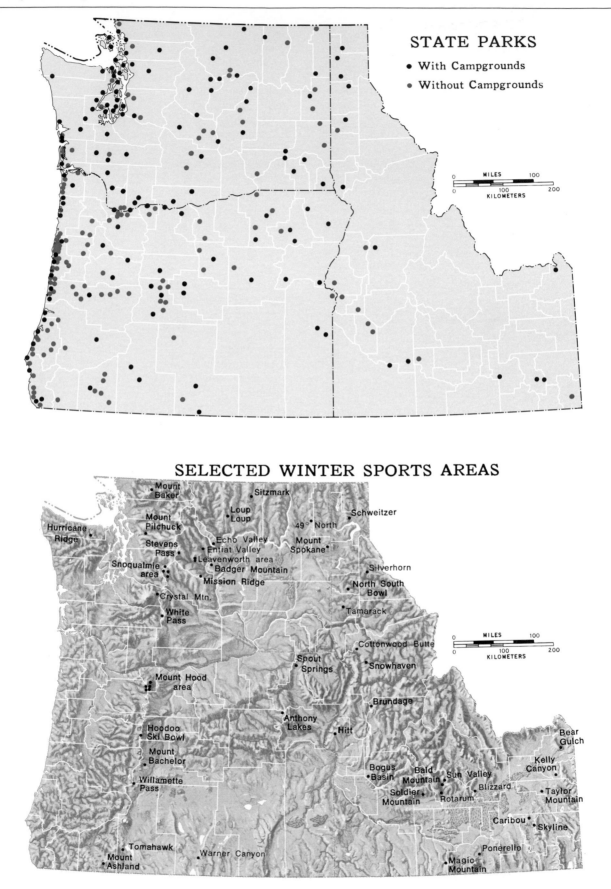

STATE PARKS

● With Campgrounds

● Without Campgrounds

MILES
0   100
0   100   200
KILOMETERS

SELECTED WINTER SPORTS AREAS

Mount Baker

Sitzmark

Loup Loup

Schweitzer

Mount Pilchuck

Hurricane Ridge

49° North

Echo Valley

Stevens Pass

Entiat Valley

Mount Spokane

Leavenworth area

Snoqualmie area

Badger Mountain

Silverhorn

Mission Ridge

North South Bowl

Crystal Mtn.

White Pass

Tamarack

Cottonwood Butte

Spout Springs

Snowhaven

Mount Hood area

Brundage

Anthony Lakes

Hitt

Hoodoo Ski Bowl

Bear Gulch

Mount Bachelor

Bogus Basin

Bald Mountain

Sun Valley

Kelly Canyon

Willamette Pass

Soldier Mountain

Rotarum

Blizzard

Taylor Mountain

Caribou

Skyline

Tomahawk

Warner Canyon

Ponerelle

Mount Ashland

Magic Mountain

MILES
0   100
0   100   200
KILOMETERS

LAPIDARY MATERIAL SITES

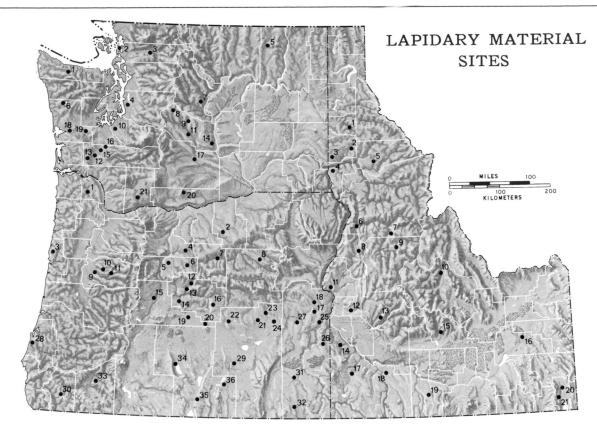

Oregon

1. Vernonia—agate, jasper (Nehalem River gravels)
2. Hardman—agate, opal in thundereggs
3. Wecoma Beach to Florence—agate, jasper, sagenite
4. Antelope—agate, jasper
5. Willowdale—thundereggs, (Priday Ranch, Kennedy Ranch, and Friends Ranch)
6. Ashwood—agate, petrified wood, thundereggs
7. Spray—jasper, agate (Corncob Ranch)
8. John Day River—agate, petrified wood (China Diggin's, Sunshine Flat, Lick Creek, Windy Point, and Howard Meadows)
9. Calapooya River—sagenite, amethyst-agate, petrified wood
10. Lebanon—carnelian, agate, petrified wood
11. Sweet Home—petrified wood, agate
12. Ochoco Mountain—thundereggs, agate, jasper
13. Crook River—plum agate (Carey Ranch and Eagle Rock)
14. Bear Creek—agate, jasper
15. Peterson's Rock Garden—rock exhibit
16. South Fork Crook River—agate "limb casts"
17. Harper—thundereggs, petrified wood (20-30 miles south)
18. Jamison—bog agates, petrified wood (8 miles N.E.)
19. Hampton Butte—agate, jasper, petrified wood
20. Glass Butte—red and black obsidian (near Hampton)
21. Buchanan Lane—agate, jasper, petrified wood
22. Burns—large obsidian flow (7 miles west)
23. Riverside—agate, jasper, petrified wood
24. Stinkingwater Mountain—agate, petrified wood (north and south of Highway 20)
25. Succor Creek—thundereggs, jasper
26. Jordan Valley—petrified wood
27. Dry Creek—petrified wood, agate
28. Bandon to Gold Beach—petrified wood
29. Harney Lake—petrified wood, oolite (2 miles south)
30. Kerby—oregonite, grossulanite garnet
31. Rome—"snakeskin agate" (15 S.W.)
32. McDermitt—petrified wood (15 miles west)
33. Camp White-Eagle Point—agate (dendrites), sagenite
34. Paisley—agate (Chewancan River)
35. Lakeview—thundereggs (Dry Creek), petrified wood (Quartz Mountain)
36. Plush—feldspar (Rabbit Creek), jasper, agate, opal (Hart Mountain)

Washington

1. Crescent Bay—jasper
2. Anacortes, San Juan Islands—jasper
3. Concrete—jade (23.8 miles east)
4. Issaquah—amber (7 miles S.E.)
5. Republic—garnet, agate (15 miles east)
6. Salmon River—agate
7. Cashmere—rose quartz
8. Lake Cle Elum—geodes, quartz crystals
9. Thorp—crystal geodes (Frost Mountain)
10. Nisqually—petrified wood
11. Ellensburg—agate (Jack Creek), petrified wood (Saddle to Kittias—one of the world's most extensive deposits)
12. Toledo—jasper, bloodstone (25 miles N.E.)
13. Adna—petrified wood, carnelian, jasper
14. Beverly—petrified wood (5 miles south)
15. Chehalis—carnelian, petrified wood
16. Tono—agate
17. Yakima—petrified wood (5 miles south)
18. Aberdeen—jasper
19. Porter—fossil crab (south of town)
20. Sunnyside-Bickleton-Roosevelt—petrified wood, agate, jasper
21. Stevenson—jasper, bloodstone (Wind River)

Idaho

1. Fernwood—garnet (in Emerald Creek)
2. Bovill—garnet
3. Moscow—garnet
4. Lewiston—opal (in rims 6 miles west)
5. Pierce—garnet (Rhodes, Oro Fino creeks)
6. Riggins—jasper, agate (John Day Creek, 12 miles north), garnet (Salmon River placers)
7. Warren—topaz, quartz crystals (Paddy Creek)
8. New Meadows—rhodonite (near Tamarack, 6 miles south), sapphire (near Rock Flat)
9. Yellow Pine—agate (Hog Creek, 10-15 miles N.W.)
10. Chehalis—jasper, agate (in low hills)
11. Weiser—agate (Hog Creek, 10-15 miles N.W.)
12. Emmet—opal, agate, jasper, petrified wood (Pearl and Willow creeks)
13. Idaho City—opal (Moore Creek)
14. Marshing—opal (Givern Springs, 15 miles south), jasper, queenstone (10 miles south on U.S. 95)
15. Bellevue—agate (dendritic and moss), sagenite (Muldoon Summit and Little Wood River Res.)
16. Firth—black tempsiki (20 miles R.)
17. Silver City—agate, corundum
18. Bruneau—amethyst, agate, jasper
19. Rogerson—thundereggs, agate (dendritic), sagenite
20. Montpelier, Bear—jasper
21. Paris—jasper

Hunting and Fishing

Gordon E. Matzke

The Pacific Northwest has wild land and water resources in sufficient supply to support substantial populations of many fish and game species. Since much of the wild land is in public ownership, even non-landowners have access to considerable hunting and fishing opportunities.

A primary management tool used by states to regulate harvest and raise revenues for fish and game work is the sale of licenses. The trend in sales of licenses in the three-state area reflects the national pattern which shows participation rates in fishing increasing substantially faster than the population while the absolute numbers of hunters has stopped growing and is actually decreasing as a percentage of the total population. The federal equivalent of the state game license is the migratory bird hunting stamp (duck stamp).

The purchase of the requisite license authorizes an individual to attempt to harvest specified fish and game species. The likelihood that an individual will participate in hunting or fishing varies according to a combination of factors including previous experience, the abundance of game, and the accessibility of recreation sites. Participation rates decline with increased urbanization of the population. In the context of the Pacific Northwest this means that Idaho residents are most likely to hunt or fish while people from Washington are least likely to participate in these sports.

Hunting

The abundance of fish and game available for harvest varies greatly from place to place and over time in any one place. The variation in waterfowl harvest is an excellent illustration. The size of the annual migration fluctuates with changing conditions on the northern breeding grounds and the hunting pressure en route. The distribution of the harvest within the Pacific Northwest is strongly associated with traditional migratory flight lines, resting and feeding areas, and the attractiveness of refuge areas. Although every county shares in the waterfowl harvest, higher than average numbers are killed in the counties along the Columbia, Snake, and Willamette rivers and the Puget Sound area. The largest harvests occur in two counties with especially large wetland habitats: Washington's Grant County (the Potholes Reservoir) and Oregon's Klamath County (the Klamath Marsh).

Wildlife management in the Pacific Northwest has achieved some notable successes in assisting the recovery of game populations which were devastated by the early part of the 20th century. All three states have large populations of deer and elk which owe their existence to extensive restoration efforts such as restocking, protection, and controlled harvests. These efforts continue in an attempt to restore several other big game species. The mountain goat now has at least a small wild population in each state, and all three states have an active program aimed at restoring the mountain sheep to portions of its former range. This animal had disappeared from most of Idaho and Washington and was extinct in Oregon. Now populations are secure enough to allow some tightly controlled harvesting of rams in all three states.

The success of restoration operations is nowhere more obvious than in the level and pattern of deer and elk harvest. Nearly every suitable piece of habitat produces harvestable surpluses of deer, while management efforts are still needed to expand the range of elk in only a few locations, most notably in western Oregon. In many places, the former problems of low to nonexistent populations have been replaced by problems of big game abundance. Hence, timber interests complain of seedling damage caused by game animals and ranchers complain of the competition for forage which results when game descends onto the limited winter range of the

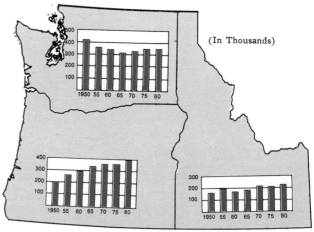

HUNTING LICENSE HOLDERS 1950-1980

(In Thousands)

DEER AND ELK HARVEST BY MANAGEMENT UNIT

Average Harvest For 1980 and 1981 Seasons

Deer Elk

6,000
3,000
1,500
750
375

No Regular Hunting Season

DISTRIBUTION OF WATERFOWL HARVEST

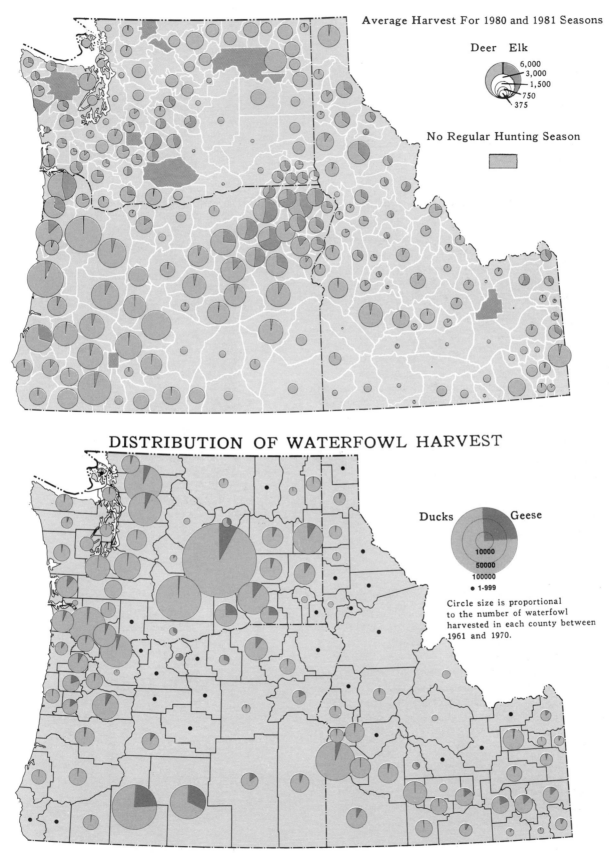

Ducks   Geese

10000
50000
100000
• 1-999

Circle size is proportional
to the number of waterfowl
harvested in each county between
1961 and 1970.

interior valleys. Harvest management attempts to balance the desire of hunters for higher deer and elk populations against the preference of ranching and timber interests for lower populations.

The spatial pattern of big game harvest exhibits several characteristics, including the scarcity of deer and total absence of elk in the driest regions, heavy elk harvests in northeastern Oregon and in a few locations in the Oregon Coast Range, and a widespread large-scale deer harvest with exceptionally heavy takes in most areas of Oregon, northeastern Washington, and the accessible fringes of the Idaho mountains. These patterns are the result of a combination of management policy, habitat quality, accessibility, and population size.

Fishing

Sport fishing is a major recreational activity in all three states. Fishing opportunities are as varied as anywhere in the world with both cold and warm fresh-water fisheries as well as the opportunities of the Pacific Ocean. In addition, nine species of anadromous fish move back and forth between fresh and salt water throughout much of the Columbia River drainage and most of the coastal streams.

The anadromous fishery, including both salmon and steelhead, shows an interesting geographic pattern. Sport fishermen compete for salmon against a heavy commercial fishing effort, especially in the ocean, and with

GENERAL PRESENT AND PAST DISTRIBUTION OF ANADROMOUS FISH

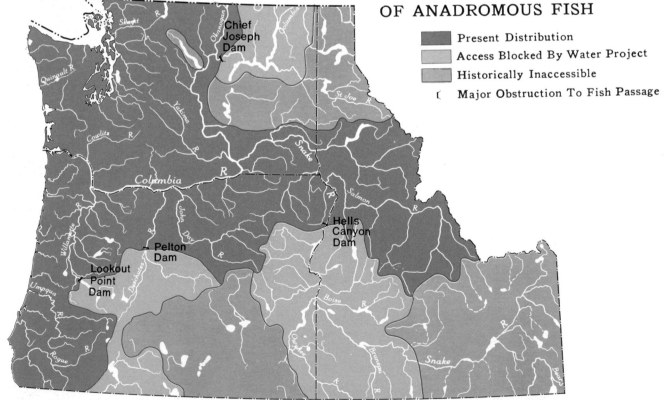

Present Distribution
Access Blocked By Water Project
Historically Inaccessible
Major Obstruction To Fish Passage

Indian Treaty fishing rights on certain rivers particularly in Washington. The near absence of saltwater steelhead catch is due to the species' ocean movements and elusive behavior. In fact, the only steelhead caught in the ocean are accidental landings by fishermen seeking other species. Since salmon flesh is in its best condition during the saltwater part of the life cycle, salmon fishermen concentrate on the saltwater harvest, and most are taken by hook and line methods before they enter fresh water.

The total anadromous fish catch declines dramatically with distance from the sea. The decline is so great that there is no salmon season in Idaho and only a few thousand steelhead are taken. This decrease reflects the combined influence of heavy oceanward fishing pressure, the dominance of downstream hatchery production in the fish reproduction picture, the destruction of river habitat, and the blockage of upstream passage by water projects.

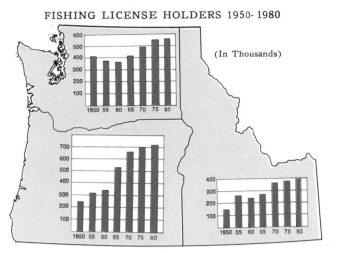

FISHING LICENSE HOLDERS 1950-1980

(In Thousands)

Bibliography

Atzet, T. 1979. Description and classification of the forests of the upper Illinois River drainage of southwestern Oregon. Ph.D. thesis, Oregon State University.

Bailey, A. W. 1966. Forest associations and secondary plant succession in the southern Oregon Coast Range. Ph.D. thesis, Oregon State University.

Bailey, R. G. 1976. Ecoregions of the United States. USDA Forest Service Intermountain Region, Ogden, Utah.

Bailey, R. G. 1978. Description of the ecoregions of the United States. USDA Forest Service Intermountain Region, Ogden, Utah.

Bailey, R. G. 1982. Classification systems for habitat and ecosystems. Pages 16-26 in: *Research on Fish and Wildlife Habitat*. US Environmental Protection Agency EPA 600/8-82-022.

Beckham, S. D. 1977. *The Indians of Western Oregon*. Arago Books, Coos Bay, Oregon.

Cooper, S. V., K. E. Neiman, and R. Steele. 1983. Forest habitat types of northern Idaho, review draft. USDA Forest Service Intermountain Forest and Range Experiment Station.

Corliss, J. F. and C. T. Dyrness. 1965. A detailed soil-vegetation survey of the Alsea area in the Oregon Coast Range. Pages 457-483 in: C. T. Youngberg (ed.), *Forest-Soil Relationships in North America,* Oregon State University Press, Corvallis.

Cressman, L. S. 1977. *Prehistory of the Far West*. University of Utah Press, Salt Lake City.

Cronquist, A., et al. 1972. *Intermountain Flora, Vascular Plants of the Intermountain West, USA*. Volume I. Hafner Publishing Co., New York.

Daubenmire, R. F. 1952. Forest vegetation of northern Idaho and adjacent Washington and its bearing on concepts of vegetation classification. *Ecol. Monogr.* 22:301-333.

Daubenmire, R. F. 1970. Steppe vegetation of Washington. Washington Agricultural Experiment Station *Technical Bulletin 62*.

Daubenmire, R. F. and J. B. Daubenmire. 1968. Forest vegetation of eastern Washington and northern Idaho. Washington Agricultural Experiment Station *Technical Bulletin 60*.

Driscoll, R. S. 1964. Vegetation-soil units in the central Oregon juniper zone. USDA Forest Service Pacific Northwest Forest and Range Experiment Station *Research Paper PNW-19*.

Dyrness, C. T., J. F. Franklin, and W. H. Moir. 1974. A preliminary classification of forest communities in the central portion of the western Cascades in Oregon. International Biome Program *Bulletin 4*.

Dyrness, C. T., et al. 1975. Research natural area needs in the Pacific Northwest: A contribution to land-use planning. USDA Forest Service Pacific Northwest Forest and Range Experiment Station *General Technical Report PNW-38*.

Federal Committee on Ecological Reserves. 1977. A directory of research natural areas on federal lands of the United States of America. USDA Forest Service.

Fogdall, A. B. 1978. *Royal Family of the Columbia*. Ye Galleon Press, Fairfield, Washington.

Franklin, J. F. 1966. Vegetation and soils in subalpine forests of southern Washington Cascade Range. Ph.D. thesis, Washington State University.

Franklin, J. F., et al. 1972. Federal research natural areas in Oregon and Washington: A guidebook for scientists and educators. USDA Forest Service Pacific Northwest Forest and Range Experiment Station, Portland.

Franklin, J. F. and C. T. Dyrness. 1973. Natural vegetation of Oregon and Washington. USDA Forest Service Pacific Northwest Forest and Range Experiment Station *General Technical Report PNW-8*.

Hall, F. C. 1967. Vegetation-soil relations as a basis for resource management on the Ochoco National Forest of central Oregon. Ph.D. thesis, Oregon State University.

Hall, F. C. 1973. Plant communities of the Blue Mountains in eastern Oregon and southeastern Washington. USDA Forest Service Pacific Northwest Region R-6 Area Guide 3-1.

Held, R. B. and M. Clawson. 1965. Soil conservation in perspective. Resources for the Future, Baltimore, Maryland.

Hemstrom, M. A., W. H. Emmingham, N. M. Halverson, S. E. Logan, and C. Topik. 1982. Plant association and management guide for the Pacific silver fir zone, Mt. Hood and Willamette National Forests. USDA Forest Service Pacific Northwest Region, R-6 Ecol. 100-1982a.

Hines, W. W. 1971. Plant communities in the old-growth forests of north coastal Oregon. M.S. thesis, Oregon State University.

Hironaka, M., M. A. Fosberg, and A. H. Winward. 1983. Sagebrush-grass habitat types of southern Idaho. University of Idaho Forest, Wildlife and Range Experiment Station *Bulletin 15*.

Hopkins, W. E. 1979a. Plant associations of south Chiloquin and Klamath Ranger Districts, Winema National Forest. USDA Forest Service Pacific Northwest Region, R6-Ecol. 79-005.

Hopkins, W. E. 1979b. Plant associations of the Fremont National Forest. USDA Forest Service Pacific Northwest Region, R6-Ecol. 79-004.

Hopkins, W. E. and B. L. Kovalchik. 1983. Plant associations of the Crooked River National Grassland. USDA Forest Service Pacific Northwest Region, R6-Ecol. 133-1983.

Irving, W. 1964. *Astoria 1836*. University of Oklahoma Press, Norman.

Johnson, C. G., Jr. 1982. An interpretation of synecologic relationships in the Billy Meadows area of Wallowa-Whitman National Forest. Ph.D. thesis, Oregon State University.

Kuchler, A. W. 1964. Potential natural vegetation of the coterminous United States. *Amer. Geog. Soc. Spec. Publ. 36*.

Lent, D. G. 1963. *West of the Mountains*. University of Washington Press, Seattle.

Little, E. L., Jr. 1971. Atlas of United States trees. Volume I. Conifers and important hardwoods. USDA Forest Service *Misc. Publ. 1146*.

Muckleston, K. W. 1977. The Columbia River. Pages 71-96 in: *Environmental Effects of Complex River Development* (G. F. White, ed.). Westview Press, Boulder, Colorado.

Munnick, H. D. 1972. *Catholic Records of the Pacific Northwest*. French Prairie Press, St. Paul, Oregon.

Oregon Natural Heritage Advisory Council. 1981. Oregon Natural Heritage Plan. Oregon State Land Board, Salem.

Pacific Northwest River Basins Commission. 1970. Water resources. Volume I, Appendix V.

Pathick, D. 1976. *First Approaches to the Northwest Coast*. J. J. Douglas Ltd., Vancouver.

Steele, R., S. V. Cooper, D. M. Ondov, D. W. Roberts, and R. D. Pfister. 1983. Forest habitat types of eastern Idaho-western Wyoming. USDA Forest Service Intermountain Forest and Range Experiment Station *General Technical Report INT-144*.

Steele, R., R. D. Pfister, R. A. Ryker, and J. A. Kittams. 1981. Forest habitat types of central Idaho. USDA Forest Service Intermountain Forest and Range Experiment Station *General Technical Report INT-114*.

Tisdale, E. W. 1979. A preliminary classification of Snake River canyon grasslands in Idaho. University of Idaho Forest, Wildlife nad Range Experiment Station *Note 32*.

US Department of Agriculture, Soil Conservation Service. 1982. Soil survey status, Oregon. Map M7-EN-22493.

US Department of Agriculture, Soil Conservation Service. 1982. Soil survey status, Washington. Map M7-PL-24009.

US Department of Agriculture, Soil Conservation Service. 1975. A basic system of soil classification for making and interpreting soil surveys. *Agricultural Handbook 436*.

US Department of Agriculture, Soil Conservation Service. 1983. Status of soil surveys, Idaho. Map M7-OL-22211-1.

US Department of the Interior, National Park Service. 1977. Preserving our natural heritage. Volume I. Federal activities. Volume II. State activities . Volume III. Academic and local activities. Government printing office, Washington, DC.

Volland, L. H. 1976. Plant communities of Oregon pumice stone. USDA Forest Service Pacific Northwest Region, R-6 Area Guide 4-2.

Washington Department of Natural Resources. 1983. Natural Heritage plan. Olympia.

Whitebrook, R. B. 1959. *Coastal Exploration of Washington*. Pacific Books, Palo Alto.

Winward, A. H. 1970. Taxonomic and ecological relationships of the big sagebrush complex in Idaho. Ph.D. thesis, University of Idaho.